Praise for

The Falling Rate of Learning and the Neoliberal Enagame

by David J. Blacker

"David Blacker provides a mordantly clear-eyed assessment of our predicament. He asks hard questions, in the tradition of our best gadflies, and reveals even harder truths, doing us and our 'democracy' (such as it is) a great potential service. Read rightly, Blacker's book, far from making you want to bury your head in the sand even deeper, will inspire you to shake yourself out of your slumber and do your part to arrest this pernicious development. We ignore his important work at our own peril."

Christopher Phillips, author, *Socrates Cafe: A Fresh Taste of Philosophy* and *Constitution Cafe: Jefferson's Brew for a True Revolution*, Senior Writing Fellow, University of Pennsylvania and founder, Democracy Cafe

"While it is no surprise that casino capitalism is in crisis and is spurring protests all over the world, few theorists connect the dots and analyze how this crisis moves through and is affected by a range of institutions. David Blacker has written a superb book in which matters of education, agency, economic justice and collective struggle come alive in both a language of critique and possibility. There will be no endgame to neoliberalism without critically thinking subjects who fight back collectively. This is the book that should be read to create the formative culture that makes such a struggle possible. —"

Henry A. Giroux, author, *America's Education Deficit and the War on Youth* and *Youth in Revolt: Reclaiming a Democratic Future*, Global Television Network Chair in Communication Studies at McMaster University, Ontario

"Invigorating pessimism"
Mark Fisher, author, *Capitalist Realism: Is There No Alternative?*

"David Blacker's book should be required reading for everyone marching circles in schools and universities."
Doug Lain, author, *Billy Moon: 1968* and host of the Diet Soap Podcast

"The notion that widespread educational attainment is the key to widespread prosperity has long been a pillar of the dominant ideology. David Blacker's central—and centrally important—insight is that the Great Recession has made this notion (which was always dubious) hopelessly anachronistic. When so many people have become superfluous to the capitalist system--mass joblessness persists four years after the recession officially ended--what have also become superfluous are these people's skills, the schools that educate them, and the spending that funds the schools. And a capitalism mired in crisis *just isn't* a capitalism that can afford to pay for what it doesn't need. But isn't this only a temporary situation? Drawing on Karl Marx's falling-rate-of-profit theory and his associated theory of relative surplus (super-fluous) population, Blacker warns that it may well be permanent and he urges us to face this prospect soberly and respond accord-ingly."
Andrew Kliman, author, *The Failure of Capitalist Production: Underlying Causes of the Great Recession*, Professor of Economics, Pace University (New York)

The Falling Rate of Learning and the Neoliberal Endgame

The Falling Rate of Learning and the Neoliberal Endgame

David J. Blacker

Winchester, UK
Washington, USA

First published by Zero Books, 2013
Zero Books is an imprint of John Hunt Publishing Ltd., Laurel House, Station Approach,
Alresford, Hants, SO24 9JH, UK
office1@jhpbooks.net
www.johnhuntpublishing.com
www.zero-books.net

For distributor details and how to order please visit the 'Ordering' section on our website.

ISBN: 978 1 78099 578 6

A CIP catalogue record for this book is available from the British Library.

Design: Stuart Davies

Printed and bound by CPI Group (UK) Ltd, Croydon, CR0 4YY

We operate a distinctive and ethical publishing philosophy in all
areas of our business, from our global network of authors to
production and worldwide distribution.

CONTENTS

Through wars and corruptions the house will fall.
Mourn whom it falls on. Be glad: the house is mined, it will fall.
-Robinson Jeffers[1]

Preface

The current neoliberal mutation of capitalism has evolved beyond the days when the wholesale exploitation of labor underwrote the world system's expansion. While "normal" business profits plummet and theft-by-finance rises, capitalism now shifts into a mode of elimination that targets most of us - along with our environment - as waste products awaiting managed disposal.

The education system is caught in the throes of this eliminationism across a number of fronts: crushing student debt, impatience with student expression, the looting of vestigial public institutions and, finally, as *coup de grâce*, an abandonment of the historic ideal of universal education. "Education reform" is powerless against eliminationism and is at best a mirage that diverts oppositional energies. The very idea of education activism becomes a comforting fiction.

Educational institutions are strapped into the eliminationist project - the neoliberal endgame - in a way that admits no escape, despite the heroic gestures of a few. The school systems that capitalism has built and directed over the last two centuries are fated to go down with the ship. It is rational therefore for educators to cultivate a certain pessimism. Should we despair? Why, yes, we should - but cheerfully, as confronting elimination, mortality, is after all our common fate. There is nothing and everything to do in order to prepare.

This book attempts a realistic assessment of what we are stuck with for the time being. Sold with hyperbolic fanfare, education "reforms" will continue: some for the better, some for the worse. We are in a period, though, where the really big changes are highly unlikely to be the products of individual or even collective volition. Those changes are coming, yes, but they will of necessity result from structural dynamics rather than volitional grit and determination.

In the meantime, we must wait. Not even the grandest experts can predict what comes next and when. This means that everyone, including the most ruddily optimistic and busiest of activists, must continually *cope* with existing systems even as conditions worsen. This is where an appreciation of fate can come in. Yet "fate" sounds intolerable to modern ears, as all we can hear is "futility." But the conflation is false. The ancients understood how fate is tied to hope and the two must come together. As the first woman on earth, Pandora, discovered, hope may need to be surrendered before it is found.

Many people have aided this manuscript, including students and audiences in the US and UK who have been subjected to talks derived from bits and pieces of it. I deeply appreciate the good work of Tariq Goddard, John Hunt, Trevor Greenfield and Liam Sprod and others at Zero Books, an extremely cool operation with which I'm very happy to be associated. I'm especially grateful for the kind attentions of Bob Hampel, Chris Higgins, Doug Lain, Alpesh Maisuria, Curry Malott, Chris Martin, Chris Phillips, Andrew Ross and the Occupy Student Debt movement. Most of all, I thank Marcia Blacker, Jessica George and Aideen Murphy for their above-and-beyond-the-call critiques of both substance and style. Please don't blame any of these people of course; all they did was suggest I make the thing better than it would have been. Finally, I am grateful for permission to use, for portions of Chapter 5, substantially revised material from "An Unreasonable Argument Against Student Free Speech," *Educational Theory* (2009): 124-143.

This book is dedicated to the memory of radical historian, activist, mother and grandmother Margaret George, who for so long saw through it all.

Introduction

The era of procrastination, of half-measures, of soothing and baffling expedients, of delays, is coming to its close. In its place we are entering a period of consequences.
Winston Churchill[1]

Controversial but central to Karl Marx's account of how capitalism falls into crisis is his theory of the "tendency of the rate of profit to fall" (henceforward, 'TRPF'). Marx himself thought this tendency to be "in every respect the most important law of modern political economy."[2] Though often misunderstood, the TRPF remains necessary for understanding the provenance and durability of the present economic crisis. Reaching deeply into social institutions such as education - more deeply than commonly realized - it gives the lie to the dream we have been sold of educating ourselves into prosperity via schools' fabrication of "knowledge workers" and their enhanced productivity. Yesterday's utopian vision of the "high tech, high wage" service economy now stands revealed as a false promise.

Due to structural features of capitalism, this promise has been *decisively* broken; there is no going back. Recapturing material prosperity via educational endeavor is simply not possible, even for those of the erstwhile middle classes of the industrialized world. Despite this reality, false hopes continue to be peddled in order to enable the ideological lie that it is a matter of pedagogically refashioning ourselves; we thereby, as sociologist Pierre Bourdieu put it, internalize the "symbolic violence" and introspect toward our sinful selves in the self-hating spirit of our dominant religious narratives.[3] If we could only make ourselves better, faster, stronger, smarter etc., in short, get our training and education right, our bright futures would once again be assured. A complete morphological makeover may be required, admittedly, but as long as we are able to adapt our perennially inadequate selves to the rapidly shifting needs of capital accumulation, a kind of market-based *eudaimonia* is ours for the taking.

But alas, we are doomed to find ourselves being held back by the new original sin of which we are perpetually guilty: our inevitable all-too human failure to keep pace with the exponentially increasing drumbeat of production. Such weak and evil creatures we are if we cannot keep up, if we prove insufficiently elastic. By way of a compensatory gesture, perhaps we allow ourselves to be "bright-sided," as in Barbara Ehrenreich's sarcastic phrase, and make ourselves believe that these adaptations count as "progress" and are good for us, thereby placing a positive spin upon our feckless twisting in the corporate winds.[4] We can become, as the education bureaucrats say, delightfully plastic "lifelong learners," in other words, infinitely malleable human material continually at the service of elite whim.

By way of resistance to this deflated conception of humanity and in order to see ourselves as something other than what Martin Heidegger called "standing-reserve" for the moneybags, it is first necessary to abandon this pseudo-perfectionism currently on offer from domination's apologists.[5] If, against fashion, we desire the intellectual and moral maturity that is captured in the grand Kantian enlightenment motto *sapere aude* (Lat. "dare to be wise"), we must at least *make the attempt* to think for ourselves. If it has any meaning at all, true self-direction demands a mentality that wants to explore beneath even the glossiest of surfaces, seeking always to be radical in that etymologically primal sense of *radix*, of wanting to get at the *root* of a thing. In that spirit we should be disposed to interrogate the proposition when we are told we are in a "crisis" that truncates our possibilities, educational and otherwise.

What lies at the root of our current predicament?

To find real answers, it is first necessary to distinguish the root from the rest of the plant. This is no trivial matter, as we are copiously beset with all manner of explanatory vegetation. We hear of personal greed and corruption among elites (and profligate consumers), regressive tax policies, financial deregulation, lack of spending on infrastructure and the like forwarded as explanations for our economic woes. While these things are all highly relevant and may even serve as *proximate* causes for specific events, they fail to fully convince as *underlying* causes. This is because it is still obviously necessary to ask "why?" regarding such would-be explanations.

Let us stipulate, say, that there is greed on Wall Street. There "greed is good," in fact, as says Michael Douglas's Gordon Gekko in 1987's *Wall Street*. But bankers and people in general have always been greedy. Did they suddenly get *more* greedy in the late 1990s when the subprime housing crisis was brewing and the many "innovative" speculative strategies were being rolled out? It is logically possible that there was some mass alteration of human nature a couple of decades ago but this possibility seems so remote that it serves as a *reductio ad absurdum* of the "greed" hypothesis.

Or maybe it is that the ancient vice of greed was merely given a freer rein of late via financial deregulation under Reagan-Thatcher, Clinton, the Bushes, Obama et al. This seems a better explanation. After all, Great Depression era banking regulations were foolishly repealed for short-term gain (i.e. "greed") and this undoubtedly caused the current economic crisis to take place in the manner it did. But even this more structural explanation insistently begs that same "why?" For why *now*? Why was there so much willingness among elites (most of the population is completely clueless about such goings on) at this point in history to abandon the New Deal era financial safeguards that were put in place *for their own good*? Are they just stupid? (Extreme short-sightedness is one form of stupidity.) Undoubtedly some of them are. Many of them are quite clever though. They are the best and brightest products of the most elite schools. They know complicated math. They may be many things but it is unlikely they are dumb - at least not as dumb as the subset of groundlings who admire them.

So the question remains: *why*?

Subscribing to explanations forwarded by Marx and American economist Hyman Minsky, I contend that there are deeper reasons rooted in the very nature of capitalist production and, to a secondary extent, collective human psychology, that together provide a far more compelling explanation of the economic crisis than greed or stupidity or the right's "big government" or other such superficialities currently being carnival barked. A grasp of these deeper reasons in turn provides a sounder basis for understanding developments concerning the largely dependent variable that is the educational sphere. If the larger context controls the smaller, one needs to understand what is happening in the former in order to grasp occurrences in the latter. As I shall explain in more detail, causality is not unidirectional here in any simple way and educational institutions are not *wholly* determined by the explanatory object of the dismal science. But they mostly are. Those who have long congratulated themselves as escapees from "deterministic" analyses of education have been celebrating far too early in the game. The 'free will v. determinism' antinomy has not been solved so much as it has been repressed. We pretend, for example, that a more generous distribution of surplus education can collectively enlighten us into liberation (so says our quaint eighteenth century voice) or that we can practice a "critical pedagogy" from within existing educational institutions by which we can bootstrap ourselves into a New Jerusalem. Trapped in a big Hollywood-like cliché, we like to think we can, through strength of sheer will, assert our humanity against a cold impersonal system - that we can rage against the machine. Perhaps. In the long run. But the machine needs to be given far greater due than many are willing. From where I sit, at present, I see only machine.

But after several generations' dogmatic slumbers, the consciousness of this "fixed" state of affairs is beginning to reawaken; the repressed is returning. And this time it is striking our children and is becoming manifest in a thousand outposts of global disquiet. People are beginning to understand for themselves that something is terribly wrong. Throughout the industrialized world, the younger generation especially is learning such lessons - as well they should, given that the massive under- and unemployment they are currently experiencing leaves these "overeducated" youths with a lot of spare time to think. From Quebec to Spain, Tahrir Square to Zucotti Park, and London to Athens, their primary teacher has become the frightening experience of their personal contingency and precariousness - what education theorist Henry Giroux aptly terms their "disposability"[6] - their placelessness in the economy that has been designed to exclude them, along with the deteriorating material standard of living entailed by such a status.

In the course of this inevitable fall downward, they are also learning that their education system had long been based on the Clintonian lie that if you "work hard and play by the rules" that is, if you allow yourself to be molded by the needs of capital, you will be granted a sure and desirable place in the economic hierarchy. They were told that they could all become technical experts, "symbolic workers," and otherwise free to fulfill their "highest potential" as creative types of infinite description. The drudgery and precariousness was to be safely offshored "out of sight, out of mind" to distant foreigners (including socially distant domestic "foreigners"), who would in turn play their own part by uncomplainingly welcoming the opportunity one day to achieve as full a humanity as their betters. In American corporate-speak, this seemed a clear "win-win" situation: doing *well* for oneself wealth-wise while doing *good* for others by "developing" them.

Yet a funny thing happened over the rainbow on the way to

this Global Fantasy Land: *capitalism happened.*

Or, continued to happen, of course. Certain of the most powerful tendencies of capitalism had just been hidden from view for a time at the alleged "end of history," among the most important of these being the TRPF. It now resurfaces with a vengeance. This is happening because, as one of this book's purposes is to explain, several of the counter forces that had been keeping it at bay are finally losing their potency, especially as we approach an alarming array of societal and planetary "limits to growth"[7]: the cheap credit and debt needed to blow massive financial bubbles, the "natural" windfall of cheap fossil fuels that still - even so it seems, after their peak - motor almost everything, the postwar bounty involving the mechanization of agriculture, the quasi-Keynesian stimulative effects of unprecedented Cold War arms spending, the intensification of labor exploitation abroad and consequent domestic wage repression enjoyed by manufacturing operations through outsourcing to the developing world and, finally, the harvesting of the "low hanging fruit" of the productivity-enhancing universal education largely in place by mid-century.[8] These and other factors served to prop up profits (and hence capitalist production) from around the early 1970s on, the point at which they really started needing to be propped up.

These counter forces were so successful that the potency of their ensemble made it seem to recent generations that capitalism was not only a magical cornucopia but it was *inevitable*, a conviction only apparently reconfirmed by the fall of the Berlin Wall and then the Soviet Union itself. Small wonder that we have now produced two or three generations notorious for their apathy about public life, like my own generically-termed "Generation X." The big battles had already been fought, the key choices already made. So why bother? In the face of this macro-ennui, it was quite sensible to conclude that the important thing, the only thing that was *real*, was to turn inward and get on with one's *own* life.

But beneath this episode of generational obliviousness and the dull whirr of politics as usual, newly triumphant global capitalism's gears kept moving and its internal dynamics kept churning, just as they had for centuries. Capitalism runs smoothest, in fact, when it is not noticed as such; this state of being taken for granted, that which is "assumed," is where ideology exists at its purest. Nonetheless, seen or unseen, it pushes forward, always, inevitably generating further contradictions. Does capitalism happen even if nobody is there to notice it? Yes indeed.

Chief among these emergent contradictions is the dynamic captured in the TRPF's interplay of production, labor and technology. Generations of critics from the left assumed that capitalism's productive drive always required more and more flesh and blood *workers* to exploit and from whom infinite value could in principle be extracted. As with the pharaohs and emperors of old, it seemed obvious that the more labor that was available for dragooning into the circuit of production, the more value there was to be extracted and hence, ultimately, the more profit there was to be made and capital to be accumulated. But labor is only part of the equation as really it always was, in the case of "primitive accumulation" whereby historically owners initially become owners simply by stealing things, "enclosing" them as property. Things are still more complicated within the modern circuit of production where the TRPF arises. Here, capital accumulates in a particular way, as an artifact of productivity gains that are reinvested into commercial operations as technological fixtures, "fixed capital" in Marxian parlance. Then, for reasons Marx explained (and I'll elaborate below), this causes the system as a whole and over time to start bleeding profits. This profit drain afflicting "normal" operations in turn precipitates business crises of various sorts. Meanwhile, the human workers enmeshed in these enterprises are of course adversely affected even though they are doing nothing "wrong" at their jobs. Ultimately, the squeeze for profits is so intense that increasing numbers are tossed out of work, as the TRPF-induced counter forces push productive capitals to outsource operations to obtain cheap overseas labor and/or simply replace workers by new technology. Tools may depreciate but they don't need pay and healthcare.

This profit squeeze at the top is then passed on to the vast majority of the population - commonly through central bank collusions with the major capitals - as chronic unemployment and government austerity. Not as many workers are needed to turn whatever profits remain and government largesse is reserved exclusively for "too big to fail" financialized capitals which have, as a result, become state-corporate hybrids that exist as government-secured monopolies evenwhile they spout neoliberal rhetoric about "freedom," "competition," and the like. Assuming more fully public and private levers of control, elites have thus consolidated themselves into a more tightly oligarchic formation than previously, allowing them a greater sway over politics than they have enjoyed for generations. And until a threshold of social instability is passed, it is proportionately easier for elites to deploy austerity policies against the general population owing to the simple fact that they no longer as greatly *need* the services of the run of humanity for winning their wealth. (Due to that same social instability, *securing* that wealth in the long run may be quite another matter.) They are either gaining it via productive processes that do not rely on the vagaries of labor as much as they once did (automation) or, increasingly, circumnavigating that messy production business altogether and grabbing it through criminality and/or cleverness in the rigged financial casino that capitalism has now become. (Properly speaking, most of the wealth generated in finance is not even "investment" in the old sense of providing capital to productive or soon-to-be-productive enterprises; it is just placing derivative bets on price fluctuations and nothing whatever to do with growing anyone's business in the old textbook sense.) Either way, the bulk of the population is no longer seen as a resource to be harnessed - as dismal as *that* moral stance once seemed - but more as a mere threat, at best a population overshoot to be managed by a self-perpetuating and therefore pseudo meritocracy.[9] If the peasants are no longer needed to work the fields, then why not go ahead and kick them off the estate? The scenery will improve.

This is where the austerity kicks in. It's a one-two punch sort of situation: fewer human beings are needed for capital accumulation *and* the public coffers are urgently needed by elites in order to continue leveraging their insatiable cash cow financial sector (almost all of the sovereign indebtedness is due to tax cuts for wealthy individuals and corporations and, more importantly, the bailouts and federal guarantees that have been tendered to the banking sector). Thus the "shit rolls downhill" nature of austerity that requires teachers and schoolchildren to pay for the solvency of sinecured bankers and their political enablers.

The financial shenanigans inherent in casino capitalism along with the rampant and structural criminality that characterizes it are maddening. And it is easy to get swept up in cathartic initiatives like wanting to regulate the banks and jail the bad bankers. All this is understandable and I am all for bankers being jailed. But it is crucial to realize amidst all this fog of financial war that the real enemy lies farther back behind the front lines: *in the ailing productive process*. We could have the most pristine regulations and clean the Augean stables of all the unscrupulous financial players and that would be good to see. But doing so would only be treating *symptoms* and would not touch the underlying causes, the reasons the casino housing the criminals was built in the first place. Those underlying causes are not going away; they can't.

Under such structurally corrupted conditions, commitments to heretofore bulwark public institutions such as public education are unlikely to be renewed. Again, as attention to the TRPF shows, technology aided productivity enhancements have merely reduced the overall need for workers - especially the expensive kind in the global North - which is leading to a wholesale abandonment of previous public commitments such as the longstanding one to the universal provision of education. Even more than this, austerity reveals what I call an educational *eliminationism*, whereby increasing segments of the population are morally written off as no longer exploitable and hence irrelevant to capital accumulation. Why bother caring for them at all, let alone educating them? Such a question is implicit in current neoliberal policies that are altering the moral status of the "unprofitable" human being toward throwaway precariousness and irrevocable degradation. There is thus no "reform" of what has become a neoliberal thanatology; it is life or death. Such is the argument of Chapters 1-3.

Symptomatic of this willingness to write people off is the new austerity in education, which makes a mockery of ideological mainstays like social mobility and equal opportunity which, as they unravel, help burst the legitimation bubble. Beneath all of this, the major premise of educational austerity is an implicit - sometimes explicit - willingness to withdraw the old liberal promise of primary and secondary universal public education as a compulsory entitlement. As Chapter 5 argues, a canary in the coal mine in this regard is an increased willingness to eliminate "students' rights" in the area of speech and expression via the legal framework that had protected it in the US for generations. When students in general are viewed as mattering less, the zeal to protect any rights they may possess decreases as well. At the level of higher education, as outlined in Chapter 4, massive student debt threatens a new era of debt servitude, even serfdom, where the very future possibilities of the young become existential carrion for the insatiably gluttonous financialized "vulture" capitals. The young stare down the barrel of a neo-feudal future that looks, *at best*, bleak and disheartening.

It gets worse. Chapter 6 describes the demise of the grand ideal of universal education that has animated enlightened capitalism since the nineteenth century. What capitalism gives, it now takes away. In the realm of education, this process represents a final *coup de grâce*: the abandonment of government provisioned and guaranteed schooling for all - after first "privatizing" and channeling those commons' erstwhile value into elite coffers. This is where educational elimination comes into its own, as one of the key moves in the neoliberal endgame. Nothing from *within* education will stop this process; it is far too powerful. Sources of internal opposition are easily managed, as most of educational officialdom, e.g. the locust-like plague of CEO-style university leaders, identifies much more closely with their corporate peers than anything recognizably "educational."

It is hard for us capitalism-soaked subjects to imagine what an "authentic" response to these processes might look like. We may not be able to at present - "intellectuals," not exempting this author, included. Perhaps as propaedeutic, as a Socratic way-clearing, we need our own kind of Naomi Kleinian "shock doctrine," an existential event that can break the crust of our ideologically enforced complacency.[10] In the Marxist materialist tradition, where there is no expectation of a *deus ex machina* as catalyst for a mass altering of human consciousness, the shock must be provided, always, via the material world. Along with the shock of labor eliminationism, the best candidate for this shock may be found in the alarmingly high potential for societal collapse due to exogenous factors such as climate change and resource depletion (including peak oil). In literally burning through our resource base, we now face a *collective* encounter with mortality that is being made vivid by a growing community of scholar-activists of the "collapse" and "transition" movements. In his early work, Martin Heidegger suggests that such an encounter need not be thought of as morose or morbid but on the contrary as necessary to our becoming more "authentic" as human beings. The idea is that proximity to one's own finitude can have a clarifying effect whether, as I am suggesting, this comes via an appreciation of natural limits to economic growth or, as Heidegger contends, an existential awareness of one's personal mortality. As I argue in Chapter 7, rather than wishing it away as we normally do via various psychological stratagems, we would do well truly to respect the overwhelming power of our situation and adopt a fatalism-inflected pedagogy of opportunism, one that watches, waits and seizes the moment when it arrives. This makes more sense tactically at present than a glorious but suicidal frontal stand like that against the Persian Emperor at Thermopylae.

Akin to the legend of the 300, though, such efforts should not be prepared with the expectation of "success," however, at least not in the sense of "sustainability" - that favorite green buzzword. Sustainability implies merely the continuation of, literally, business as usual - only with new eco-friendly technologies. A green capitalism full of solar, wind, and Apple products. We just need a grand "techno-fix," a clever invention that will enable us to "sustain" our current mode of living.[11] But *ex hypothesi*, what if it is our current mode of living and its associated mentalities (including capitalist ideology) that are *themselves* the culprits? What if our typical approach to problem-solving is itself a problem? This would be a strange situation indeed.

What we need instead is a new *amor fati* (Lat. "love of fate"), as Friedrich Nietzsche termed it, that will enable us fully to understand the magnitude of the ongoing environmental devastation wrought by capital and how this perhaps irreversible cataclysm *will in fact* alter humanity's existential possibilities. Nietzsche writes: "I want to learn more and more to see as beautiful what is necessary in things; then I shall be one of those who make things beautiful. Amor fati: let that be my love hence-

14

forth!"[12] Scholars and activists in this area are extremely unlikely to "change" things on such a vast scale and should understand their role as more akin to a John the Baptist: preparing the way for what is surely to come. The collapse may be concentrated and acute or drawn out and "stepwise" or, in the happiest (and most unlikely) case, gradual and smooth.[13] All we can do now is, like Marx after his own fashion, brace for the historical inevitability and do what we can by way of preparation. As capitalism has gone so far as to implicate the entire planet, this fatalism - dour or cheerful - is the only real "environmentalism" and the only true educational endeavor still available. Still-relevant aspects of the philosophical tradition such as ancient Stoicism and individual figures as Seneca, Lucretius, Spinoza, and Nietzsche - and many others - can be scavenged for insight as to how we might conceive a post-capitalist fatalism that is coexistent with a non-extractive stance toward nature and each other. If you'd prefer it without the name dropping: it might finally be necessary to try *getting over ourselves*.

Chapter I

Endgames

Capitalism is a suicide pact.
-Noam Chomsky[1]

Education and sustainability

My thesis is that the neoliberal endgame is precisely that, an endgame. The neoliberal phase of capitalism advances a series of moves the execution of which causes the game to end; upon completion of its final sequence the players cannot continue. Though ultimately merely a symptom, neoliberalism represents capitalism's moving beyond its traditional concern with extracting labor's surplus value, i.e. worker exploitation, into a posture of worker *elimination* and, ultimately, elimination *simpliciter*: we ourselves, future generations, and much other life on earth. "All that is solid melts into air, all that is holy is profaned, and man is at last compelled to face with sober senses, his real conditions of life, and his relations with his kind."[2] This searing sentence must once again be read in its most literal sense.

Traditional Marxist eschatology is thus correct to posit that, driven by its own contradictions, capitalism will finally enter a terminal phase. Yet few have understood until recently just how literally that "terminal" needs to be taken. As the ideological expression of the latest mutation of capitalism - a *systemically* hybridized monstrosity of state subsidy and oligarchic monop-olism - at its deepest structural level neoliberalism amounts to an uncompromising thanatology. It is a death wish that has taken hold of our collective mentality. It will eliminate first the poor and otherwise vulnerable and then it will kill all of us as it destroys the capacity of our planet to sustain human life. I mean this not as hyperbole but as a sober extrapolation from present economic and environmental trends. As John Bellamy Foster and colleagues, in their study of capitalism's effect on the environment, warn: "the stability of the earth system as we know it is being endangered. We are at red alert status."[3]

There are more optimistic scenarios. But at the moment these seem less probable. Unfortunately, sometimes it turns out that the news is bad and it may even lack the silver lining we seem almost hardwired to try to locate. So many of us proceed like we *deserve* a happy ending, as if by birthright. This sense of cosmic entitlement has a long intellectual history: from the Judaic self-understanding as God's "chosen" people, to the Aristotelian *scala naturae* where humanity serves as biological *telos*, to the Calvinist-Puritan-American conviction that God will prosper his elect, to today's suitably banal expectation for technological fixes that "they" will figure out in order to deliver the Hollywood happy ending upon which "we" the audience insist. Human beings may even be hard-wired for a certain degree of psychological ruddiness; speculative evolutionary rationales for the survival positivity of "high hopes" are easy to imagine (though depression may have its own evolutionary rationale as well).[4] But clearly optimism can delude, too. This calls to mind Friedrich Nietzsche's dangerous insight that at times truth can be *inimical* to life. "Is wanting not to allow oneself to be deceived really less harmful, less dangerous, less calamitous?"[5] This attitudinal ambivalence pervades every worthwhile discussion of the realities of the neoliberal predicament in which we now find ourselves.

Take the critical notion of "sustainability" that is often quite reasonably offered in opposition to the present annihilative path. Every reasonable person should be in favor of sustainability. But as a guide for action it can be misleading. Sustainability is largely a strategic notion. It tends to assume as static the desirability of certain outcomes and therefore frequently frames problems as technical malfunctions needing appropriate technical fixes. If I decry our present oil usage as "unsustainable," implicit in that message is an imperative to locate an alternative energy source in order to sustain the same activities fueled by the old energy source. What tends to be assumed is that our general way of doing things, our "lifestyle," needs to be preserved but by alternative means, in this case, say, by developing sources of renewable energy; *we* are not the problem, it is only our current way of doing things that is to blame. As essayist Paul Kingsnorth pointedly puts it, "It means sustaining human civilization at the comfort level that the world's rich people - us - feel is their right, without destroying the 'natural capital' or the 'resource base' that is needed to do so."[6] Admittedly, this is *not* what is meant by "sustainability" by our most enlightened activists (one hopes); nonetheless, it is what is *heard* by an ideologically degraded consumer culture that ultimately sees *itself* as the universe's center.

In this crucial respect, the rhetoric of sustainability is inadequate for describing the magnitude of what is at stake with neoliberalism and the comprehensive - and compounding - damage it currently wreaks. The problem with "sustainability" in the larger context of human survival is that it tends to understate matters. When resource depletion and environmental destruction are factored in, the neoliberal phase of capitalism is more than merely unsustainable. If it is allowed to play out its endgame, it will not just alter our lives and cause us to seek new ways of achieving what we currently desire. It will *eliminate* us, and when we exit, so will the sustainability question, as the question of what is to be sustained and how to sustain "it" - namely, *us* - will no longer remain. In this sense, neoliberalism's endgame is not just another problem for clever humanity to figure out and from which to move on. In the parlance of our now endless war against "terror," it represents an *existential* threat, not a threat against specific practices or even our particular way of life as a whole. It is a threat against life itself: *our* lives, certainly, and also much other precious nonhuman life as well.

To illustrate the point, I could frame a life-or-death struggle against an assailant as a conflict over the "sustainability" of my life. Once again this would be true but it is misleadingly understated. It would be more accurate to say that I am engaged in a struggle against being eliminated, where I may face the harsh survivalist disjunction of either killing or being killed. The more chronic question of sustainability (and its strategies and solutions) rightfully comes into play only once this more acute life-or-death existential question has been decided. I contend that this is where we are now finding ourselves with capitalism in its neoliberal phase; we have been enduring a chronic condition that has recently turned acute in the life-or-death sense. Consequently, we are subject to that harsh survivalist disjunction: *we will have to kill it before it kills us*. And soon. For the powerful imperatives for which neoliberal ideology provides cover are actively destroying everything in their path, in a congeries of extractive processes that go well beyond the "creative destruction" ambivalently identified by Marx and celebrated by capitalism's dead enders as an always right and necessary manifestation of market forces. For creative destruction has given way to just plain destruction - alone and for its own sake. Driven by its own kind of internal optimism, Marxist dialectics might see in this rape of nature yet another, though perhaps the final, Hegelian master-slave reversal, where we end up debilitated and conquered by that which we created and over which we thought we had control, like the situation with capital itself writ large. For its part, the Christian tradition might see in all this destructive nihilism the figure of Satan making an audacious apocalyptic move. The scientist simply measures again and sees more and more clearly a planet in peril, one already ominously exceeding life's limits across what leading environmental scientists have identified as nine key "planetary boundaries".[7]

This book focuses on the one area that, broadly construed, almost all oppositional forces agree is the *sine qua non* for any possible salvific response: *education*. Education comprises a highly ambivalent set of practices in this connection: everything from servicing capital accumulation as additive "human capital" to providing a potential seedbed for real resistance against the same. Temporally, it is both a lagging and leading indicator, by its very nature showing us both past and future. Much that it accomplishes merely reproduces the existing social order while at the same time it also provides sites for the development of the inevitably altered rising generations. Further, it functions at both the smallest scale of personal experience - from gestalt "aha!" moments to (reported) individual spiritual awakenings - while it also scales up as a sociologically larger phenomenon having to do with mass government schooling, public awareness campaigns, policies having to do with the societal flow of information, and the like. Education exists both formally in schools, workplaces and other institutions yet also informally in group and intimate settings and in an almost infinite variety of popular media - all of the above instantiating education in its widest anthropological sense as the transmission of culture. Of course it also goes beyond transmission in a static sense as well. The very act of transmission often generates novelty, as what is learned has its own appropriative autonomy. And education is also almost always - perhaps merely *always* - what sets the scene for innovation and discovery. It is among the largest and most varied human phenomena and the approaches to it are infinitely varied. There are "educational" aspects to everything. So some specificity is required in order to make meaningful claims.

Accordingly, a specific focus will be on education in one of its most formal and largest-scale aspects, namely, the enterprise of universal public education that has become a definitive component of the world's most developed economies. The qualifiers "universal" and "public" are of course perpetually contested and have both meant different things in different eras and different things to different parties in the same era. For example, there are always to be found unresolved but basic distributive questions about *who* exactly gets this education and similarly unresolved substantive questions concerning *what* precisely it is that "they" are to get. Be all that as it may, the shorthand term for this unwieldy grab bag of phenomena may be reduced accurately enough to "schooling": a selective formalization of ongoing educational practices. Schooling itself has been around a long, long time, perhaps in some form since the advent of the settled communities made possible by agriculture some 10,000 years ago. It obviously far predates capitalism. Its modern institutionalized form, however, arose along with the labor needs of nascent industrial capitalism, in the US things really took off with the rise of factory production in the nineteenth century. Though not alone, capitalists quite clearly and deliberately built the institution of schooling as we now know it - along with the ancillary legal framework of compulsory education that supports it. Although it contains plenty of its own internal peculiarities, schooling's structural core has always consisted of its economic functionality, including its service to the economic and political elites who typically coordinate that functionality. So nobody should become doe-eyed about any alleged golden era where schools were bastions of authentic learning and civic ideals. They have always been sites of both domination and, to at least some extent, resistance - now no less than in earlier times. Schools therefore provide an interesting and ultimately telling vantage point from which to observe the depredations of neoliberalism, as they function both as symptoms of those depredations yet also as staging areas from which resistances constantly arise, just as in the realm of production itself. It is in the nature of the thing to be both symptom and cause.

This traditionally dual aspect of schooling is also reflected in the more personal experiences of education that are possible. As the practices of teaching and learning, it reflects the range of human beings' moral capabilities and ambivalences. On the one hand we are causally determined playthings of larger forces who can do no other than as we do. But on the other hand, from within our own experience we ourselves *undergo* our lives as if we possess the personal capability to exercise our will. Spinoza says that free will is merely an illusion caused by ignorance of the causes of our actions.[8] That may be true. But still, it is also true that we nonetheless *feel* that we can act and probably are not capable of ridding ourselves of that experience, however finally illusory it may be, save perhaps in the extraordinary and fleeting epiphanies said to be achieved by the world's aesthetic and spiritual masters. As our illusions may surely damn us, it may well prove that suitably transformed they may save us too. This contradictory pedagogical "workshop where ideals are manufactured," to use Nietzsche's phrase, are thus an appropriate primary focus.[9] It matters how we see ourselves.

I offer little uplift, though, and certainly no Boy Scout techniques for sustaining our current activities. As a philosopher I am committed to the deepest intellectual pessimism, in Hegel's sense that if it flies at all, the Owl of Minerva alights only at dusk.[10] And after dusk is darkness.

Falling rates, instability, extraction

Neoliberalism deals eliminationist death in two interrelated modes:

1 *as a function of **internal** economic contradictions rooted in capitalist production*
2 *as a function of **external** environmental contradictions occasioned by capitalist production*

Current and future prospects for education must be understood as profoundly shaped by both of these phenomena. Educational practices and institutions have some ideological autonomy. But education at all levels currently labors under mercilessly severe constraints supplied by neoliberalism along these two axes that have become definitive of capitalism's current and so far most desperate phase.

First the internal economic contradictions. I will address two interrelated themes that are, I believe, driving contemporary events, including the recent economic crisis:

The first of these is identified by Karl Marx as the counterintuitive TRPF. Though typically hidden by an array of counter forces, the TRPF is the first of three root causes that I will discuss that all but guarantee late capitalism can only lurch from one crisis to the next, to such an extent that it should be understood that crisis is actually a "normal" part of today's capitalist system. There is no easy fix for the TRPF for, as I explain below, it is arises from within the very internal dynamics of capitalist production, namely the interplay of technology and labor in the form of productivity and in the long-term ability of rising productivity to generate the profits that fuel the entire system.

The TRPF had experienced its own falling rate of popularity, even among otherwise sympathetic thinkers such as David Harvey, until its recent resuscitation by prominent Marxist theorists such as the late Chris Harman, Guglielmo Carchedi, Alex Callinicos and Andrew Kliman.[11] Unusual for high Marxist theory, the TRPF and associated ideas also enjoy an able popularization in the compelling educational videos created by YouTube sensation Brendan Cooney as part of his *Kapitalism 101* project.[12] Through careful analysis of the relevant texts, especially the later volumes of *Capital*, as well as supplementary empirical work on the best available recent economic data in this very difficult area (see especially Kliman's analysis of relevant data on profitability), these theorists in the ensemble make a convincing case that since the 1970s, world capitalism has experienced an epochal change due largely to technological change and its effects upon productivity. As shall be explained below, via the TRPF, these productivity increases have generated a crisis of profitability first in manufacturing and later in other sectors. To be sure, as Marx himself immediately pointed out, there are many counter forces, to the extent that the counter forces become in some sense a larger story - neoliberalism itself being one such. And it is, in my view, undecidable as to the *precise* extent the TRPF drives events. Economics simply isn't that "hard" a science as it claims to be - let alone predictive - beyond a certain level of confidence. Some Marxist proponents of the TRPF err in fact in this scientistic direction. I have no stake in the "intestine wars" of Marxist economics and there is good reason to be as wary of Marxist sectarians as one should be of all sectarians because, by definition, they tend to end up valuing doctrinal purity over truth. As a cautious philosophical outsider, then, I will content myself with a weaker and more defensible claim than is advanced by some of the theory's proponents: the TRPF matters, and if it is not *the* reason capitalism is morphing into its death spiral neoliberal phase, it is surely *a* reason.

The TRPF along with its counter tendencies provides the best available general framework within political economy for making larger sense of this vast interplay of forces. While not always purely "wrong," leading popular explanations for the financial crisis are either inadequate on their face (e.g. personal character flaws that certain "greedy" bankers just happen to have) and/or they supply only proximal causes - they are correct as far as they go (e.g. widespread criminality and short-sighted deregulation in the financial sector) but they immediately beg larger questions. Why the myopic drive toward deregulation in the first place? Why was that perceived by elites as so necessary, in the US by both Republicans and Democrats, and in Europe by conservatives, labor/liberals and even many (nominal) socialists? Why despite ostensible ideological differences, such a united and zealous deregulatory front? Why was it so irresistible to move capital out of traditional productive sectors and into the financial casino? In the end, the TRPF fills a void of explanation and becomes indispensable for helping answer such larger questions. It needs supplementation, however, as I begin to describe in the next section. But it provides a core part of the reason why piecemeal reforms are inadequate to a problem that is rooted in the structural dynamics of capitalism itself. Like any good idea, though, if taken in isolation and pushed too far, it can become misleading. It must be integrated into a larger account and not treated as a magical explanatory pill.

At any rate, the TRPF has helped spawn what we now refer to as "neoliberalism": a catchword that signifies the ideological management of a set of phenomena that are symptomatic of the failure of "normal" productive capitalism to make a profit. Let me be clear on this: neoliberalism is an ideology, a *story* that is advanced - explicitly and also, more powerfully, implicitly as "common sense" - to justify the machinations of today's global capitalism. It is, as economist Andrew Kliman puts it, "the tail, not the dog that wags it."[13] If capitalism is the client, its new and spectacularly effective public relations firm (since the 1970s or so) is neoliberalism. It is a rebranding of capitalism, not unlike the ads unleashed to sell us on the idea that, say, post Gulf oil spill BP is really an environmentally conscious "energy" company that just happens to dabble in a bit of petroleum. In this sense, *neoliberalism does not actually exist*, in that economic realities such as the state-aided monopoly of capitals and the debt-servitude among the populace does not match the ideological fairy tale where worldwide liberty advances via rugged, self-made entrepreneurs, fairly winning their spoils in a free market through their ingenuity and hard work. This is just what is told to people to avoid the legitimation crisis that looms any time rational individuals get a glimpse of how fatally rigged the system is against them. Like legitimating "noble lies" from time immemorial, the neoliberal lie greatly helps both victims *and* perpetrators accept their respective roles in the mechanisms of domination.

Keeping its unreality as a justificatory fantasy firmly in mind, the four key symptomatic features of the era of the neoliberal lie are:

1 the globalization of labor and consumer markets under the banner of "free trade" and the like; and

2 the propping up of demand (and therefore profits) for those products through the massive playground pusher-like extension of consumer credit (viz., credit cards, autos, student loans and, most importantly, home mortgages /refinancing); and, consequently,

3 the mass migration of capital from production to finance and, within the latter sector, from old-style growth-oriented *investment* in actual businesses that create saleable commodities to the quicker and easier money within the highly leveraged phantasmagoria of speculative finance (including the proliferation of hedging and derivatives schemes) in the casino that now becomes the center of world capitalism; and, as an effect of the degenerate gambler's short-sighted rapaciousness,

4 an increased adventurism toward accumulation by dispossession as stressed elites seek to marketize, financialize and finally burglarize erstwhile public resources such as criminal justice, health care and education systems that must be dragooned into providing the liquidity insatiably needed by the "too big to fail" to cover their old bets and further leverage their new ones. The titans of finance are at this point, literally, gambling thieves. Complementing this *domestic* adventurism aimed at taking over unsuspecting schools is a continuation of more or less old-fashioned *imperial* military adventurism. This too feeds the gamblers' permanent addiction by securing perpetually outsized war

profits while creating lucrative disciplinary grids against resistance, as attested by heightened...surveillance (e.g., as revealed by whistleblower Edward Snowden about the US National Security Agency) and ridiculously overwrought "tactical"-style police gear now regularly deployed against peaceful protesters.

What Marx's theory of the TRPF offers is a key component of a deeper structural analysis of these neoliberal developments, an analysis not content with an emotive condemnation of personal "greed" and the like that so often poses as *the* explanation. Yes, the bankers are greedy and the regulators corrupt. Lots of them anyway. But decrying such individuals would be, as they say, like handing out speeding tickets at the Indianapolis 500. *They speed because they have to*. In the ensemble, any group of human beings will always possess an abundance of good and bad qualities across the full spectrum of human capabilities. For present purposes, what needs explaining is not the existence of those behaviors but why we have built institutional traps for ourselves that emphasize certain of those behaviors and not others. The perspective provided by the TRPF helps satisfy this acute diagnostic need.

My specific focus on educational institutions supplies a case in point. In sum, because of these changes in capitalist production occurring over the last several generations, we have moved roughly from an era in which the predominant telos of worker subordination involved *exploitation*, i.e. as per Marx, the extraction of abstract labor value pursuant to capital accumulation and capitalist profit. From the capitalist's point of view, in the best case there existed a "surplus army" of workers whose existence would help ensure that labor market competition was kept internecine among the workers (i.e. worker vs. worker) rather than amongst the capitalists themselves *for* workers (capitalist vs. capitalist). In the former scenario, wages tend to fall and in the latter they tend to rise. The traditional capitalist, of course, wants wages to fall in order to maximize workers' exploitation and hence, ultimately, profits. It is in short all about worker exploitation. In capitalism's neoliberal phase, however, the "more is better" mania for exploitation is replaced by a technologized "less is better" mania for eliminating labor costs. Both tendencies have certainly always been present in capitalist production, but the overwhelming contemporary drive toward automation signals the decisive ascendency of the sentiment that wants to eliminate human beings from the production process. They are merely "costs" to be overcome via the latest technology or, in the second best scenario, outsourced overseas to far cheaper labor. At this point, one should be so lucky as to be exploited.

This economic eliminationism sets the stage for the eliminationism we are now seeing in education. In the industrialized world, public discourse on education has always had its economistic side but once upon a time the discussions also appear to have at least been tinged with larger concerns of a civic and moral nature. Of late, however, education policies are almost always justified by virtue of their economic utility alone, especially in the US and the increasingly Gradgrindian UK. We should fund X because it is an "investment" in our future; we need Y because businesses require it; we need Z so we can keep up with the global competition. Educators have usually been happy to play along with this mode of justification because, well, it worked to make it rain resources. For a time. But: live by the sword, die by the sword. For what if, instead of businesses needing to see X, Y and Z in their workers, it turned out that they wanted to see - domestically at least - drastically fewer of them? What if, instead of criticizing schools for not producing workers with enough X, they started criticizing schools for their very existence? This, I contend, is exactly what is happening. Eliminationism in the economy is quite predictably morphing into eliminationism in what was once, in the good old days of

28

exploitation, the primary conveyor belt for supplying human capital: the public school system. A situation in which there is a surfeit of workers becomes one in which there is a surfeit of students, who in turn are well on their way to becoming part of the surfeit of humanity logically slated for elimination.

No longer possessive of much exploitability, these are the people seen purely as costs, redundancies, superfluous, "extra" people, regrettable instances of systemic waste and excess. As I shall discuss in the next chapter, the best place to see these coal mine canaries is in the "planet of slums" overtaking the developing world in places like Kinshasa where almost everyone there exists outside the "normal" economy and subsists ever more desperately. Closer to home, large swaths of African-American youth in such inner cities as the Baltimore depicted on HBO's *The Wire* provide domestic examples of individuals caught in the grips of a savage proto-eliminationism. For many of these no-longer-exploitables, family life and schooling have effectively ended, and the method of elimination for them is to be tracked via the sinister "drug war" into the largest carceral network in the world, one that has grown by 500% in the last thirty years and now holds more black men than were antebellum slaves.[14]

Supplementary to Marx's theory of the TRPF is a second root cause of capitalist financial crisis identified a generation ago by American economist Hyman Minsky and later refined by Australian economist Steve Keen (one of the very few to have predicted the US housing crash). Influenced by Marx yet also departing from him, Minsky defends a "financial instability hypothesis" in which modern hyper-financialized capitalism's tendency toward instability and crisis is due to *"upward"* forces, namely, the behavior of an elite speculative behavior - the 1%, if you will, or perhaps more accurately, the 0.1%. *Pace* Marx, for a variety of factors, it has turned out that it is not so much the working classes that are positioned to precipitate a terminal economic crisis and are destined then to seize historical agency and destroy capitalism. Sometimes the good guys don't win. Instead of the essentially downward instability predicted by Marx ("downward" in the sociological sense of the economic ladder) it is instead an *upward* turbulence ironically generated by elites themselves that is the proximal cause of contemporary economic instability and is thus one of the primary threats to capitalism.[15] In an interconnected speculative environment that allows high levels of leverage-based risk taking (*ex hypothesi* that deregulatory environment having been created by dearth of profitable opportunities in productive sectors), elites can be counted on simply to go too far - especially when government backstops allow them to utilize public wealth in order to hedge their bets, in effect to gamble with the house's money. Former US Assistant Secretary of the Treasury for Economic Policy Paul Craig Roberts summarizes this rigged game:

It is ironic that the outcome of financial deregulation in the US is the opposite of what its free market advocates promised. In place of highly competitive financial firms that live or die by their wits alone without government intervention, we have unprecedented financial concentration. Massive banks, "too big to fail," now send their multi-trillion dollar losses to Washington to be paid by heavily indebted US taxpayers whose real incomes have not risen in 20 years. The banksters take home fortunes in annual bonuses for their success in socializing the "free market" banks' losses and privatizing profits to the point of not even paying income taxes." Roberts then asks, "Will the disastrous consequences discredit capitalism to the extent that the Soviet collapse discredited socialism?"[16]

Given the global interconnectedness of the financial system, this increasingly top heavy speculative behavior causes both an intensifying cycle of crises in which, in a three steps forward two steps backward manner, an increase in the overall amount of debt, as the deleveraging that occurs during the crises never resets all the way back down to zero. Massive - and, really, unimaginable - debt accumulation thereby becomes the shadow twin of capital accumulation. This debt is simply unpayable. All the "austerity" in the world will not repay losses from the 2008 financial crisis that the Bank of England estimates to be between $60 *trillion* and $200 *trillion*.[17]

The Minsky financial instability hypothesis proceeds from the inherently cyclical boom-bust nature of capitalist economies, where capital expands and contracts in an almost respiratory manner (as Smith, Marx and others saw from the beginning). For Minsky, however, the analogy stops there. For among elite money managers there are interesting goings on of a psychological nature during these swings. During the growth or boom part of the cycle, especially as memories of any previous serious downturn fades (such as the Great Depression of the 1930s), investors tend to experience success in venture after venture and come to see themselves as immune to any downturn, their confidence only increasing as they go from triumph to triumph in what Minsky called a "euphoric boom economy."[18] This is essentially equivalent what even former Federal Reserve Chairman Alan Greenspan famously termed "irrational exuberance."[19] In this environment, the customary psychological hedge of risk aversion may vanish to an almost zero point, as investment bankers note that the more leveraged ventures are the ones that have been making the most money; simply put, in this euphoric environment, more leverage means more profits. Cautious investors are seen to be punished by the market, if not literally by stockholders demanding ever higher returns like "the other guys" are enjoying. This collective experience sends the overall amount of leverage in the system skyward. This mentality extends to average consumers as well, who come to feel as if asset inflation is a law of nature, one conveniently designed to reward them - as if they were all little landed lords collecting rents - for the mere fact of ownership. Never mind that all the while it is the bank holding the actual mortgage lever. (I remember being told by a mortgage loan officer during the housing boom of the 2000s that the main mistake borrowers make is "not getting enough house.") In sum, this boom period creates a general financial climate of ever-greater risk taking, where "ownership" becomes a mere means toward collecting one's ordained high rate of return.

Previous safeguards against what seem by now to be ancient and irrelevant market downturns are ignored or overturned - on the largest scale such as the US New Deal era's Glass-Steagall Act (The Banking Act of 1933), which separated consumer and investment banking in the wake of the Great Depression and was designed to prohibit banks from speculating with their depositors' money. All this leverage and lessening of risk aversion then sets the stage for a harbinger of financial doom that Minsky calls the Ponzi financier, who meets his current cash liabilities by increasing his amount of debt outstanding (so new creditors pay back current ones), in a trajectory of perpetually augmenting liabilities. The Ponzi financier is crucial because he creates a situation even beyond the casino-style speculator where assets and liabilities no longer match up in a one-to-one correspondence; *per impossibile*, as a result there is actually more overall debt in the system than there are covering assets. There is no "other side" there to cover investors' losses when the Ponzi strategy inevitably comes crashing down of its own inverted pyramidal weight. When this kind of thing happens on a large enough scale, as in 2008, where various Ponzi-like hedging, insurance, and derivative schemes went awry - via a vast armada of obfuscatory financial instruments that nobody really fully understands - the entire global capitalist system is placed under threat. The system is so, literally, top heavy with inequality and leverage that it threatens to topple of its own weight at any moment.

Depressingly, as Minsky saw, the cycle of upward financial instability into which we now appear locked creates a situation in which it is darkest not just immediately *before* dawn but right in the middle of the day: any inkling of a salutary boom or boomlet gears up the whole euphoric leverage machine once again, with consequences that bring great devastation the next time. The 1987 stock market crash becomes the 2000 dotcom crash which becomes the 2008 housing crash which will become, presumably, even worse without urgent corrective action, of which there appears to have been very little. According to Minsky, the only thing we can count on is that there *will* be a next crash and it *will* be still worse than the preceding one. For the Minskian Keen, the only saving move is the radical one of what he calls a "modern jubilee," where debts are forgiven and savers are awarded cash in order to minimize the moral hazard of pre-jubilee savers being effectively penalized as their holdings are liquidated when borrowers' debts are canceled. Jubilee policies are of course highly improbable - for now - but the intensity of an anticipated and even more acute economic crisis might well change some minds.[20] The alternative is chronic stagnation if not outright collapse and, most significantly for present purposes, a continuation of the eliminationist program.

What might be the educational correlates of this frightening upward financial instability phenomenon? Education mirrors this economic system in which the rich have grown richer and moreover have increasingly insulated themselves against the rest of the population via a geographical stratification where they inhabit a very few US counties in Manhattan, Silicon Valley and a handful of others. As such, public schooling is not really a direct problem for them because of their location and because of their financial ability to opt out of the public system altogether via expensive private schools. However, the influence of this top heavy group is felt less directly, though powerfully, in several areas. First among these are the proliferating schemes to suck wealth upward from what were once public institutions like schools into private hands in order to make them available for speculation. Schools are to be drained of resources and then restructured to function more fully as "extractive institutions," to use the provocative phrase from political scientists Daron Acemoglu and James Robinson's influential study of elite rapaciousness, *Why Nations Fail* (2011): "Extractive political institutions concentrate power in the hands of a narrow elite and place few constraints on the exercise of this power. Economic institutions are then often structured by this elite to extract resources from the rest of society."[21]

A favored long-term extractive strategy is accumulation by dispossession via the strategy of privatizing schools in various ways. The championing of school voucher schemes (and precursor "charter" schools), where public money is doled out so that parent-consumers can make school "choices" among, ultimately, private providers, is a prominent policy initiative along these lines. This accords quite nicely with the casino mentality of the too big to fail banks: take educational risks not only with other peoples' children but with public money as well. A second best strategy in the US is to champion so-called "charter schools," which are public only in the sense that they are government funded but they are exempt from many state regulations. The ideology here is that such hybrid schools will demonstrate the wonders of educational competition where the invisible hand will then guide everyone closer to educational success. In the spirit of "follow the money" detective work, the telos of these operations is to funnel money into private and ultimately for-profit hands. Like social security and the prison system, the school system is too big a potential treasure house for the money funnels of the great investment houses to ignore. The money will flow upward and there will be that much more to play with.

A second set of strategies involves student loans in the lucrative higher education sector. This is no small scale operation, having recently passed the landmark $1 trillion mark, making US student loan liabilities total more than consumer credit cards *and* auto loans. This market is even more directly tied to the financiers than the K-12 privatization schemes, especially given the growing segment of that market governed by private as opposed to government loans. However, again, just as in the case of the too big to fail banks, the "private" nature of these student loan creditors is rather illusory given that they are either government-backed in case of borrower default and/or non-dischargeable for borrowers in bankruptcy. What this phenomenon shares with upward financial stability are its bubble-like characteristics: the overhyped rhetoric and hyperbolic claims about the coming age of "knowledge workers," "symbolic analysts etc., the outsized expectations for the remuneration associated with the personal "investment" in college, and the credential inflation that fails to keep pace with any actual underlying societal economic needs and where a decreasing amount of formal learning is taking place. Surveying a half century of data, for example, economists Philip Babcock and Mindy Marks report broad based declines in the amount of studying done by full-time US college students, from 40 hours/week in 1961 to just 27 hours/week by 2003.[22] My own experience as a college instructor leads me to feel safe in assuming that since then study rates have remained low or are falling. What to make of such a severely inflationary situation where students are paying more but getting less in every respect? Specifically targeting the rising generation, this sad situation is the subject of Chapter 4.

Finally, there is the rise of what has been termed "venture philanthropy," as exemplified by initiatives such as the Bill and Melinda Gates Foundation, the Broad Foundation and Facebook founder Mark Zuckerberg's $100 million "gift" to the Newark, New Jersey public school system. These lordly dispensations have an inevitably coercive element because they are carrots offered amidst the sticks of chronic and, in more and more cases, emergency levels of underfunding by states and localities of public schools, especially those in poor urban minority areas. The premise of venture philanthropy in education is that public education policy is not to be seen as a matter of public deliberation among ordinary citizens but rather should be directed by the mega-rich, who are presumed to be experts not just in Microsoft and Facebook but in all policy matters, merely on the grounds that they are rich. Wealth is its own justification. Education scholar Kevin Kumashiro further explains:

> Unlike traditional philanthropy, which sought, at least in principle, to "give back" to society, venture philanthropy parallels venture capitalism in its goal of investing capital in ways that earn more. In contrast to venture capitalism, one benefit of venture philanthropy is that it operates under different incorporation laws, providing tax shelters for what are really financial investments. Whereas the financial returns may not be as immediate as those of corporate transactions, the policy foci of today's venture philanthropists indeed reveal the economic incentive of their investments. They overwhelmingly are pushing for the privatization of public education, creating new markets worth hundreds of billions of dollars, as well as for the prerogative to direct how public tax dollars get spent. They target the large urban school districts, experimenting with models they hope eventually to "scale up" nationally, as they have done in Chicago, where the Gates Foundation alone has spent millions on small-school initiatives, school turnarounds, youth organizing, and parent organizing.[23]

Though there are some outliers, predictably, these initiatives tend always to amount to pushing some corporate structure as panacea , including efforts to make over school leaders into CEO-like "managers," provide various Pavlovian material "incentives" for teachers to "add value" to their student-products, "empower" parents to act more like "customers," and the like. The Obama Administration has jumped into the ring and offered its own version of this kind of thing with its "Race to the Top" initiative, whereby cash-starved schools are thrown money in exchange for further corporate style reforms, with an emphasis on those pretending that standardized test scores can stand in as sales numbers or whatever other quantitative measures of productivity are said to be analogous in the hallowed and infallible business world. As a result, as Kumashiro summarizes, the "result is a philanthropic sector that is inseparable from the business sector, advancing school reforms that cannot help but to be framed by corporate profitability."[24] We can fully expect that these corporate reforms will accomplish for American education what JP Morgan Chase, Goldman Sachs and AIG have for the American economy, which is to say they will suck it dry of resources, pocket the proceeds and then stand back as the whole thing crashes and burns.

Educational externalities

The second set of neoliberal calamities is to be found in capitalism's often unacknowledged externalities. These include both what one might call the "upstream" externalities that are necessary for the system's performance, in other words, its required *inputs*, and also the "downstream" externalities that result from the system's operations, its *outputs*. These are both externalities in the sense that they are widely (and mistakenly) thought to be outside the ambit of economic activity proper.

Absent government regulation, the capitalist's power plant smokestack spews, say, mercury into the air that drifts off into the surrounding area and goes on to have whatever poisoning effects. Yet absent some sinister covert plot, the mercury (or greenhouse gasses or whatever) is merely a *byproduct* of the coal-burning plant's production of the commodity of electricity, rather than that production's intended goal. In this example, the mercury output constitutes a downstream externality vis-à-vis the power company. There are also of course the inputs. The resources going into the plant, in this case, say, coal and/or natural gas, water etc., are typically considered only in their aspect as commodities themselves, i.e. how they in turn factor into the costs of production and ultimately profitability and so on. It is assumed that resource inputs necessary to maintain operations in general will always be around in some form and that there is no inherent scarcity that cannot be dealt with by the simple laws of supply and demand: the market will find the proper price and discipline resource use appropriately.

Thus understood, any form of productive activity, as it requires both inputs and outputs, can be said to generate both upstream and downstream externalities. Yet the narrow focus of traditional economic models considers only the latter, and then only as potential short-term costs. This comes at the expense of a larger contextual understanding that would include upstream externalities and also long-term externalities across the whole range of spheres of human activity, including where those effects' economic characteristics might be neither direct nor easily observable nor especially prominent at the moment of production. For example a rare aquatic species might be jeopardized by the power plant or some mercury-induced form of cancer might arise in surrounding populations, but only decades later.

This myopia concerning both types of externalities may prove capitalism's real undoing. Marx certainly did not ignore environmental aspects of production and described the relation between humanity and nature as "metabolic" in the sense of their mutualism and their co-creation of one another. But catastrophically debilitating environmental effects and, especially, the finite nature of currently indispensable resources like liquid fossil fuels are not a primary focus. Since just after Marx's time, capitalism has enjoyed a bonanza of what might be the world's most astonishing upstream externality: cheap fossil fuel energy, mostly in the form of oil and gas. Oil and gas provide an extremely richly concentrated, versatile, efficient and consistent source of energy that is not remotely yet matched by renewables such as biofuels, wind or solar, or even nuclear (which obviously has other externality problems). They provide the *sine qua non* of both industrialism and globalization. But these are finite resources and they will not last. "Peak oil" is a controversial idea because some equate it with a sudden running out of oil and hence a rapid and spectacular collapse of contemporary civilization. But all it signifies is the unimpeachable reality that at a certain point finite oil reserves will reach their peak and then it is all downhill as far as oil's existence for our use. There should be no controversy about this; peak oil is a certainty. Increasing global usage of a nonrenewable energy source logically entails it. The controversial part is the timing. Has it already occurred? If not when will it? Will the down side of the slope be steep and precipitous or smooth and gradual - or some hybrid, such as stepwise? These essential questions are strangely missing from "serious" public discussion.

Just a moment's glance at modern lifestyles is enough to appreciate what is at stake here. Living without cheap fossil fuel is obviously possible (human beings did it until a few hundred years ago) but it is no longer something most of us in the industrialized world can even really contemplate. Unless one lives wholly self-sufficiently and sustainably (a negligible percentage of the population), just about all of one's activities are based upon fossil fuels: almost all the food we eat depends on petroleum-based fertilizer, mechanized agriculture and gas-driven transport, our water depends on the same in terms of motorized public works and even most of those with wells require electric pumps. Electricity, it should be remembered, is created in power plants that burn fossil fuels, mostly coal and natural gas. Our jobs and transportation systems are obviously petroleum-based. So are all of our modern institutions, including schools, prisons, hospitals, police and the military. Without this energy input, and even with it in a compromised and/or substantially more expensive form, modern life would be unthinkable. But it is running out and it is only a matter of time. The same can be said in mitigated form of other indispensable resources whose easy abundance can no longer be assumed, such as unsullied fresh and ocean water, usable topsoil and certain minerals needed (and not merely optional) for agriculture.

For the present analysis, the point is that neither capitalism nor even, really, its historical critics, have made the reality of the finitude of relevant natural resources central enough to their worldviews. This is, I think, the ultimate externality problem in both its upstream and downstream aspects. Upstream, the models created in classical economics have assumed the infinite availability of energy and other natural resource inputs. Downstream, the potentially catastrophic effects of running out (or effectively running out, for example, when the costs of extraction become too high) are nowhere factored in; these are other peoples' problems, and future others at that. This standard corporate attitude of deliberate indifference to these larger questions is simply unacceptable. We have come to grasp the externalities question with regard to obvious pollutants and it is now time *quickly* to extend that understanding to the question of the scarcity of key natural resources - if it is not already too late.

Would that resource depletion were the only large environmental externality problem. But there is still pollution and other forms of industrial toxicity along with *their* byproduct, perhaps the most fearsome and intractable externality of them all: climate change. For libertarian ideologues and capitalist apologists, this problem cannot possibly exist. It seems too grim a twist on the old invisible hand story, allegedly providing only salutary effects. This time, however, the invisible hand represents the deleterious ensemble of CO_2 emissions resulting from the aggregation of our individual economic choices. And yes, regimes carrying the label "socialism" have had significant emissions-related problems, too, to wit, Chernobyl in the twilight years of the former Soviet Union. By general agreement, though, capitalism is far more productive and therefore proportionately presents by far the largest danger. Yet, please excuse the pun, climate change presents an almost perfect storm of difficulty as far as our ability to address it. As behavioral economist Dan Ariely argues, the problem of climate change seems almost "designed" to depress human motivation toward addressing it. It occurs (so far) relatively gradually, it is not (yet) perceived to be effecting us directly, there is just enough cultural noise from corporate media outlets to cast sufficient doubt in the minds of "low information" types and, as Ariely suggests, the relevant issues are so complex that they discourage the conviction that one can mount a meaningful personal response; everything one might do seems to be a mere "drop in the bucket."[25] Add to the equation that those on the other side of the issue, the climate change deniers, are often intensely motivated (by ideology and money), and we have a recipe for almost certain inaction.

Meanwhile, just as with many of the resource depletion problems, the frog in the cooking pot is not noticing as the water temperature rises around it.

The larger point is that capitalism as presently constituted may be unable to handle these kinds of environmental externalities, owing to the deliberately-produced ideological fog surrounding them and their relatively long time horizons. This concern is pointedly articulated by investment analyst Jeremy Grantham of GMO Enterprises. For Grantham, "the current US capitalist system appears to contain some potentially fatal flaws."[26] These he identifies as roughly the above two types of externalities I have discussed thus far: climate change and resource depletion. With regard to the latter, emphasizing topsoil problems, he writes:

> Damage to the "commons," known as "externalities" has been discussed for decades, although the most threatening one - loss of our collective ability to feed ourselves, through erosion and fertilizer depletion - has received little or no attention. There have been no useful tricks proposed, however, for how we will collectively impose sensible, survivable, long-term policies over problems of the "commons." To leave it to capitalism to get us out of this fix by maximizing its short-term profits is dangerously naïve and misses the point: capitalism and corporations have absolutely no mechanism for dealing with these problems, and seen through a corporate discount rate lens, our grandchildren really do have no value.[27]

He concludes that capitalism's necessary fixation on short-term growth at all costs - literally *all costs* - presents its greatest Achilles heel. Present trends - which are accelerating, especially as China, India and others come online - concerning both resource depletion and climate change are bleak. Above all else, then, the neoliberal endgame appears to involve an energetic and almost completely heedless destruction of the biospheric preconditions of human existence. This is why the imagery of mass death is neither hyperbolic nor hysterical but appropriately reflective of a sober extrapolation from present trends. "Capitalism, by ignoring the finite nature of resources and by neglecting the long-term well-being of the planet and its potentially crucial biodiversity, threatens our existence ... My conclusion is that capitalism does admittedly do a thousand things better than other systems: it only currently fails in two or three. Unfortunately for us all, even a single one of these failings may bring capitalism down and us with it."[28] This is from an enlightened lifelong *champion* of the system, from within its very center.

How does education stand regarding these grave matters? The question admits of different approaches.

First there is the question of *institutional form*, a.k.a. the question of schooling. Resource depletion has enormous ramifications across the board and it is important to begin engaging in something like scenario planning as the effects of various resource peaks begin to be felt. For starters, something like a rudimentary counterfactual exercise might make sense. Take peak oil. What would the US school system look like under different peak oil scenarios? Let's take a moderate forecast, one in which there is no short- or medium-term "running out" of oil but where the next decade or two see huge price rises that are a function of increasing scarcity, speculation and diminishing "energy return on investment" (EROI), sometimes simply called "net energy." EROI is a crucial but often neglected concept reflecting the distinction between the simple presence of, say, oil of whatever grade and what the cost might be of extracting it, refining it, and otherwise making it usable. There is much excitement about shale deposits and tar sands, for example, and there is certainly oil there. But it is of a lower grade and far more expensive to reach (not to mention far dirtier and therefore climate destructive), to the extent that in some scenarios it would not be worth it in terms of energy and financial input even to bother. If it takes more energy to extract the oil than the oil itself provides, in other words, if the EROI falls below zero, it would make no sense to proceed. (An analogous point applies to the economics of energy extraction; if the extraction costs more to accomplish than it would generate in profits it is not financially rational to continue, any more than it makes financial sense for a farmer to grow crops that sell for less than it takes to produce them.) Bearing such considerations in mind, then, it is important to understand that "peak oil" is a much more multifaceted concept than simply the sheer quantity of oil left in the ground. It represents the possibility of a hard economic limit as much as anything else. It would therefore be advisable for scenario planning, which should of course involve an assessment of the most basic necessary physical resources, to factor EROI into forecasts for the drastically worsening economic constraints upon an already highly stressed public school system.

Like much else upon which we depend, the current US public school system makes sense only under the conditions of cheap energy, the gargantuan energy windfall that has made industrial capitalism possible in the first place. This is so clearly the case that it would seem appropriate to describe the currently predominant arrangement as *petroschooling*.

Let us take some of our system's most obvious features in this regard. First are the historically consolidated factory style schools that we have come to favor due to their economically efficient batch processing of relatively large numbers of students. As distinct as they could be from their largely non-age-graded one room schoolhouses that were much smaller and per capita far more numerous, a typical American high school enrolls thousands of pupils because it is able to draw from a geographically wide catchment area. Especially in rural areas, the school itself may be many, many miles from most of the students who attend it. As a result, a gigantic transportation system has developed in support, and there is no icon more instantly recognizable in America than the yellow school bus that that has been making its rounds here for generations. Among many other things, this transport system makes compulsory education possible, as because of it even the poorest and busiest parents lack the excuse that they cannot get their children to school. It also underwrites the entire extracurricular life of the school and the culture built up for generations around that in America: inter-school competitive athletics and other activities, for example.

All of this is possible because the costs of providing free and convenient transport to all students is regarded as economically feasible and a good return on investment, given durable (perhaps until now) education policy goals having to do with universal education. But what if, as per the peak oil and diminishing EROI type of scenario sketched above, vehicle gas prices rose, say, five- or ten-fold? At current prices (2013) this would mean a five- to ten-fold rise (from ca. $4.00/gallon to $20-$40/gallon). Would US school districts be able to afford this? Would bus transport still seem like such a winning investment? It is hard to imagine that it would. One would then have to factor in the costs of staff getting to work as well. And the situation would be greatly compounded when one considers the climate control (HVAC) costs for these large buildings as well, especially in certain geographical regions, considering that many of these large schools were built under the standard assumption of cheap energy, e.g. a multi-storied school building in south Florida which would need to be cooled not just for comfort but to be habitable. All this is worthy of more detailed research, but even the tip of the iceberg of such considerations is sufficient to accentuate the present point: the material infrastructure that makes possible our current school system rests, like so much else, on the alarmingly precarious basis of cheap and abundant fossil fuels. One does not have to be much of a "futurist" to see how this could easily go very, very wrong. At the very least, the paradigm of what I am calling petroschooling might be in for some severe shocks where we might have to rethink what makes sense in terms of the physical arrangement of schools. Maybe homeschooling becomes more attractive. Or a return to more numerous but walkable/bikeable small schoolhouses. More dramatically, might face to face rural education largely be given up upon so that public schooling becomes more of an urban affair? And how would that reshape the American social and physical landscape? Questions upon questions.

Obviously, whatever its particularities would actually happen to be, this kind of shift would be sure to have huge ramifications for American society as a whole, let alone just education policy. This is an enormously complex set of changes about which to speculate and a useful analysis would require intense and thorough multidisciplinary study. But very few are even close to considering all this. We prefer to proceed under current assumptions. It is easier for the moment and requires less thought. Unfortunately, education reform's traditional pattern of muddling through and "tinkering" may not be adequate to future constraints dictated by our vanishing energy resource base.

An even scarier thought begins with the recognition that the last century's fossil fuel bonanza was a necessary condition for the past century's momentous gains in universal education (just as this same energy windfall may have been a necessary condition for industrial capitalism itself). This is true both directly, in the above sense of the net energy inputs necessary to efficiently get children to the new consolidated and hence farther-distant schools, but also indirectly in the sense that powerful energy inputs around, especially, mechanizing agriculture, reduced farm labor needs such that kids could be sent away during the day to learn. (The American system retains vestiges of this previous era in its antiquated school calendar that still allows for two to three month summer "vacations.") From the point of view of extending public education, this freeing of agriculturally laboring children was no trivial matter. In 1910 the population share of rural America was 72%, most of whom also *worked* in their local areas (especially farms), whereas today the rural population stands at just 16%.[29] Liberating these farm families from ancient human labor needs made universal education possible. In 1900 only 6.4% of American kids graduated from high school. By 1960 that number had grown to 60%, peaking at around 80% a decade later.[30] This revolution in secondary school attendance was made possible by the productive efficiencies wrought by cheap fossil fuel. These efficiencies were realized in the technologies that then came online to exploit the energy windfall: from affordable tractors and petroleum-based fertilizers to vast government projects such as New Deal rural electrification and the extension of telephone service. The current structure of mass schooling in the US is unthinkable apart from its mutualism with cheap fuel.

From the point of view of public education, the disquieting thought thus occasioned is that the literacy gains achieved during this 6%-to-80% explosion of universal education was an exercise in plucking most all of what economist Tyler Cowen refers to as "low hanging fruit."[31] As this metaphor suggests, once the easy gains are achieved, further educational fruits are available (e.g. greater amounts of higher education) but they are increasingly difficult to obtain and require higher expenditures of resources; the returns start to diminish. One imagines a plateau regarding the economic yield brought about by the achievement of universal literacy and the like. As Cowen notes, taking "a smart, motivated person out of an isolated environment and sending that person to high school will bring big productivity gains."[32] The trouble is that once those initial large productivity gains have been reaped, the return on the human capital investment levels off, perhaps to the point of unfeasibility. Ironically, while technological development made universal basic education possible, those same technological developments and consequent productivity increases render further education for the masses mostly a waste.

Sure there is an ongoing need for a small percentage of the population to reap the spoils accruing to those with the technical background to run the machines. Such people do well. As the machines get better, however, by definition even a smaller percentage of the machine-maintainers are ultimately needed. This level of expensive educational investment simply does not "pay" with regard to most people, because more and more of us are not exactly *needed* for much of anything. No longer needed as workers, the domestic masses are needed as open mouths into which to force feed as much consumption as possible, an irrational strategy that purchases short-term overconsumption at the price of long-term underconsumption (due to the inevitable ensuing debt overload) and hence is defeating of its very purpose. Domestically at least, neoliberalism really needs consumers and otherwise neutralized types (e.g. the incarcerated) rather than the industrial era of capitalism's skilled and semi-skilled labor. For the dirty little secret of the high tech economy is that, despite incessant boosterism to the contrary, it does not need *widespread* technical competence; most jobs in the high tech environment demand stultifying activities that require nothing beyond basic literacy - if that. The "cashier" at the high tech fast-food restaurant no longer needs to figure anyone's change, as was the case for yesteryear's cashiers using the earlier, lower tech machines. She doesn't even need the skill and minimal mental wherewithal to fill drinks properly: all she has to do is push the small, medium or large icons on the soda machine. For every "high tech, high wage" worker enjoying a cool workplace at google.com, there are many, many more who are "enjoying" the inverse proportion between high tech and their job demands: the higher the tech, the dumber the worker can be and, ultimately, in the best case neoliberal scenario, phased out altogether where possible (via outsourcing and/or further automation). Just like the industrial age factories of yore (and in today's developing world), the labor is almost purely de-skilled and reduced to simple timing and motility. Such people - the lucky ones who have even *those* jobs - merely need behavioral training and not education in any substantive sense.

Educationally, it has been a long run but it is finally over for them. They can now expect to revert to their traditional status as a kind of non-waged and economically precarious peasantry and/or imperial military fodder. The future to which they can look forward is comprised of a carceral circuit of police state schooling, poverty-level ad hoc jobs that are radically un-steady, military service in any one of our perpetual wars (one cannot predict *which* war only that there will *be* war), and consequently a life shorn of all the basic cultural elements of what was once considered a "decent" life, such as stable family units - let alone the American dream. The chaotic recent unrest in capitals such as London and Paris offer a glimpse of the future public life of this element that Marx called the *"lumpenproletariat,"* i.e. those who find themselves outside the loop of "normal" capitalist wage labor. As will be discussed in later chapters, these unexploitables are already a massive presence globally in our growing "planet of slums" and they are rising, ineluctably, here at home as well. There is nothing to romanticize here, no place to look for "inspiring" stories of "slum dog millionaires" "against the odds" that can warm and reassure the bourgeois heart that "life goes on" despite all. (One just needs to be plucky and clever!) It is an intolerable human tragedy writ large.

Despite the epochal evil they have wrought in these regards, one should never make the mistake of giving elites too much credit for planning and foresight. A central theme of this book is how resource depletion - the "limits to growth" - may reshuffle *everyone's* deck. It is even possible that such phenomena as peak oil, whose predominant effect in the coming decades is likely to be rising energy costs rather than a simple running out of anything, may bring back the need for higher quantities of good old-fashioned manual labor right here at home.

For the moment, though, because of the technological productivity heights it has now reached, capitalism simply no longer needs as many workers, particularly of the expensive North American or European kind. Absent countervailing vestigial cultural forces, it is predictably therefore likely to care proportionately less about yesteryear's costly enterprise of mass schooling whose economic rationale always did lie in the upstream externality it provides to commerce and industry in the form of skilled labor. However, as per the general TRPF hypothesis, as profits dry up long-term due to the decreasing labor component of production, and as fossil fuels simultaneously grow scarcer and more costly, any imagined post-petroleum capitalist elite stands to discover that in fact they need other human beings after all. The scary thought is that it may be too late by then. If social unrest due to economic turmoil doesn't do it, the apparently inexorable downstream externalities of climate change and resource depletion may propel events beyond anyone's control. Current systems of social control may not even function. Under "collapse" conditions, the project of universal education may seem quite the quaint relic of more innocent times.

A second set of educational considerations has to do with much more general *pedagogical* question of the desirability of and prospects for altering human self-understanding toward repairing what Marx called the "irreparable ... metabolic rift" we have created between ourselves and our environment that industrial capitalism, beginning with mechanized agriculture, has greatly widened. Marx has often been mischaracterized in this area, largely due to distortions during the Soviet era after Stalin's ascendancy. As John Bellamy Foster shows, Marx is actually clear and prescient on this point, developing a kind of "interactionism" between human beings and nature that was centrally concerned with long-term sustainability and future generations, especially with regard to modern agricultural practices and their impact upon soil fertility.[33] The point is that there is an enormous pedagogical challenge involved in repairing this metabolic rift toward a more defensible conception of the relation between human beings and nature, much of which involves understanding how our own (capitalist) social relations are implicated. As Foster puts it, "a potentially fatal ecological rift has arisen between human beings and the earth, emanating from conflicts and contradictions of the modern capitalist society. The planet is now dominated by a technologically potent but alienated humanity - alienated both from nature and itself; and hence ultimately destructive of everything around it. At issue is not just the sustainability of human society, but the diversity of life on Earth."[34]

But what would it take to overcome this monumental "alienation"? What would this even mean? The difficulty is that attempts to articulate "getting back to nature" and the like quickly spin out into vagueness and, usually, essentially contested notions of spirituality and associated religious stances.

Yet there are four general moves that seem to me in the right direction. I explore these at various points throughout this book, especially in Chapter 7.

The first of these has to do with challenging our stance toward technology and our workaday conviction involving what I would call a "principle of sufficient technological reason," according to which we assume there exists a technical solution - out there somewhere - to every problem we encounter. The only uncertainty is whether we will be bright and clever enough to come up with it. Disguised as an unimpeachably modern attitude of "better living through science," this attitudinal stance is really an atavistic form of magical thinking: little better than a faith that "those in the know" in the priestly caste (for us, the technologists) will conjure up *something*.[35]

Second is taking steps to recognize and alleviate the purely extractive stance toward nature and each other that has come to govern our collective unconscious, providing us what we take to be "common sense." The Heideggerian admonition "to let beings be as the beings which they are" takes on a new urgency in a finite world of rapidly approaching natural limits.[36] This includes examining how intersubjective relations might be rendered less extractive, for example, in practices of "gift giving," long recognized as fundamental to pre-capitalist forms of social organization by anthropologists such as Marcel Mauss and outside-the-mainstream contemporary thinkers such as Charles Eisenstein.[37] Another world is indeed possible because it has actually existed.

Third and more philosophically is questioning our sense of control regarding the effecting of future outcomes, where we see ourselves fundamentally as *choosers* who exercise free will and so are not wholly subject at the micro-level to causal forces and at the macro-level to anything like "fate." This is a strategy associated with ancient Stoicism, one that has and continues to take many forms. I explore a couple of relevant ones in the last chapter.

Fourth, and perhaps most fundamentally, there is interrogating deep yet lightly examined assumptions we carry about human and even biological exceptionalism. Paradoxically, our predicament might best be addressed by attempting to alleviate both anthropocentric *and* biocentric mechanisms of problem framing, the outlines of which are being supplied in the developing object-oriented school of ontology. One such deflationary iconoclast, philosopher Levi Bryant, explains: "The point is to recognize how we are dependent for our agency and existence on broader networks of entities, that we aren't little gods legislating everything in our image, and that if we wish to do well we better attend to these things. The stakes are not to defend science over culture, but to reconceptualize the very nature of ourselves, nature, our duties and obligations."[38] This weird and discomfiting constellation of philosophical concerns goes against most of what everyone has been taught about the uniqueness of human beings: our consciousness, reasoning abilities, ethics, etc. But we may need to be willing to explore some way down this rabbit hole if we want actually to counter that which animates the neoliberal endgame sequence currently underway. Nobody said it was going to be easy - or even likely.

Chapter 2

The tendency of the rate of profit to fall

Yet for all its stinginess, capitalist production is thoroughly wasteful of human material, just as its way of distributing its products through trade, and its manner of competition, make it very wasteful of material resources, so that it loses for society what it gains for the individual capitalist.
Karl Marx[1]

A Marxist account of the crisis

On a weak Marxist theory of correspondence between school and society, I argue that "long wave" historical economic trends are associated with complementary movements in educational ideology, i.e. the set of societally hegemonic basic assumptions about education's aims and purposes.[2] I say it is a "weak" theory of correspondence because, as has long been recognized in the Marxist tradition and by common sense, there persists as a matter of degree a relative autonomy that characterizes all social institutions and human endeavors. There is no simple causal connection between economic base and any given super-structural element and further, social causality is not mono-directional and economic relations do not pull every string of human life. While often in the controlling position, there is no guarantee that economic activity does so always and in every case. (Much of my own work defends this proposition in detail.[3]) Nonetheless, this should not lead one to underestimate the powerful economic forces that usually do, in fact, shape important social institutions. Indeed, despite the public relations fog of rhetoric to the contrary, we are currently experiencing a powerful case of what might be termed "spherical capture" - on the analog of "regulatory capture," where regulators become

53

compromised by the object of their attentions - wherein capitalism's financial sector is achieving such aggressive preeminence that it ventures a comprehensive makeover of all other spheres.[4]

Sometimes termed "market fundamentalism" or the more anodyne "globalization," this geographical and pan-spherical corruption engendered by all-encroaching capital accumulation is the essence of the neoliberal phase of capitalism. To be sure, it is still capitalism. And capitalism has always had its underwriting ideologies, from imperialism to the notion of progress itself. Neoliberalism, though, represents a specific justificatory ideology, one that subsumes everything ultimately to finance and to the inexorable yet (allegedly) freeing logic of "the market." Neoliberalism does more than merely celebrate capital's spanning of the globe in search of far away "spatial fixes" for heretofore localized profitability problems, e.g. the relocation of factories pursuant to a global labor arbitrage.[5] It also exercises a kind of internal social extortion ("we'll relocate unless you capitulate but then eventually we'll relocate anyway"), where the leading edge of capital functions to make over in its own image an array of domestic social spheres in order to ready them for profit extraction, "relentlessly jamming its blood funnel into anything that smells like money."[6] The often significant cultural disruption left in the wake of this fluidity - "switching crises," as David Harvey terms them - commonly generates significant difficulties for endogenous educational institutions.[7] Such effects are hardly surprising, given that not even life itself is immune from a metastasizing neoliberal "biopower" that embarks upon new and radical ventures in medicine, agriculture, brain science, genetics and everywhere. Widely felt in folk psychology to be unmediated touchstones of reality, the body, the mind, the land, and even mortality itself have all become objects of corporate strategy.[8]

The sphere of education hardly stands apart from these larger forces. Again to be clear: it is not possible to trace every educational problem back to neoliberalism or even capitalism generally. Education qua social reproduction is a basic aspect of human existence which, even in its organized forms, long predates capitalism and will, if humanity itself does, necessarily survive it. There are vestigial elements representing the long and diverse experiences of humanity nestled within our educational practices, much like the sequence of pre-human stages gone through in the development of the fetus, as reliably coiled within our collective ideational DNA as are our mitochondrial ancestors. This complexity necessitates basing one's analysis on a weaker correspondence theory than any simple mono-causal economistic conception would allow. The general structural shape may be visible enough but we should not thereby be fooled into, to paraphrase Schopenhauer, an overconfident "principle of sufficient (economic) reason" where for *every* educational effect there is an identifiable and determinate economic cause.[9] The fog of complexity is usually too thick for that level of precision, though a certain clarity of connection is still possible in a given instance: imaginative empirical research, investigative journalism and the like might uncover often deliberately obscured connections (e.g. correlations involving wealth and school success or uncovering a standardized test maker lobbying for self-serving state assessment policies). Such investigations have value but they provide little toward explaining the overall systemic trajectory. For this one needs the "big picture" which *at this time and in this place* involves the gravitational pull of global neoliberal capitalism in its hypertrophic financial phase. This monolith has now grown so strong that it sucks all other endeavors into its orbit, including educational institutions, so that they now move not on their own volition but exclusively according to the financier's logic. Now there was always a lot of this; one searches in vain for a golden era of "education for itself." It's just that it's getting *more* that way than it has been.

In my view this recent intensification - made more visible in the late economic crisis - can only be understood in light of unfolding contradictions within capitalism itself, just as the neoliberal phase was itself an "answer" to the previous generation of capitalism's internal contradictions. The relevant Marxist thesis here is that major economic crises such as the current one are not the result of greedy individuals who are breaking the rules (though there is plenty of that). Neither is the crisis to be solved by progressive regulatory reforms of the financial sector nor even by a redistribution of financial institutions' continuing hyper-profits. Such measures, even unto large scale New Deal-like settlements, while they may certainly be defended contextually on humanitarian grounds, will only *defer* the continuing resolution of capitalist crises rather than durably eliminate them. As has always been true, cyclical economic crises are not incidental imperfections in an otherwise smoothly running capitalist totality; they are fundamental structural features of this system and are crucial for this form of economic organization's dynamism and resilience. Far from aberrations, they are, as Alex Callinicos relates the Marxist position, "to some degree functional for the system."[10] A central thesis of any form of Marxism is that capitalism develops according to its own internal logic, in part by means of periodic crises, such that it continually alters itself; like any social phenomenon it is not static. It mutates and changes according to its own arising tensions, eventually reaching a point where further mutations lead to successor systems that may be unrecognizable from the point of view of their progenitors. The processes of this transformation could be evolutionary or revolutionary or both and, depending on one's axiological framework, the newer forms could appear as "better" or "worse." In the long run of history, the exact timing of the mutation does not matter much, although it matters a great deal to those actually living through one of them at a given time and place. Furthermore, nothing is *predetermined* in any simple way;

the only metaphysical guarantee is that stasis is not an option and that systemic mutations are bound to occur. There is no "end state," no final u-or dys-topia wherein resides a closed and total system unabraded by its own internal friction. An end state equilibrium, even one of a socialist or communist variety, makes no sense within the Marxian dialectical framework inherited from Hegel.

Worse, traditional Marxist eschatology is typically overly optimistic that a *better* world will eventually result from large-scale changes; there is still a residual Hegelian metaphysical comfort in the thought that the further-developed will be in some never-quite-fully-articulated sense *preferable* to the less-developed. Running counter to this teleological conception, the deeper Hegelian insight is ultimately "to recognize reason as the rose in the cross of the present and thereby enjoy the present," meaning that purpose is to be found neither in an inevitably narcissistic narrative of the past (where events allegedly "lead up" to ourselves) nor in an equally spurious psychological projection of some future preferable world (for which, John the Baptist-like, we prepare the way) but in the unstable developmental energy that is always roiling under our own very feet in the here and now.[11] This is where his rational mysticism saves Hegel from his own teleological impulses and he ultimately embraces his famous image of philosophy as the Owl of Minerva that only alights at dusk.[12] Other Marxists may gasp at the atavistic heresy and potential quietude of Hegelian philosophical reconciliation, but in this respect Hegel's oddly radical notion of temporality is more defensible than that of his most famous dialectician-heir. "The philosophers have only *interpreted* the world, in various ways; the point is to *change* it" - and all of that.[13] This bumper sticker aphorism is much better rhetoric than it is analysis. As much as activists understandably and by definition want to know "what we can *do* about it," theoretical understanding can neither reliably prognosticate nor provide sound concrete plans for action. Warning: philosophers *always* disappoint; and it is far better that one should be disappointed by a philosopher than it is that one should "follow" one. Ironically, despite the surrounding noise, Marx's oeuvre itself provides a telling case in point: long on diagnosis, short on cure. Hegel sees that this is as it should be for the philosopher and why philosophers are indeed formally useless. In fact, the sophist who purports to see the future and provide concrete plans should not be trusted at all. As in André Gide's aphorism, "one should always seek those who search for truth but always beware those who have found it"[14]

The only world historical certainty is merely that something *different* will emerge. It may be a better *or* a worse something, depending on the axiological framework of such a judgment, which will itself be a historical product and as such not immune from further judgment, *ad infinitum.*

If the play is not predetermined, then neither are the players. In the struggle against capital's dominion, there is no guarantee that oppressed persons are the exclusive agents of evo/revolution, as much as this fits the comforting biblical template of the meek's just inheritance of the earth. It is entirely possible that global elites have for the moment seized historical agency and they could lead us down into something backwardly atavistic like neo-feudalism or something altogether new and worse. In this sense I advocate a Marx tempered with the Dantean ability to counsel despair: clear-eyed dialectics should always proceed with an abandonment of the hope for a Hollywood happy ending. Marx's own dialectician, Hegel, emphasizes this, describing the "education of consciousness" as the pathway of *doubt* or, more precisely, as the way of "despair."[15] Recognizing the psychological cheat of projection should render one suspicious of any "end times" analysis portending a world that just happens to accord with the one desired by any would-be Nostradamus.[16] The psychodynamics of eschatological projection are no more plausible in other spheres than are the very terrestrial political revenge fantasies fobbed off by the author of the Book of Revelation.[17] It is a salutary psychological check and a safe wager that what actually comes to pass will be something other than exactly what one wants.

All of the preceding is by way of saying that we should indeed look *within* current processes of production in order to ascertain what is going on elsewhere in society such as in education. But we should do so bearing two key caveats in mind: (1) there should be no expectation that every specific alteration in education policy will be found directly to have been wrought solely by neoliberalism or any other economic development; and (2) the analysis will not necessarily lead to a resolution of educational problems that either a) takes on a familiar form that has been pre-approved as desirable, or b) identifies either schools as preferred venues or educators as preferred protagonists. Vanity may have to be wounded. Education is certainly responsive to tectonic changes in the economy but not always at the micro-level of particular administrative or pedagogical practices or ad hoc news items. And although educators have become very jealous of the idea that they possess high levels of "agency," there is nothing written into the fabric of the cosmos assuring that they are pre-positioned at the crux of history. Maybe they are; maybe they are not. But this cannot be known *a priori*.

A precondition for any Marxist account of the financial crisis is that it is not ultimately caused by individual bad actors such that we could punish the culprits and/or re-regulate the banks and all will be well again. More significantly, neither was it caused by the repeal of regulations such as New Deal era legislation like the Glass-Steagall Act (1933, repealed in 1999) that separated commercial and investment banking operations. While deregulation certainly hastened the crisis and so is highly germane to any analysis of the late domination of the economy by the financial sector, it still begs the question, *why?* Why the neoliberal zeal for deregulation or, perhaps one should say, why did this simple market idolatry suddenly become so appealing to so many? Why, then, the mortgage crisis, itself enabled by that very deregulation in the form of an array of exotic leveraging instruments and, shall we say, "creative" practices in accounting, insurance and banking? Why for that matter the wildly dispro-portionate growth of the finance-insurance-real estate (FIRE) sector? Why the rise of the neoliberal matrix in the first place?

These are of course large questions beyond the scope of this essay on education. I only wish to point out that what distin-guishes Marxist analyses of these developments is that they resist surface explanations and aim for an account that is rooted in the dynamics of the capitalist system itself. This sounds like very heavy weather, admittedly, and humility counsels one to proceed cautiously. But humility also requires one to recognize the inade-quacy of system-preserving proposed remedies like reigning in personal greed, merely re-calibrating the regulatory parameters on finance or even redistributing corporate profits. All of these may be fine things to do and defensible ad hoc in context, but piecemeal melioristic approaches share the unfortunate assumption that the extant underlying forces of production are static and legitimate. The current iteration of capitalism must appear as if natural and inevitable, just as propagandists for whatever form of domination have always made similar natural-izing apologia. Many reform-minded critics play this game too. There is often a "realist" insistence on putting aside larger critical questions in order to rush in and simply help the suffering. This is psychologically understandable at an interpersonal level at the moment of an emergency. But as the "emergency" undergoes repetition after repetition, in the long-term the "let's just shut up and do something constructive" sort of response becomes simply another strategy for naturalizing the situation so that everyone treats economic devastation as natural, something that we do not question or blame - any more than we blame the tornado or hurricane, in whose aftermath it is bad form to do anything other than drop everything and uncritically rush in to help. "There will be time for that later!" the would-be critic is admonished; or, in the infantile inflection of American politics, "don't play the blame game." All the while, elites are perfectly adept at utilizing shock doctrine reforms to reshape our world while we have turned our backs and/or are psychologically primed through fear and desperation to accept their dictates.[18] Emergency reactions, yes, but sustained efforts to channel strong moral sentiments into anodyne pathways are counterproductive and are key factors in mass quiescence. So yes by all means let's not let ideological debates induce practical catatonia amidst actual human suffering. But it is only rational to look at causes as well. Otherwise, all the emergency responding begins to look a bit Munchausen by proxy and psychologically self-serving.

The tendency of the rate of profit to fall

Once again it is evident that even between major crises, 'the market' has no answer to the major problems confronting the twenty-first century: that unlimited and increasingly high-tech economic growth in pursuit of unsustainable profit produces global wealth, but at the cost of an increasingly dispensable factor of production, human labor, and, one might add, of the globe's natural resources. Economic and political liberalism, singly or in combination, cannot provide the solution the problems of the twenty-first century. Once again the time has come to take Marx seriously.
Eric Hobsbawm[19]

The biggest "shock" of all may be that capitalism no longer works as advertised. Since the early 1970s a range of productive and distributional efficiencies have rendered human labor - at least in the global North - a decreasing portion of the industrial production process and consequently of what Marx called the "organic composition of capital" (more on this below). Everyone knows about job losses due to outsourcing and the global labor arbitrage generally (more on this below also). But what is less appreciated is how not only workers' livelihoods but also, ironically, capitalists' profits are themselves under long-term assault by the very efficiencies that have become necessary strategies for accumulating those same profits. Marx identified this counter-intuitive predicament as the "tendency of the rate of profit to fall" (TRPF). This tendency has been with capitalism since its inception. Yet in recent decades it has come to the fore and brought in its wake a severe diminution of the need for labor - at first "expensive" global North labor and then eventually all labor - and consequently, eventually, an abandonment of the ideal of the universal distribution of education. After the Marxist phrase, I call this wrenching educational de-leveraging process "the falling rate of learning." What capitalism gives, capitalism also takes away; and it turns out that the universalist aspirations for all children in this area, including the twin mechanisms of compulsory education and schooling as a right, are artifacts of the erstwhile industrializing phase of capitalism that hungered initially for a disciplined and appropriately skilled (or, as the situation may require, de-skilled) domestic labor force. There is lag time whose length is due to many factors, including plain institutional and political inertia, but as the good jobs are irrevocably lost via globalization, so is the education.

Though often absent from discussions of Marxist crisis theory, Marx himself held the phenomenon of the TRPF to be "the most important law of modern political economy." Despite its complex and controversial status among many Marxist theorists, the general priority Marx gives to the TRPF seems more and more justified amidst the current economic crisis, where unemployment and underemployment in the global North - particularly among young people, where it approaches 60% in some areas -continues to deepen with apparently little hope for amelioration. We seem to face an economic future in which there is a decreasing need for an increasing proportion of the population. An understanding of the dynamics of the TRPF helps explain the peculiar perniciousness and durability of this unemployment crisis and, among other things, decisively gives the lie to the dream we have been sold of educating ourselves into prosperity via schools' fabrication of "knowledge workers" and their enhanced productivity. The utopian vision of the "high tech, high wage" service economy stands revealed as a false promise. This latter was always a product of willful ignorance concerning the confluence of capitalism, technology and education.

Marx's description of the TRPF is found in the third volume of *Capital* (Ch. 13). It builds upon his theories of the composition of capital itself and the fluid roles that labor and technology play in that composition. Yet the basic theory can be relayed relatively clearly. Under Marx's famous "labor theory of value," profit derives ultimately from the surplus labor value provided by workers in the course of their manufacture of a given commodity. Even as workers become vastly more productive due to organizational improvements - not only technology but also schemes such as vertical integration and just in time delivery - the human worker remains the fount of profitability. As much as the capitalist would like to rid himself of his fellow human beings and his dependence on their labor, he cannot. That this is impossible has nothing to do with humanitarianism but, as TRPF helps illustrate, gives rise to some of the more subtle and interesting contradictions at the very heart of capitalist production.

One obtains profit by selling a commodity for more money than it took to produce it. For Marx, the expenditures necessary to produce a commodity can be divided into two main categories: "variable capital" and "fixed capital." Variable capital, sometimes called "human" or "living capital," refers to the labor costs, the expenses incurred by paying and otherwise maintaining the workforce. Primarily this involves wages along with other costs associated with securing workers' labor, e.g. benefits, training, safety compliance. It should be noted also that there are many additional costs that are external to the capitalist's operation, costs that are often hidden - or willfully ignored - such as the securing of the workforce's basic literacy in public schools, the maintenance of roads, police and fire protection etc. Perhaps the largest external cost that the capitalist does not have to pay in full is that arising from nature, as when the capitalist deploys his capital to extract oil from the ground but the oil itself is already there and cannot be fabricated out of nothing. The other main category of expenditure, fixed capital, has to do with the inanimate in-house aspects of production that the capitalist controls: the factory machinery, the warehouse, the shipping trucks, the computers in the office cubicles etc. Fixed capital is all the "stuff" owned by the capitalist whose utilization augments his productive capacity. Taken together - variable plus fixed in whatever resultant proportion - we have what Marx referred to as the "organic composition" of capital.[20]

It is the investment in fixed capital that really makes the capitalist a capitalist. One could imagine a primitive "factory" where assembly of X is done purely by hand. Let's even imagine a balmy climate where the work can be done outside, not even needing a shelter for the laborers (which would be an item of fixed capital). Whether the laborers were slaves or wage-earners, such an operation would be almost all *variable* capital, i.e. "pure" human labor (or, if you like, "human capital," after the Chicago school).[21] Conversely, we could imagine the opposite: a fully automated factory where we have, at most, a human technician to monitor the machines or, even less visibly, some sort of remote oversight and/or troubleshooting by an off-site human operator. Such an operation would be almost all *fixed* capital, the direct flesh-and-blood contribution of human effort minimized ideally to a vanishing point.

From an individual capitalist's point of view, if all other things are equal (a big "if") it would seem advantageous to maximize the proportion of the operation's fixed capital. The variable capital provided by labor is called "variable" for a reason: its costs can be fluid and unpredictable. Pharaoh may not need to worry about an endless supply of captive, cheap labor. But a modern capitalist must purchase that labor. This can temporarily function to the advantage of workers, as during a boom period in which rising labor costs augment workers' bargaining powers and consequent job opportunities, remuneration, working conditions etc. Other factors can increase the amount that must be spent on variable capital, such as unionization or religion, which could cause workers to agitate for more holidays and/or better working conditions (more expensive for the capitalist) or, ultimately, halt production altogether by means of the workplace strike. Since the capitalist's profit on commodity X is the difference between X's sales price and the costs of producing X (and bringing it to market), the capitalist has every incentive, of course, to lower the cost of X's production - including the variable capital labor part of the equation.

Labor costs can be lowered by raising productivity, say, paying one worker for what two once did or simply by raising the rate of workers' exploitation, i.e. paying them less and/or making them work harder, longer, and so on. In the contemporary US, this squeeze on workers has been achieved primarily by: a) *reducing the costs of labor* by union busting and outsourcing, first to non- or less-unionized domestic regions such as the US South and eventually to the global South where labor is vastly cheaper, literally pennies on the dollar as compared to domestic rates; and b) *augmenting workers' productivity* through technology. Especially considering global South remuneration levels, these twin strategies have helped reduce variable capital costs almost to its "optimal" low point, which would be workers' mere subsistence or, even better, temporary subsistence for a portion of the surplus army of labor who, when exhausted, may be replaced by the next cohort - and so on, ad infinitum. The massive numbers of displaced rural peasants in China and India fit this pattern quite nicely. After the labor value is sucked out of them, the disabled, sick, old and otherwise infirm will be cycled out and off and die somewhere, preferably as rapidly as possible.[22]

It is important to remember that it is still the laboring human being - somewhere - who persists as the value-soil from which this worldwide system of capital accumulation grows.[23] Out of the sight may be out of mind for most in the global North, but the latest Apple products most obviously do not fall from the sky. The laboring masses of the global South still underlie them. Thus, despite its name, even the Apple iCloud is still very much tethered to the good earth.[24] However, although their wages approach a near zero-point, from the point of view of capital they are still paid too much, which is especially troubling because heretofore quiescent Chinese workers are beginning to assert themselves and push back on a large scale against the savagery of their exploitation, their traditional "iron rice bowl" (*danwei* system), having been shattered.[25] Such developments underscore how globalization, outsourcing and the like are merely second-best solutions to the chronic problem of capitalists' dependency on labor and its all-too human inadequacies. By way of extrapolation, the ultimate dream of techno-capitalism on the production side is the elimination of variable capital completely, that is to say, achieving independence from the inconvenience of reliance upon actual human beings as part of the production process. Implicit in capitalist production from its inception, the perennial dream here is of a true "rise of the machines," a total automation of production where the presumptively obsolescent human beings would no longer be needed—however incoherent the implied vision of a workerless and hence largely consumerless economy. This is one key aspect of the eliminationist dream that increasingly haunts late capitalism.

But at this precise point, we encounter one of those key

contradictions in which the Hegelian-cum-Marxist tradition so delights. Though capitalism dreams of driving human beings completely out of the production process, it simply cannot succeed in doing so in a general manner. Reminiscent of a prisoner's dilemma sort of decision matrix, where self-interested defection comes out on top, the ideal situation from the point of view of an individual capitalist would be a positional advantage where he is the *sole* producer in his sector who has *per impossibile* transcended the need for variable capital/labor in the production process. This imagined competition-free and labor-free capitalist would then enjoy the windfall due to him from the eradication of his erstwhile variable capital costs. This seems logically possible. Insurmountable problems arise at a *systemic* level, though. If not only within a sector but *across* sectors, *all* of the capitals were fully automated and labor-less, then, by the logical property of identity, there would be no laborers. Unless they were conveniently "disappeared," there would certainly be *people* around, but they would not constitute *laborers* in the context of capitalist production. This lack of laborers gives rise to two main and interrelated problems that, in a sense, *doubly* guarantee the unsustainability of the imagined labor-free system:

(1) given the TRPF, as explained below, profits would *in principle* start to vanish and with them the point of the whole productive enterprise, and

(2) absent some work-free redistributivist techno-utopia (which would be hard to call "capitalism" anymore), a state of affairs of such massive inequality would leave precious few human beings with disposable resources.

There would only be the capitalists themselves, say, the 1%, and whatever crumbs of purchasing power they allowed to be distributed to the 99%, perhaps just enough to avert acute social instability (if they would be able to avert it). In such a situation, there would exist no consumers for even discounted (labor-free) products and in turn no sales or profits. Underconsumption would therefore undermine the imagined labor-free system. Techno-utopias frequently ignore this point. The wonders of technological development must be given their due, and it is sensible to imagine how the very economic problems with which we are struggling themselves might change due to future techno-logical development.[26] But the question of what potentially billions of economically surplus people are supposed to do with themselves in the techno-wake must be acknowledged. Is a problem "solved" if its resolution augurs greater destruction and misery than if it had not been tried?

Let us look more closely at the TRPF. Under Marx's surplus labor theory of value, profits inevitably derive from the extraction of workers' surplus labor, viz., that portion of their labor over and above what it takes to recoup the initial capital outlays (as they depreciate), along with associated production and distribution costs, and also the amount paid to the worker as wages. Wages in turn will be a function of supply and demand in the labor market as well as whatever constraints are supplied by pertinent local laws and customs such as taxes, a minimum wage, or mandated worker benefits. At a bare minimum the wage must provide subsistence for the workers, unless they can be allowed to drop dead and be continually replaced by "new recruits" from a surplus army, as per the Nazi operations at Auschwitz and other camps, where over 400 "good capitalist" German companies – including BMW, Siemens, Daimler-Benz, Volkswagen etc. - all happily profited from their conveniently ever-replenishing slave labor force.[27] It is important to note that the situation obtaining in many areas of the global South, such as China, is structurally similar to such a scheme of mass slave labor. Here, traditionally rural inhabitants are made to leave the countryside and present themselves for industrial use (mostly manufacturing export goods) where, after the inevitable physical and mental breakdown guaranteed by ferocious working condi-tions, the used-up ex-workers are then recycled back to the countryside for lifestyles of bare subsistence.[28] Industrial slave labor is instructive as it vividly illustrates the telos of capitalist surplus labor extraction, i.e. the direction it inevitably heads if left to its own devices and unchecked by other forces such as law, custom or morality. Whatever its size, though, the segment of the value produced by workers over and above the costs of production, that all-important remainder, is appropriated by the capitalist as his "just" profit. Capitalism is thus unthinkable without worker exploitation, aggregated and concentrated into the capital that is necessary to keep the cycle running and expanding.

This sliver of profit-yielding labor is for the most part the goal of the entire enterprise from the individual capitalist's point of view. It is taken and reinvested (in more land and/or equipment, a capitalist-capitalist transaction) or taken as personal remuneration. Marx's great discovery is that while profits may fluctuate all over the place due to a range of counter forces, the general tendency created by increasing worker productivity is for the rate of profit actually to *fall*.

Why would this be? It would seem that augmented productivity would generate increased profits. If distributed equitably, this could even be an unmitigated boon for everyone, more wealth to spread around, a "win-win." And so it might. For a time. (This in fact is the dream of many liberal reformers: maintain the current relations of production, only ask the owners of capital to be less greedy and "spread the wealth around.") But temporality is key here: over time it is in the nature of capital to run, like water falling, into the arenas of production with the highest profits. If a neighboring sector is far more profitable than my own, I will do everything in my power to convert my operations in order to set up similar shop there and begin producing *my* own competing products. Acme Widgets is now joined by A-1 Widgets. Maybe Acme and A-1 are then joined by a third company, and so on. Now the race is really on for productivity enhancements. In the ensuing productivity arms race, each worker must be made to generate a greater amount of surplus and any technological edge is welcomed. This might be achieved by a variety of means: organizational efficiencies (e.g. vertical integration of supply and distribution chains), doing more with less (say, layoffs), ratcheting up the exploitation (more hours, lower wages), and/or, for present purposes the most interesting strategy, augmenting the pace and quality of productivity through technology and automation.

The problem for profits becomes acute when this latter strategy becomes predominant. When the automation of production reaches a certain level, it does indeed provide a temporary respite for the capitalist from his dependence on living labor provided by workers. Fewer of them are needed. The computer now does the work of three erstwhile workers. So far so good. However, as Acme Widgets successfully employs this strategy, it is only a matter of time until A-1 Widgets notices and adopts it too. This sounds innocuous enough: textbook competitive capitalism. Everyone wins according to classical models, especially consumers who enjoy the fruits of all the competitive pricing and innovation. But remember that the whole point of capitalist enterprise is to turn a profit. It is not ultimately to make wonderful products; production is at best a means to an end. And profits come from the surplus labor of *workers*, not from the machines or from the commodities by themselves. Assuming there is real competition among capitalists, profits cannot durably come from the machines, because the other capitalists have - or will shortly have - those same machines, too. This means that, absent monopoly or functional monopoly (e. g. collusive price fixing), to keep up with one another, Acme and A-1 have to sink more and more of their profits into those machines i.e. into their fixed capital. This in turn causes a proportional shrinkage of that all-important profit-producing piece of the production pie. In Marxist shorthand, the organic composition of capital changes as the ratio of fixed to variable capital grows. Absent countervailing forces, profits must fall under this scenario, at least in the long run, because as automation increases the profit-bearing segment made up of surplus labor shrinks. It is not a *technical* limit that comes into play but rather one of economic *incentive*. There comes a point where technology-fueled competition and consequent price drops render it unprofitable to continue making DVD players. One either retools in favor of some new innovation or one dies.

In an age of intensive automation, the best an individual capitalist can hope for is a *temporary* and *positional* advantage vis-à-vis other capitalist competitors. And indeed, gigantic fortunes are to be made during the pendency of these profit-taking interregna. The problem is that while an individual capitalist may gain huge *temporary* market advantages by being the first to, say, automate a factory, eventually other competitors will automate too. (Unless of course the initial advantage is so swift and decisive as to drive competitors out of business completely, thereby setting up the optimal situation for the capitalist: an ascension beyond capitalism proper into monopoly.) Whether through industrial espionage, copying or merely the general societal diffusion of knowledge, those competitors will find ways to catch up or even surpass the efficacy of the fixed capital possessed by our original capitalist who will, in turn, try to stay "one step ahead" of the competition. This positional fluidity is the essence of competitive capitalism. It is the part of the system that is most celebrated in official ideology and, arguably, that part of capitalism that is most lauded by individual consumers who get to sit back and enjoy the product innovations and price drops.

But just like a military arms race, this fixed capital arms race, while necessary (innovate or die), is also very costly, as more and more resources go toward the stock of fixed capital. Even more important than the overall absolute cost, the *ratio* of fixed/variable capital is altered by this dynamic. This might sound like a technical point but it is absolutely crucial, for it means that the organic composition of the capital (the proportion of variable to fixed) has altered such that the variable capital constitutes a diminishing portion of the capitalist's productive operation. This matters because, simply put, it affects the capitalist's bottom line: profits. Profits, it will be remembered, *ex hypothesi*, come from the extraction of workers' surplus labor value that is "congealed" (Marx's term) into the variable capital. With a greater proportion of operations being automated (high tech or otherwise), there is less and less surplus to extract and there are fewer and fewer profits. This surprising inversion - which is the heart of the TRPF - occurs when the capitalists' competitors *also* invest their operations with higher percentages of fixed capital (by definition at the expense of variable capital). The ring of competition in a particular industry thus becomes akin to a circular firing squad where profitability is the victim.

This point is often overlooked by those distracted by superficial aspects of a particular capitalist's enterprise or by a new segment of industry that seems - as it often does - that it is so novel that it seems to break all the old rules (think "internet," "social networking," "biotech"). Initially DVD players reaped high profits for early bird manufacturers. But in the course of time, due to advances in productivity (i.e. fixed capital associated with high tech production), everyone started making DVD players, profit margins begin to fall, and it is on to the Next Big Thing: HD, 3D or whatever.

Lots of people made lots of money making DVD players. Marx's point is not that money is not made this way. But the riches are not from the making of DVD players generally but from being the *early bird* who is making the DVD players; one is not going to be able to keep raking in the profits by making DVD players in the same old way. For a while one might be able to maintain profits by augmenting productivity (more automation, more fixed capital). The problem for profitability only appears *diachronically*, as a *temporal* phenomenon in which, *as time goes on* and more and more competitors come on-line with the latest productivity enhancements, there is less and less surplus labor around (qua variable capital) to be extracted for each of them. Via temporal early bird advantage, individual capitalists can win enormous individual battles. For an obtrusive contemporary example, think of the iPod/iTunes/iPads/iEverything that have made Apple into the richest corporation in the world. Marx's view is that in the ensemble, though, and over time, they and all their competitors will lose the war. The TRPF is most apparent not as a phenomenon that besets individual capitals ad hoc; rather it is a tendency that becomes visible in the system *as a whole*, as a generalized crisis of profitability. There is no more blood to squeeze out of the labor stone. Or is there?

Insofar as there are "laws" in economics, it is perfectly defensible to characterize the TRPF as one. However, there are two main points to emphasize in any deployment of the idea:

First, as just mentioned, the TRPF is a *systemic* property rather than a property of individual firms and their specific environments. *In the long run and in general*, the manufacture and sale of different iterations of the personal listening device, say, portable radio - boom box - Sony Walkman - Apple iPod, will tend, along with the electronics industry generally, toward exhibiting the TRPF. However, along the way this does not at all preclude Sony and Apple from making a killing due to their early bird advantages and the maintenance of those advantages. An example would be the cornucopic symbiosis between iTunes and the iPod. So even if things eventually press downward long-term, plenty of livelihoods and fortunes are to be made in the short and medium terms.

Second, the lawlike nature of the TRPF explains little by itself, especially given all the counter forces that are perpetually at play such as the various strategies of wage repression. Consider an analogy with the law of gravity. We know that in a vacuum bodies will fall at $9.8m/s^2$. Yet this tells us very little about how, say, a particular airplane will function. Gravity will be *relevant*, but not by itself very rich in explanatory value if we are assessing, say, whether the airplane will arrive on time. While still relevant, neither will it tell us which mattress is the most comfortable or how high an athlete can jump. Marx recognized this fully on his original formulation of the TRPF, where he draws immediate attention to the many counter factors that, in the teeth of the TRPF, might prop up profits for individual firms, economic sectors or even the economy as a whole indefinitely.

Thus, contrary to common opinion about his alleged "mistake," as Andrew Kliman points out, Marx did not believe that the TRPF would cause "the collapse of capitalism."[27] Rather, due to the accompanying counter forces, the TRPF is merely an inevitable *shaper* of capitalism's eventual long-term - maybe *very* long-term - demise. Marx in fact explicitly and repeatedly emphasizes that the counter forces typically inhibit the fall in the rate of profit so as to "delay it and in part even paralyze it ... [t]he law operates therefore simply as a tendency, whose effect is decisive *only under certain particular circumstances and over long periods* [emphasis added]."[29]

Idenfitying the operation of the TRPF is thus akin to how astronomers identify black holes. They are not so much identified by direct observation - one doesn't really "see" a black hole - as they are by the observation of adjacent phenomena. The black hole can be detected via the patterns of movement and other indicators of matter it creates within its orbit. Likewise, the TRPF, as one of the most truly "macro" of macro-economic phenomena, is perhaps best detected by how, to continue with the analogy, its gravitational force is evident in the behavior of bodies around it. Under ideal conditions, in vacuum as it were, where all counter forces could be controlled, we could directly observe the TRPF. We would have perfect competition, so firms would have to keep investing in fixed capital in order to keep innovating. They would not find new ways to exploit labor, including outsourcing overseas so as to enjoy an epochal windfall in labor cost reductions. They would not be able to inflate financial credit bubbles in order to prop up consumption. They would not be able to eliminate "natural" competition by utilizing government to place themselves into a comfortable rent-collecting monopoly position. And so on.

This is today's strategy for success: evade the TRPF by winning a commanding Google-like monopoly position in order to "win" in this high stakes game of king of the hill. But king of the hill has two parts: 1) winning the place at the top and 2) staying there. And the latter point is very often where the game is rigged, as firms not only win a monopoly position but use the levers of government to ensure competitors are kept down. An example would be a giant agribusiness interest that via campaign contributions and the like secures passage of new "food safety" regulations, the real purpose of which is not the stated one of protecting the public, but rather of making it too expensive for smaller less-connected competitors to afford compliance. (Thus we have bizarre spectacles of aggressive government raids on allegedly nefarious small-scale organic "raw" milk producers and the like.[30]) State policy is utilized as a means by which to destroy competitors. The same monopoly advantage may also be secured by purely business means, as when a giant software manufacturer parlays its commanding market share into a coercive instrument with which to force hardware manufacturers to collude with it in keeping competitor software products out. And so on.

In the ensemble, there are so many of these situations that the actual competitive capitalism of free market booster lore seems difficult to locate; we have in this respect entered an age of what Paul Baran and Paul Sweezy generations ago termed "monopoly capitalism."[31] By definition monopoly capitalism constitutes a situation where a given capital lacks competition, so the above description of Acme and A-1 no longer applies. Monopolization thus represents perhaps the historically grandest counter force strategy for staving off the TRPF. Without competitors one has so much less to worry about. One especially doesn't have to worry about the kind of over-investment in fixed capital that drives profits down, as per the above. If the monopoly is secure enough, one also may be insulated to a great degree from wage competition among other capitals for workers. One becomes the only employer in town so to speak. Competition then becomes a matter for the little people, the workers wanting *you* to hire them, and not the ongoing existential threat of other capitals' competition wherein one must innovate or die. It is a neat reversal that only aids in solidifying those already at the top, as the arena of economic competition is shifted from occurring primarily among capitals to occurring primarily among workers. All in all, a monopoly can buy much more time in which to sit atop the hill and collect the all-but guaranteed rents (including "imperialist rents" on a global scale), all while enjoying the ancillary advantages of workers' intramural globalized competition and consequent diminished bargaining power.[32] (As both Marx and Lenin theorized, imperialist "ground rents" also had the bonus effect for monopolists of preventing competition from arising among the developing areas, their gains being extracted through oppressive rent payments rather than their own capital accumulation.[33]) In this world, we depart decisively from the textbook fairytale of neo-classical economics. And the vaunted "competition" that is allegedly such a virtuous hallmark of capitalism. Here capitalism leads to less innovation, higher prices, lower wages, in short, nothing good for anyone but the capital owner.

As Marx explains in the original articulation of the TRPF, massive counter forces such as monopolization may keep the gravitational downward pull on profits at bay almost indefinitely. In fact there are so many countervailing forces and they are of such variety that normally the "downward pressure on profits" exerted by the TRPF can be largely invisible. The existence of these counter forces is why Marx emphasizes that the TRPF is in context only a *tendency*.[34] These often hugely powerful forces might involve anything from foreign trade to overpopulation. Among the most important are:

a) as presently being discussed, the monopoly/near monopoly position of certain capitals that prevents competition and thus serves as a brake on the "normal" inter-firm fixed capital arms race;

b) an intensification of worker exploitation and wage reductions, fueled especially - as Samir Amin has long argued - by a global labor arbitrage, the enclosure and extraction of indigenous natural resources and neo-imperialist strategies of sovereign indebtedness in the global South and on the developed periphery such as Greece;[35]

c) an augmentation of organizational efficiencies such as vertical integration, an iconic example being Wal-Mart's dominance over its global supply chains;

d) a further and often covert externalization of the past and future costs of production, like offloading environmental problems such as pollution onto the public, training workers through such means as public education and the erection and upkeep of public health, transportation and safety infrastructures without which capitalist production would halt;

e) and perhaps most significantly of late, a large-scale migration to un-productive but high profit sectors such as finance, a move whose symptoms include the creation of ever more menacing credit and debt bubbles and accompanying state subsidization of banking elites. Not a new phenomenon, none other than Marx himself described the situation: "If the rate of profit falls ... we have swindling

77

and general promotion of swindling, through desperate attempts in the way of new methods of production, new capital investments and new adventures, to secure some kind of extra profit, which will be independent of the general average [profit determined by the average rate of profit] and superior to it"[36]; and,

f) more determined intra-national efforts at what Marx called "accumulation by dispossession" or a kind of "primitive accumulation" redivivus, where heretofore public assets are privatized and made into profit-bearing capitals for their newly minted owners. The most spectacular recent example of this latter is the fire sale of former state assets during the collapse of the former Soviet Union, where state assets were essentially stolen by well-placed ex-apparatchiks. Less dramatic but still profitable examples may be found in the US Powell Doctrine-like "cut it off and kill it" strategy of savage austerity to soften targets such as schools and prisons, followed by a final *coup de grâce* of privatization and corporate desiccation.

Each of these strategies is best contextualized as a *response* to the relentless gravitational pull of the TRPF, and ultimately endemic boom-bust crises are themselves responses qua readjustments of the array of counter forces needed to counteract the TRPF. For individual firms they represent a quite rational menu of moves for maintaining and temporarily - always only temporarily - increasing profitability. As an economic necessity, the TRPF is the mother of many inventions. In fact, neoliberalism itself should be seen precisely as an ideological expression of the aggregation of the most recent round of such inventions. There is very little to it other than that. No less than the divine right of kings, neoliberalism provides merely another textbook example of Marx's famous proposition that

[t]he ideas of the ruling class are in every epoch the ruling ideas: i.e. the class which is the ruling *material* force of society, is at the same time its ruling *intellectual* force. The class which has the means of material production at its disposal, has control at the same time over the means of mental production, so that thereby, generally speaking, the ideas of those who lack the means of mental production are subject to it. The ruling ideas are nothing more than the ideal expression of the dominant material relationships, the dominant material relationships grasped as ideas; hence of the relationships which make the one class the ruling one, therefore, the ideas of its dominance.[37]

Whatever localized relative autonomy it may obtain, education on the whole is hardly exempt from this ideological tether. The historical timing of universal schooling is not coincidence. It arose originally as a function of the labor intensive industrializing capitalism that needed "all hands on deck" for colossal manufacturing enterprises. Those labor needs in turn gave rise to an expansive ideology of universal public education in the US from the mid-nineteenth century onwards.[38]

Live by the sword, die by the sword, though. When labor needs expand, so does education. But when labor needs contract and do so *chronically*? The previously unthinkable begins to occur for an education sector that has enjoyed so many consecutive prior generations of unremitting growth that institutional memory houses no other possibility. Workers in general are less and less needed, *a fortiori* educated ones (though from the employer's point of view it is always helpful to maintain that fratricidal competition among Marx's "surplus army of labor" job aspirants). As the relentless logic of automation and offshoring renders more and more domestic workers superfluous, universal education becomes less and less of a priority - though we are still treated *ad nauseam* to vestigial and at this point Orwellian rhetoric about education reforms premised on the idea of "no child left behind." The truth is that neoliberal capitalism has left more and more children behind, approaching a 50% jobless rate among post-graduates in increasing swaths of the developed world. It turns out that leaving children behind is a neoliberal specialty.

Yet all this human superfluity leaves in its wake a persistent economic problem that compounds what I just described. Following the logic dictated by resisting the gravitational pull of the TRPF, individual capitalists pursue their own best interests of reducing and ideally eliminating labor costs altogether. Perhaps *mirabile dictu* an individual capitalist achieves the Holy Grail of getting wholly rid of his labor dependence. The most beautiful of the bosses' dreams: fire them all! And let's say technological conditions allowed this. And as previously discussed, for a time workerlessness might in principle be possible in some sector. However, by virtue of the TRPF, it is impossible for the system *as a whole* to achieve the beautiful eliminationist dream, the ultimate telos of austerity. Why? The answer is rather simple: in a word, *underconsumption*. Capitalists might sell to one another for a time but ultimately even capitalist-to-capitalist sales (i.e. fixed capital that makes other fixed capital such as factory machine tools or mining equipment) are dependent upon a set of eventual consumers whose purchases will prop it all up; in the end someone down the line has to buy the stuff that all the fixed capital is churning out. Perhaps the 1% or so could simply manufacture and sell to one another as a kind of Robinson Crusoe restart of the pre-history of human exchange. Though logically consistent, such a development would presuppose a science fictionalized world so different from our own that very little could be said about it that might apply to this one. Billions would somehow have been eliminated from it, for starters.

But back to the premise that sellers need buyers: even if, *per impossibile*, all production were to be automated - i.e. subsumed under fixed capital - then simply put there would be no one left with the ability to purchase the products. No one would have the requisite income-generating jobs. And approaching this zero limit there would be systemic and sustained unemployment such that there would be precious little purchasing power on the demand side of the economy as a whole, thus robbing the capitalist's profit motive for automating production in the first place. Marxist economists sometimes label such a situation - arguably the one we are currently in - a crisis of underconsumption. Underconsumptionists argue that the current crisis is due to an imbalance between the production of goods and services and buyer demand; too much stuff is being produced to sell it all. A century ago, this problem was famously anticipated and judiciously countered by Henry Ford, who bestowed higher wages on his workers so they could afford to buy his cars.

This Fordist solution to underconsumption has long been an important component of American capitalism - until recently, that is, when the old enlightened capitalists' lessons seem to have been forgotten. Short-term profits may indeed be gained (1970s-present) by reducing workers' wages and rendering them ever more precarious. Yet this quite obviously kills the geese that lay the golden eggs: there are too few left with steady employment and confidence about the future to buy (and enter into indebtedness to buy) all the wonderful new products. This includes the impoverished workers in developing countries who have been on the receiving end of outsourced US jobs. Workers in Mexico, India and China make so much less than their counterparts in the global North (their main attraction to the outsourcers) that, while they indeed save X Inc. and Y Inc. money, once the outsourcing reaches a critical level, the underconsumption problems become acute once again, this time on its new global scale. (Domestic underconsumption is widely acknowledged to be a looming problem in China, for example.) At the moment, profits are (temporarily) up, as the workers that have jobs have never been more productive. But due to widening un- and underemployment, wealthy countries' workers can no longer buy what their compatriots and, especially, the rest of the world are working so feverishly to produce for them. To paraphrase the title of Raj Patel's book on related agribusiness themes, there is a sense in which we are simultaneously "stuffed and starved."[39]

Copied by most in the industrialized world, the great American solution to all of this has of course been debt: personal and institutional. Through clever mechanisms originating in the bowels of the large banks' more adventurous departments, the financialization of the economy through credit cards, student loans and, perhaps most importantly, home equity, has for the past generation stepped in to "solve" the underconsumption problem. This worked for a time, until 2007 when the housing bubble burst and the ongoing financial crisis ensued. Suddenly American *homo suburbiensis* could no longer tap the equity in its home in order to exercise its divine right to escalating levels of consumption - consumption upon which much of the world depends at this point.[40] To paraphrase economist Richard Wolff, that is where things start to hit the fan.[41] To be sure, through socializing their losses upon the taxpayers (via bailouts, loan guarantees and the like), banking elites have mostly insulated themselves from direct personal financial harm. In fact, they have done very well, as evidenced by their reported bonuses and the boom in luxury items in the very midst of the downturn. But the wealthy 1% can only buy so much, and they certainly cannot by themselves prop up enough consumer demand to sustain the entire world economy. The super profits that neoliberal globalization has allowed them to accumulate over the last generation only adds to the problem, as the super rich find decreasingly attractive havens for investing their "giant pool of money."[42] They must therefore attempt ever more "creative" financial innovations in order to avoid seeing their own capital disintegrate.

This is the point at which our elites have turned wholly predatory, like the sharks that must constantly move forward or die.[43] With colossal lack of wisdom, they have built a machine that forces them into the "smash and grab" neoliberal strategy of maximum short-term gain while, literally, mortgaging everyone's future. And this neoliberal machine is only getting started, its fake rhetoric about "free markets" and "competition" now fully exposed for what it is. As the bursting of the credit bubble continues to rain its toxic residue, the strategy of propping up demand through consumer debt is all but foreclosed. What is left is a short-term strategy of further social-izing bankers' "debt overhang" spreading it out as widely as possible by transforming it into public debt via the magical mechanism of central banks' "monetizing" (or "quantitative easing," which essentially amounts to money printing). This in turn helps exacerbate enormous sovereign debt levels, leading to austerity and the rest of it in order to close the gap.[44] And somehow, through all of this, the financiers continue collecting during the "de-leveraging," which, it turns out, is only a temporary moment after which they start re-leveraging once again. Criminals often cannot resist returning to the scene of the crime.

Now, with "normal" capitalist profitmaking options foreclosed, what we are left with now is an all-out assault on anything in the system that might still have a little exchange value, a little liquidity with which to re-leverage. One might term this the "searching under the couch cushions for loose change" phase of late capitalism. One of the main areas to find the loose change is in previously less accessible precincts such as schools, infrastructure, public health and safety - anywhere, really. All that is solid is liquefied and sucked up into the financial upholstery vacuum, to be consumed by the megabanks. As per Marx's famous vampire image, the latter perform no function whatever except a kind of super rent collection, a permanent life-crushing tax on all forms of human activity. The long field-tested imperialist rent strategy now comes home to roost in American states, municipalities and school districts. One wonders if American localities will relish their new structural role as honorary members of the long-ago enclosed and dispossessed global South. How will it play out when they see up close how the most vulnerable among them - like their own children - are dragooned into a system of public peonage where the debt becomes an existential state that can never be repaid? (More on this in the next chapter.)

Thus the time has come to grab the education sector, hold it upside down, and shake until whatever change falls out of its hapless pockets. As during the Soviet economic collapse, where public assets were directed into private oligarchs' hands, we are now witnessing a further and, given the relatively small change involved, intensely pathetic phase of the post-debt bubble cleanup: accumulation by dispossession, a neo-enclosure movement of neoliberal privatization, where what were heretofore public assets are transferred over into private for-profit and rent-seeking hands.[45]

American higher education supplies a prime relevant example. Explicitly abandoning their nineteenth century land-grant public service missions, our great public universities are now "public" in name as they now receive, at best, only a small and ever-diminishing percentage of their operating funds from public sources. This has been a creeping decades-long process, one of neoliberalism's crown jewels. Big State U. was not put up for sale at auction one fine day. Its "publicness" has been bled out of it over decades. In what ways are these contemporary universities "public" anymore? In what ways do they stand for anything other than *themselves* and their corporate donors? Indeed, they seem no more "public" than do Microsoft or J.P. Morgan Chase (and indeed are proud to form "partnerships" with such). They may even cause a greater amount of private indebtedness via the decreasingly repayable student loans that keep the whole system afloat. (To think: it was once thought that the "long march through the institutions" was being accomplished by the *left*!) Similar processes have been playing themselves out in US K-12 public schools through charters, vouchers, and also direct subsidy to private (including for-profit) schools. The latter option is now even more available in the US, via recent legal developments, most notably the *Zelman* case (2002) from Cleveland, that have cleared the way constitutionally for private religious schools, to receive public funds via parental vouchers. This development is significant because some 80% of private school students attend religious schools.[46] The accumulation by dispossession/enclosure pattern is simple: divide and conquer. What was once held in common must now be privatized so as to be forced into the individual "entrepreneurial" mode, only with the "deeper pockets" of a whole school or school district. Even under austerity, even a poor school district still has more money for the taking than do most individuals.

More, this neoliberal value-extraction project in education has global ramifications. A group of Chinese education scholars, well-positioned at the receiving end of it, explain how these extractive and what they view as "Eurocentric" characteristics are exported and result in a wholesale repurposing of educational institutions, a tighter alignment of them with the needs of capital:

The substance of modern Eurocentric education, duplicated by developing countries in the twentieth century and continuing today, mainly serves capital's drive to turn human beings into a factor of production in order to obtain surplus labor value. Modern education is also part of a superstructure that strengthens governments' power based on urban culture to implement pro-capitalist policies, whatever "ism" is claimed by the country. It requires that knowledge be

standardized and homogenized for convenient dissemination
... Such education benefits mainstream scholars and turns so-
called intellectual circles into interest groups allied with
capital. Institutional education controlled by mainstream
scholars has also commercialized itself as a worldwide
business. The globalization of such institutional education
shares the enormous profits from human resources...[47]

Not just the educational institutions and their budgets but also
the *inhabitants* of those institutions are to be streamlined and
otherwise more effectively deployed toward the capital accumulation of the rent collectors who have seized them. The "capital"
part of "human capital' becomes ascendant.

And it literally *ascends*. This process of redistribution upward
- one-sided class warfare from above - operates of course on a
vast scale that is hardly limited to education. It includes the sale
of public lands and resources; persistent privatization schemes
involving pensions and, ultimately, social security, health care,
and even formerly sacrosanct public preserves such as prisons,
the post office, and the military. This is the neoliberal period of
capital in all its fetid glory: the ruthless marketization of everything existing - including *itself*, in the sense that the marketization is itself marketed as, among other things, "natural," "fair,"
"win-win," "progress," and other empty signifiers. The
marketing of marketization has been so successful, though, that
at this point, as Slavoj Žižek famously remarks, "we talk all the
time about the end of the world, but it is much easier for us to
imagine the end of the world than a small change in the political
system. Life on earth maybe will end, but somehow capitalism
will go on."[48]

The comprehensive nature of its dominion can, however,
make us lose sight of the fact that *neoliberalism is a solution to a
problem*, namely, the TRPF, this time appearing in especially
potent form due to the globalization-enabling technological

developments of the last generation. Despite its manufactured air of naturalness and inevitability, the neoliberal global power play is also a world historical act of desperation.

Boiled down, it is a gigantic attempt once again to solve a problem that previous capitalisms failed durably to solve, namely, that *"normal" production cannot durably turn profits.* Due to the robust technological development that capitalist production inevitably engenders (ingeniously building in its own internal necessity in the form of inter-firm competition), it ends up by necessity squeezing its own profitability. Once again, this does *not*, by itself, cause capitalism to collapse. Instead, it causes it to *adapt* via various stratagems (deliberate or not) and stumble into whatever is to be the next mutation. What we observe, then, is a series of attempts to adjust for this crisis-impelling TRPF, the outcome of which is regularly acute enough to be labeled a "crisis." This jarring economic rinse and repeat cycle is not due to incidental bad luck or the contingent bad behavior of individuals or the weather or God but, as Andrew Kliman explains,

> the tendency of the rate of profit to fall and economic crises are instead rooted in a relationship that is "internal" to capital, the internal contradiction between physical production and the production of value that is built into the very functioning of capitalism: as physical productivity rises, commodities' values fall. As a result, their prices tend to fall, as does the rate of profit, and this leads ultimately to economic crises and the destruction of capital value.[49]

Capitalism from its inception has been one with its crises; they are not aberrations but are integral aspects of its self-adjusting mechanisms. And each time the "solution" for going forward created large changes to the world as a whole: the amazing windfall of cheap fossil fuel to motor the entire expanding enterprise, the misery and destruction of the world wars themselves, government war spending and Cold War at mid-century vis-à-vis the Great Depression and, since the early 1970s, consumer credit and debt bubbles to cover for wage deficits and, currently, the neoliberal societal makeover under the twin death heads of globalization and the bankers' stop-loss austerity programs that collectivize their debts.

Complicating matters, amidst all this is the spectacle of a clueless political right wing that dreams of a mythic return to a ruggedly individualistic capitalism, where virtuous Ayn Randian "Job Creators" use an allegedly "free market" to discipline if not eliminate unsavory actors - those whose villain role in the mythic story is to be the lazy, the impulsive, and the weakly parasitic who see themselves as being "owed a living." But we are long past this hallucinogenic quasi-libertarian collage of self-serving images.

Chapter 3

Upward instability and downward elimination

The fundamental instability of capitalism is upward.
Hyman P. Minsky[1]

[M]ore and more people are being permanently excluded from the economic system because it no longer pays to exploit them.
Hans Magnus Enzensberger[2]

Upward instability

At this point capitalism's many escapes from the TRPF have altered it irrevocably. In fact one might say that the counter forces to the TRPF have become more the thing than the erstwhile thing itself (which is one way of appreciating how the dialectics of change allows both for necessity and surprise). Of late, the neoliberal form of capitalism, even amidst its self-referential hysteria, has in reality become an inversion of what the right wing dreams it is. The allegedly arch-individualist titans have somehow banded together with a group solidarity that would be the envy of the most fervent syndicalist in order to rig the financial game for themselves. As Marx himself puts it, "capitalists form a veritable freemason society vis-à-vis the whole working class."[3] There is still plenty of competition, in fact, arguably more than ever, including, on an intra-sector basis, among the capitalists themselves. Due to widespread monopolies, though, the arena of competition is now to be found mostly among the *workers*, not the capitalists. Whereas we once had more widespread competition among capitals, who together confronted widespread solidarity among unionized workers, we now have the reverse: a pan-monopolist solidarity among capitals that confronts a globalized mass of anomic, consumption-focused workers who have been successfully pitted against one another. It is a dazzling world historical jiu-jitsu move, where competition and solidarity have switched class positions.

Back to that Hegelian 'no guarantees' caveat. There is an irony that Marx would have appreciated but he did not emphasize. While class antagonisms *are* indeed causing the disintegration of capitalism, it is not the proletariat who is the agent of change. That potentially fearsome entity has for the moment been tamed. Rather, in the long battle of their rational self-interest against the steady pull of the TRPF, it is the capitalists *themselves* who are destroying the system that once enriched them. As a laying hen will do over a lifetime, capitalism's productive system began yielding fewer and fewer eggs. Along aforementioned lines, strategies were put in place to try to counteract this epic profit slowdown. But these too began to fail. Most prominently, the purely banking and financial sector - as distinct from the traditionally productive sectors - began to rise as a proportion of the economy in an epic corrective quest for elusive profits. Depending on how one calculates it, an extractive FIRE sector currently accounts for a third or more of the US and developed economies and, in economist Michael Hudson's striking estimation, absorbs 75%-80% of US workers' wages (viz., housing payments, loans, insurance), "even before employees can start buying goods and services."[4] The speculative thrust of these operations, including the various hedge and outright Ponzi schemes, has illustrated how, as the renegade but now resuscitated economist Hyman Minsky put it a generation ago, "the fundamental instability of a capitalist economy is *upward*."[5] The instability is "upward" because it is the finance capitalists' chasing of outsized expectations for profit - expectations that develop during boom periods - that generates the systemic instability. "The tendency to transform doing well into a speculative investment boom is the basic instability in a capitalist economy."[6] Allegedly facilitative of the efficient movement of capital, contemporary hypertrophic finance ironically causes the opposite: a top-heavy wooziness among the bankers who are supposed to be in control but are actually more like a bar drunk stumbling around before finally toppling over, sleeping it off, and then repeating the process. All the while, the rest of us perpetually stand by to repair the damage and pay the costs. Repeatedly.

Influenced by Marx - though ultimately more sanguine about the possibility of "stabilizing the instability"[7] - Minsky argues that not only did this upward instability account for the nature of the contemporary boom-bust cycle, where the post-war period of stable growth was actually anomalous from the long term point of view, but it created a longer-term macro-problem as well. Since the amount of debt leverage undertaken by the financiers never resets all the way back down to zero during the de-leveraging bust phase (hair of the dog: the drunk never *fully* sobers back up), over time the system *as a whole* becomes more leveraged (i.e. indebted) in a three-steps-forward-two-steps-backward kind of way.[8] This means that although there continue to be mini-booms that follow mini-busts (e.g. the "tech bubble" of the early 2000s), with global finance capital now ascendant - especially after it began to be unfettered in the 1990s from New Deal-era regulations - it is only a matter of time until debt levels are radically unsustainable and a final, gigantic de-leveraging event (aka a crash) is inevitable, perhaps even the "terminal" crisis of capitalism always envisioned by the more ruddily apocalyptic Marxists. More frighteningly, the other historical solution to this problem has involved the outright destruction of fixed capital on a massive scale, with World War II being the major example, following as it did - non-coincidentally - in the wake of the Great Depression.[9] Just as the US permanent war economy - so-called "military Keynesianism" - has provided a crucial ballast for the system as a whole in the post-war period, outright war itself is *the* tried and true method for a capital re-set, one that capitalists can be regularly counted on to favor.[10]

Until the war solution dawns on them once again, the controlling financiers proceed along as if, in their desire to set a speed record, they are blind to that ninety degree turn in the road up ahead. All the while, strapped into the back seat is an isolated proletariat enjoying the scenery provided by the pre-fabricated ideology and yelling at the driver to speed up his own personal indebtedness. The point is that the financial capitalists are *themselves* doing the world historical work of bringing down their own system, abetted by a corporate ownership structure that encourages short-termism and practically demands that they behave this way, otherwise the expected high rate of short-term return simply will not materialize. In this ironic sense one can only applaud investment mega-firm Goldman Sachs CEO Lloyd Blankfein's notorious statement that he is just a banker "doing God's work." Onward march the financial soldiers.

To be sure, financialization and monopoly have fattened God's workers up with Gini coefficients (i.e. measures of inequality) that would be the envy of the emperors of old. But capitalism as we once knew it is now dead. And it is the capitalists who have killed it. They have counterintuitively killed their own *summum bonum*, the very God they claim to worship. As Nietzsche has his Madman say, "This prodigious event is still on its way, still wandering; it has not yet reached the ears of men. Lightning and thunder require time, the light of the stars requires time, deeds, though done, still require time to be seen and heard. This deed is still more distant from them than the most distant stars - and yet they have done it themselves."[11] As with Nietzsche's death of God, even though the deed is already done, the old patterns of thought may still persist for some time ("I am afraid we are not rid of God because we still have faith in grammar"); there is a lag time before ideology catches up. But the capitalists have now killed their dearly beloved. Until we collectively recognize the capitalists' murder-suicide, what we have at best is what the late Chris Harman termed a living-dead "zombie capitalism" that still walks the earth on government support and terrorizes us through austerity and other blood curdling measures.[12]

In the near term, to be sure, the monopoly strategy may "work" for the few cash-bloated individuals who can remove themselves to their gated communities, islands, and the like. But the system that enriched these individuals is now devolving into something more akin to the robber barons of the nineteenth century or, perhaps, into what might better be termed a neo-feudal arrangement where a monopolist rentier class, insulated from competition, sits back and watches the *bellum omnium contra omnes* reigning among the paupers on the outside. From the point of view of duties to the public at large, today's putative neo-feudal overlords are arguably quite a bit worse than their medieval predecessors. Cruelty was certainly widespread, but at least there was a common religious morality to provide some measure of restraint. Plus, as a practical matter, medieval castle walls were typically a place of refuge for the surrounding residents in case of war. By contrast, our neo-feudal lords' walls provide no refuge as they are built solely to keep the peasants *out*. There remains neither *noblesse oblige* nor any other animating ideal or restraining set of customs; there is only consumerist vainglory gorging itself on its "More! More!" This revolution from above has been won by a monopolist rent-extracting class that no longer dreams of Christendom or Imperium but rather of escaping completely from the rest of humanity. They have erected and are perfecting a new finance-based, technology-enabled and geographically stratified pathos of distance.

This fantasy of escape - "the possibility of an island" as in novelist Michel Houellebecq's evocative title[13] - represents a departure from an ancient ideal of civic-mindedness that has been influential since it was hyperbolically depicted as the guardian class in Plato's *Republic*. The legitimacy of Plato's idealized elites is based in large part on: a) their ability to *reject* a personal escape (into philosophizing), along with b) their inability as guardians to own personal wealth.[14] This latter was a bargain with at least some moral symmetry, i.e. those who rule cannot have, those who have cannot rule. Our bloodlessly acquisitive neoliberal overlords thus turn the traditional ideal around 180 degrees; they base their legitimacy on what they personally *own* and their ability to sequester themselves from the rest of us. They take and they consume - and we are to love them for it.

The signal difficulty is that they have now taken the decisive step of occulting themselves from the mass of the population - physically and in terms of the mechanisms of their rule. This severance has been made possible through technological innovation, especially in the areas of automation and computer and communications technology. These processes have in the short term provided a sort of neoliberal fantasy world for the few: less geographical proximity to ordinary people as well as less general dependence on them. Servants for menial and personal tasks are still needed, admittedly, but those from whom the surplus labor value is extracted in direct production are located farther and farther away, in Mexico, China, India and points beyond. It has never been easier to cultivate indifference to these distant toiling others and to remain willfully ignorant of the provenance of one's commodities, the "made in..." label being essentially part of the background noise of everyday life. At "home," whatever that means any longer, fewer and fewer of these "extra people" are still needed; they are simply too expensive at this point - with their unions, health care and family needs - and they appear now to be so expensive precisely because it is the *surplus* aspect of the surplus army of labor that has come to the fore. There is no place for these people; they are no longer needed. *A fortiori* there is no place for their legal freedoms, their health care, their infrastructure, their physical environment, their public safety or, indeed, their education. Capitalism is now finally done with them.

Elimination as the neoliberal endgame

No longer do they want to exploit you; now they want you gone.

Though the capitalists may be on the downward slope of the TRPF, one might think that the rising productivity that is part of the equation would augment workers' value and hence their job security, wages and benefits. Alas, this is true only *positionally*, i.e. for a worker who is *relatively* productive vis-à-vis his fellows. If I can outsmart and/or outpace my competitor job-seekers, all other things being equal, I ought to be able to command proportionally higher compensation. This dynamic works nicely for superstar athletes as via contract superstar performers enjoy a prodigious transformation of their athletic "productivity" into money because what they have to offer is either unmatched or very scarce. Yet *per impossibile* when *all* quarterbacks become Tom Brady this situation no longer holds; as the market becomes flooded with Bradys, the price-per-Brady drops proportionately as Brady-supply begins to outpace Brady-demand. And so it is that college graduates become barristas and PhDs drive cabs.

Such is the fate of the average worker in an age of increasing productivity: temporary positional gains for a lucky few, steps forward for selected individuals that help to legitimate the turning of the hamster wheel, but a long-term weakening of everybody's position vis-à-vis employers. Economists Robert Frank and Philip Cook term this dismal race the "winner-take-all society" in their book of the same title.[15] Frank and Cook explain how productivity gains from technology (with education as an important additive) overcrowd labor markets. This in turn allows employers to be more selective about whom they hire and reward. What follows is an environment where ever smaller differences in workers' productivity (or at least perceived productivity) begin resulting in widening gaps in compensation;

such employees are *worth* ever more relative to their fellows. An employee who is *slightly* more productive, say $1/100^{th}$ as much as her co-worker, receives not just $101.00 as against the co-worker's $100.00, but may receive $200.00 and/or an entirely better position in the company altogether. Since so few are able to eke out that extra $1, when it comes time for the very few to be differentiated, it is that small group of extra-$1-earners who stand out and not only "win" but win big. This phenomenon of small differences providing outsized gains in productivity and in turn outsized gains in compensation has many ramifications. Among them is the perceived linkage of one's educational credential, an alleged marker of the quality of one's education and/or class competence, with one's productivity. For example, whereas generations ago an applicant may have been asked only if he possessed a college degree or not, or even merely "some college," now he is asked precisely *where* he obtained that degree, if not also *what* he majored in. Ivy League, state school, community college: these are perceived as vastly different entities. Smaller differences matter more and more. Such super-competition is the fate of those condemned to fight over an ever shrinking portion of the pie.

As workers are thus divided and conquered, employers' leverage is further compounded by the massive downward pressure on wages wrought by globalization. To use an anachronistic manufacturing example, the Michigan assembly line worker no longer competes merely against other Michigan workers, or even those from Ohio or Alabama, but against the nameless, faceless (to him) toiling masses of India, Mexico and China who by US standards earn sub-poverty wages.

This creates an interesting situation for the school system in its traditional role as vocational conveyor belt, what one might think of as a kind of *upstream vertical integration* of human capital. "It is fully in keeping with the capital concept as traditionally defined to say that expenditures on education, training, medical care etc, are investments in capital," writes one of the most prominent mouthpieces of neoliberalism, Nobel laureate economist Gary Becker.[16] In fact, Becker allows that "education and training are the most important investments in human capital."[17] And capital, whether of the human kind or of any other variety, must be made to pay. It must be rendered malleable and serviceable toward its *raison d'être*: the accumulation of still more capital. Like fixed capital, human capital must be *shaped*, and not in ways that are necessarily congenial to the *capital* which, as part of whatever production process, may need to be re-purposed, transformed or eliminated altogether. The *capital* doesn't get to decide its own usage, the *capitalist* does.

Labor will thus be utilized or, more pertinently, *not* utilized. Simultaneous with the winner-take-all narcissism of small differences at the shrinking top of what Mikhail Bakunin (and later Lenin and others) called the "labor aristocracy," there grows at the bottom a mass of neo-peasants that is rendered structurally less and less employable - no matter what their standardized test scores and what good boys and girls they've been.[18] It seems that technologically-generated increases in productivity have allowed for a massive overaccumulation of human capital. One no longer just gets a decent and steady job by simply following the societal rules, as per the Clintonian rhetorical trope of championing those who "work hard and play by the rules." So at the diminishing top there is escalating incentive (and pressure) to succeed at school, whereas at the widening bottom there is diminishing economic incentive to care.

Just about every American kid, and certainly every middle class one, knows the promised (or threatened) chain of causality: do well on this exam *for* a good grade in the class *for* a good GPA, *for* a good college *for* a good job *for* a good salary *for* a good life *for* one's children's good life, etc. Reflecting on his working class youth in the American Midwest, John Marsh memorably elaborates what so many of us have always heard on the receiving end of this train of reasoning: "They put the fear of McDonalds in you. Either you studied hard and enrolled in college, or you took your chances in the local labor market. And for those with a high school diploma or less, those chances led, more or less, through the Golden Arches to a minimum wage job."[19] So there is constant striving at the apex for very real stakes at the same time that cynicism, alienation and despair spreads throughout the student body writ large. In its job-yielding role, one imagines the school system as a capsized and sinking ocean liner, where survivors scurry upwards to the remaining above-waterline areas, even as those areas disappear. Some have huge head starts and even their own life boats while some are all-but-doomed from the start. But nobody is really safe. There are no guarantees anymore. Not even McDonalds is always hiring.

What do these developments portend for education policy? With a certain economic instrumentalism regarding schools having almost completely saturated our political life, we can expect macro-economic conditions roughly to determine the outlines of education policy. (Hence the relative school/economy correspondence asserted above in the Introduction.) Not that this is airtight : as indicated earlier, the school system is vast, serves a number of interests, has its own internal imperatives and so enjoys a degree of relative institutional autonomy.[20] Nonetheless, a relatively crude economism holds sway overall and is manifest across a number of fronts, from the "accountability" craze to the commodification of schooling (higher education included) as a purely personal "possession" rather than any kind of public good that speaks to collective as opposed to individual/consumerist aspirations.[21] As the global economic plate tectonics shift in the direction of efficiencies of outsourcing, vertical integration, and the incessant augmentation of technologies of production, it is reasonable to expect education systems eventually to align themselves (or to *be* aligned) with economic needs. Via whatever policy levers are available to money-sniffing potentates, this has ever been the case.

Though it is unglamorous for educators who like to think they can by their everyday activities "change the world" (who like other Americans are taught this morale-booster as a birthright), history establishes that school systems track fairly reliably the socio-economic system within which they are ensconced. It is a correspondence thesis too dull even to say much about it: Nazism yields Nazi schools, Communism communist schools, apartheid apartheid schools, capitalism capitalist schools etc. And within those school systems, predictably, individuals are slotted for the cultural and economic roles that their environing society makes available for them, an iron law of correspondence recognized from Plato and Confucius to Horace Mann. The weak countercurrents that are commonly observable - however locally strong they might be - in the end only help to emphasize the direction in which the main body of the river still ineluctably flows: downstream. For every Deweyan Chicago lab school or holistic Waldorf effort, there are the other 99.9% of American schools; ditto for every freedom-loving Summerhill vis-à-vis the English system and every child-centered Reggio Emilia vis-à-vis the Italian. As per the cliché, these are the exceptions that prove the rule.

Understandably, many critical educators find this correspondence picture lacking in psychological uplift and therefore offer an imaginary, kill-the-messenger, deflationary sort of objection that school-society correspondence is bad for pedagogical morale; the lack of "agency" it seems to offer is regarded as depressing. A kind of reverse Tinker Bell logic is offered against any kind of structural analysis: if X makes one feel bad and is "disempowering," then X must be untrue. Unfortunately, one's emotional reaction to a possible state of affairs proffers nothing either for or against its existence. As Nietzsche understood, truth may be inimical to life and still be what it is. Besides, whether or not a given truth is inimical to life requires a separate argument.

If the truth strikes one as deterministic, this may lead to quietism, yes. But it may also lead to activism. Consider the Calvinists-cum-Puritans-cum-Pilgrims: as Max Weber famously described it in *The Protestant Ethic and the Spirit of Capitalism*, the world has rarely seen such a deterministic theology as Calvinist predestination. Yet "the Puritan ethic," holding that God would prosper his "elect" and show material evidence of His favor, counter-intuitively yielded one of world history's most energetically activist psychological orientations. One could make this same argument regarding ancient Stoicism (and Roman fatalism generally), for example, those versions associated with Cicero and Marcus Aurelius. One simply cannot assume the psychological directionality of a worldview.

Unjustified optimism may also lead to improper target selection. This is the classic Marxist position: while it may have a measure of relative autonomy, as a superstructural element, education is not where the real action is. The scene of resistance is the class struggle. In fact, an excessive focus on education, say, in the form of advancing an allegedly liberatory pedagogy, *in the absence of a broader and enveloping social movement*, is ultimately going to be delusional; at best it will help create even more delightful personal experiences to which the children of the bourgeoisie already feel entitled.[22] Marsh's above-quoted study *Class Dismissed* presents an updated statement of this thesis, reminding his readers of the sociological tradition from James Coleman to Christopher Jencks that shows the severe dependency of educational attainment on family background, aka social class. For Marsh, "we cannot teach or learn our way out of inequality." In the American context, this observation is reminiscent of FDR's "second bill of rights," and above all its declaration that "opportunity, including educational opportunity, emerges from a foundation of economic security."[23] More, the consistent faith that education is the cure for our national economic woes, as well as for individuals "*the* path to economic prosperity," has long performed the crucial ideological function of distracting citizens' attention away from unjust economic *outcomes* in favor of a focus on allegedly omnipresent economic *opportunities*, helping everyone maintain what Marsh sardonically calls "the belief in a just economic world":

> Education, you might say, is what allows people to sleep at night. Because Americans have built schools and funded loans and scholarships, anyone who wants to get ahead can. If people cannot or do not get ahead, however, that is on them. Indeed, the nineteenth-century faith in hard work and industriousness on the job did not disappear so much as it did migrate to a belief in hard work and industriousness in school. Those who succeeded must have worked hard in school. Those who failed must have not taken school seriously.[24]

Move along from the economic crime scene, children, nothing to see here. Nothing at all. In this respect, belief in the efficacy of schooling ultimately helps keep everything just as it is.

Marsh is right, in my view. But the situation is even worse than the Sisyphean picture of educational futility that he imagines. For the ideological cover schools provide is already being blown. Notwithstanding the place in our political tradition that Marsh rightly ascribes to it, even the pretense of education as the source of legitimate economic opportunity cannot be sustained in the face of chronic youth unemployment and youth disposability. The very economic forces that Marsh rightly places in the driver's seat are currently driving an entire generation off a cliff (minus a few privileged types who get to watch). The era of exploitation is ending. Enter the era of *elimination*. Say goodbye to social reproduction, "working class kids getting working class jobs" and all the rest of what was once thought by the left to be the most outrageous of injustices: the lie of equal opportunity and social mobility. Say hello to uselessness, disposability, precarity and whatever other dismal synonyms might describe the growing - and disproportionately young - ranks of the super-surplus humanity that has been squeezed out of a world that simply does not need even their hardest and most degrading labor. It simply wants them gone. They thus have *less* than their mere labor power to sell, as Marx imagined as the ultimate existential nadir for industrial capitalism's proletariat. All they have is their mere *humanity*.

Back to fatalism, then, this time both figuratively and literally. First, as in the Calvinism example, it is important to keep the lack of necessary connection between fatalism and inaction firmly in mind because the picture at present of large-scale human obsolescence is scary and bleak. Across many areas, especially in technology, many milestones are being passed, new vistas are being opened and new discoveries are being made. But from the point of view of the non-rich these milestones are likely to translate into new lows, the vistas are terrifying and the discoveries offering little cause for optimism. It was once thought that the worst thing that the capitalists did was to exploit you such that you ended up as less than a fully flourishing human being, your very mind and body turned into another productive gear. Yet as British economist Joan Robinson once remarked, "the misery of being exploited by capitalists is nothing compared to the misery of not being exploited at all."[25] In retrospect, it may look as if we never had it so good as back when they were exploiting us. In that same vein, we may retrospectively comprehend that the only thing worse than undergoing exploitation via schooling is *not* finding a way to undergo it.

With the advent of the globalized marketization of everything, we have now collectively crossed a rhetorical threshold beyond which the traditional left critique of education as exploitation seems quaint by comparison. Neoliberalism triumphant presents us with the more frightening specter of what I am calling *educa-*

tional eliminationism, by which I mean a state of affairs in which elites no longer find it necessary to *utilize* mass schooling as a first link in the long chain of the process of the extraction of workers' surplus labor value. It has instead become easier for them to cut their losses and abandon public schooling altogether. Any remaining commitments are purely vestigial and have more to do with social stability than with education proper, as vast swaths of our school system (particularly in urban areas) are decisively repurposed as holding facilities for (putative) proto-criminals, lost within what Henry Giroux decries as a "youth crime-control complex," with a special layer of legal menace for urban kids in what Michelle Alexander pointedly terms "the new Jim Crow."[26]

I adapt the term "eliminationism" from the very dark context of Holocaust scholarship, specifically the work of Arno Mayer and Daniel Jonah Goldhagen.[27] These historians trace the rise of what they call "eliminationist anti-Semitism," which is to be distinguished from the more practical "instrumentalist" orientation to be found among a segment of Nazi officialdom. The instrumentalists were ascendant at the outset of the War. They championed using Jewish and other prisoners as slave labor so as not to waste this valuable resource toward the war effort. It is the eliminationists, however, who won out at the notorious Wannsee conference (1942) with their advocacy of outright genocidal elimination of the Jews.

This ambivalence was reflected throughout the concentration camp network. The Nazis themselves distinguished between, on the one hand, mere concentration and forced labor camps (*arbeitslager*) and, on the other, single-purpose death and extermination camps (*Todeslager, Vernichtungslager*). Treblinka and Sobibor were largely examples of the latter, whereas Dachau and Buchenwald were of the former type. The lines were sometimes blurred. One could find both types of operations, for example, in the large camp complex comprising Auschwitz-Birkenau, where there existed both a series of labor camps (where untold numbers perished) alongside outright extermination operations for those considered unfit for work. The labor camps reflected the Nazi instrumentalists' desire not to "waste" this exploitable human mass, whereas the extermination camps reflected the exterminationists' desire for a "purer" genocidal elimination. Hybrid situations like Auschwitz were in this dark context a kind of compromise between the competing Nazi factions: work them to death. A "win-win" for both sides. Drain away as much labor value as possible and then when the slaves are expended, murder them. First exploit, then eliminate. Given the fundamental moral depravity of the genocidal world view that divides people into "human" and "sub-human," this is an eminently "rational" solution.

To those standing by to misunderstand this alarming comparison, let me make it clear that I am *not* saying that being unemployed in Flint, Michigan or enduring a dilapidated school in East St. Louis, Missouri is equivalent to being shipped to Treblinka. Given the choice, anyone would choose the former over the latter. My point is that *the two situations share a similar moral structure*: both involve persons who have been ideologically constructed as surplus humanity vis-à-vis the reigning power structure. The range of eliminationist possibilities open to someone in such a predicament is not inviting. It is, however, still a wide range, one whose spectrum encompasses wholesale neglect (e.g. disabled children a few generations ago, the street kids of the sprawling favelas of the global South) through to mass incarceration (e.g. young African-American males in the US, 1 in 10 of whom are actually *in* jail and in major US cities an estimated 80% have criminal records and so are subject to various forms of legal discrimination, including disenfranchisement, an internal form of statelessness) all the way through to the extreme endpoint of programmed mass genocide.[28] The point is that even though the *quantitative* difference between two states of affairs can be decisive, just as too much medicine can make it poison, a special vigilance must be maintained where the phenomena in question are *qualitatively* homogeneous. So while the ideational stance of eliminationism admits of a wide spectrum of responses, once people are consigned to social categories such as "useless," "disposable," "parasitic," and the like, history demonstrates all-too clearly that this is a slope that can become slippery very fast.

Note also the complicating factor that austerity and policy eliminationism are rarely advertised as such. The publicists for these efforts are much too effective to allow such crudeness. They are of course typically advertised in the opposite terms as efforts to *save* schools and children and so on, akin to how budget cuts to education, including such programs as Head Start for impoverished preschoolers, are advertised as for the benefit of "our children and grandchildren." This bizarre hypocrisy calls to mind Slavoj Žižek's point that consumption seems always justified in terms of *saving* money. The ads don't directly say *"SPEND! BUY!"* etc. but instead they say *"SAVE!"* and present themselves paradoxically as the embodiment of frugality. You cannot afford NOT to buy our product! As part of this effort "free" items are ubiquitous: 30% more - absolutely *FREE!* Žižek jokes that he would like to ask for only the free 30% of the toothpaste and leave the rest at the store for someone else to buy.[29] We see precisely this rhetoric at work with regard to today's educational eliminationism: We must destroy today's schools in order ultimately to help future children, who will somehow emerge for the better from the damage done to their current education (which if true would justify further destruction). This is reminiscent of the notorious reported quote from a US Army officer speaking about the Vietnamese village of Ben Tre during the Tet Offensive: "We had to *destroy* the *village to save it*." One of course notes the irony of moving from "it takes a village to raise a child" to destroying the village in order to raise the child. Which, I wonder, do we think will actually raise the child?

The exsanguination of public goods and collective life in order to enrich banking elites, otherwise known as "austerity," is one such location along the above-named strategic spectrum. Pressing examples of the starvation diet of what might be termed "austerity eliminationism" would include the devastating higher education fee hikes in Britain and the massive K-12 public education cuts at the state level in the US. The other side of the same coin might be termed "policy eliminationism," with leading examples being the designed mass failure of US schools under No Child Left Behind and the ongoing and multifaceted attacks on public school teachers' working conditions. It should now be clear to everyone that neoliberal education policy is not about reforming public schools. It is about obliterating any remaining vestiges of the public square via a market discipline that is officially supposed to apply to everyone but in reality is selectively applied only to those lacking sufficient wealth to commandeer state policy; ironically, the sacred market applies to public schools not to megabanks. It is in essence the strategy of the gated community, where those at the top "have theirs" and withdraw from the educational commons and into their state-backed corporatist enclaves. Our elite captains are abandoning the public educational ship in whose hold still lie nearly 90% of US school children.[30]

A caveat about how we should understand this new educational enclosure. In my view it is a misunderstanding to say that what we are witnessing is a "withdrawal" or "retreat" of the state from the public sphere *simpliciter*. There is indeed a push toward "privatization" and Orwellian named "public-private partnerships" in schools and elsewhere (especially in universities), but as in the case of voucher (and many charter) schemes, these are still to be funded by public money and as such they are better understood as reallocations of public resources such that they are available for private capture by elites. In this sense it is a *redistribution* (upward of course) of public wealth, in a sense a vast theft and a form of domestic accumulation by dispossession.[31] On the largest scale, the processes before us might be described, in Hungarian-British Marxist philosopher István Mészáros's terms, as a "systemic hybridization" of state and private sectors where, ironically, the state attempts to protect elites from the vagaries of the marketplace through massive bank bailouts, loan guarantees etc.[32] Regarding the latter, even the oft-used phrase "casino capitalism" is misleading. In our current situation of socialized risk and privatized gain for those at the system's "commanding heights," it is tails they win and heads we lose. Imagine a casino in which you play with the house money and if you win you get to keep all the winnings to yourself, whereas if you lose, the house covers your bets. The literally astronomical public sums required to continue this arrangement for the minutest percentage of the population is the proximal cause of the squeeze on public resources. Schoolchildren, the poor, the sick, the disabled, the elderly etc., must all sacrifice so elites no longer have to undergo the risks that are officially supposed to be inherent in their role as fearless capitalist risk-takers. But the zombie lives on in the cherished ideology of "competition," whose virtues are conveniently to be reserved only for the masses. Competition and risk is for *small* businesses and other little people like private and public sector employees. Populist conspiracy mongers such as radio host Alex Jones are quite right in this sense to fear a "socialism" that they equate with government-enabled neoliberal globalization and enslavement by world banking cartels. On this point, the critique is not so different from that of the Marxist Mészáros (above) who indicts systemic hybridization. Simply put, what we have currently is the worst of both systems: a "lemon socialism" that provides a genteel monopoly and social safety net for elites while it simultaneously increases austerity, meanness and heartless competition for everyone else.

Can this eliminationist strategy be opposed? Identifying and naming it helps, I think, but that is only a start. A great deal more than argumentation is needed actually to challenge the eliminationist trend, but argumentation is part of it. As a preliminary step, it is helpful to grasp as fully as possible what it is that one opposes; weaknesses in conceptualization tend to manifest themselves in the course of political struggle. There is of course a dialectic in which one grows clearer about one's goals as one actually engages in the struggle, just as one becomes clearer about the nature of a roadblock as one tries to remove it. But one must start somewhere, otherwise there is blind lashing out and inadequate self-awareness. As Immanuel Kant put it in his first *Critique*, "thoughts without content are empty, intuitions without concepts are blind."[33]

In this spirit, I contend that traditional left narratives of opposition have generally framed their concerns - either explicitly or implicitly—within what I would call a neo-Kantian moral framework. Specifically the familiar "formulation of humanity" version of the categorical imperative, where Kant advances his famous dictum that one should treat human beings never merely as means but also as ends in themselves.[34] One does not have to self-identify as a Kantian to be generically "Kantian" in this regard; there is a strong sense in which we are all Kantians now, particularly when it comes to near-universal lip service given to some notion of human rights. In Kantian terms, for example, slavery is understood to be uniquely morally abhorrent because it represents a comprehensive reduction of human beings to tools for someone else's projects, the zero point of human exploitation. The simple moral argument against this kind of dehumanization is rendered in the iconic "I AM a MAN" placards carried by the Memphis sanitation workers in the 1968 strike. Upon such general moral bases, canonical left critiques of education have tended - rightly - to focus on education's exploitative aspects which, in the Marxist analysis, means exposing the extent to which schooling is at the service of capital both directly, qua supplier of labor, and indirectly via social reproduction of existing class relations.[35] And analogs have emphasized how racial, ethnic, gender and other identity configurations are similarly implicated in the reproductive dynamic.

Yet despite the diversity of legitimate concerns, the moral outrage still flows from a sense of violation that is most coherently understood under the aspect of the Kant-like imperative to resist states of affairs that reduce human beings to mere means. If systems of work and schooling are exploitative, the root moral concern is that in some crucial sense they rob people of their full humanity (again: the Memphis sanitation workers' strike). If those systems are vicious regarding persons' particular identities, the violence (symbolic and real) being perpetrated implies a diminution of those persons' dignity in precisely the Kantian sense. As anti-colonialist existentialists such as Frantz Fanon and Aimé Césaire emphasized, identity-based forms of violence constitute yet another way of reducing a person to a thing-like status and therefore represent a denial of core constitutive features of our shared humanity:

> Between colonizer and colonized there is room only for forced labor, intimidation, pressure, the police, taxation, theft, rape, compulsory crops, contempt, mistrust, arrogance, self-complacency, swinishness, brainless elites, degraded masses … No human contact but relations of domination and submission which turn the colonizing man into a classroom monitor, an army sergeant, a prison guard, a slave driver, and the indigenous man into an instrument of production.
>
> My turn to state an equation: colonization = 'thingification.'[36]

Whatever "civilizing" rationale was provided as pretext, it seems clear that colonialism was motored first by the economic exigencies of exploiting the labor of indigenous populations (concomitant with the resources of the "discovered" land itself). The oppositional moral core of the intergenerational anti-colonialist project was one of basic recognition, the human right to be self-determining, autonomous, and a chooser of one's own destiny.

A fundamental part of the dream of emancipation remains the "negative freedom" not to be coercively subordinated by some powerful Other.[37] Abolitionism is therefore also a dream of non-exploitation. Along with the many poems and songs of the Arab Spring, from Tahrir Square and elsewhere, the most poignant and now iconic example of this dream remains the Tunisian fruit seller Muhammad Bouazizi's self-immolation, December 17, 2010. Harassed, robbed and otherwise pushed to the edge by corrupt and petty government officials, Bouazizi felt he had no other gesture open to him than that of publicly taking his own life, the ultimate "illustration" of his thing-like status vis-à-vis ruling elites. The power of Bouazizi's desperate moral lesson - in a way the purest imaginable "pedagogy of the oppressed" - can be seen by the near-universal sympathy it evoked among Tunisians and later Egyptians, and eventually protesters across the region and the entire world and remains widely credited for the Arab Spring revolts that overthrew the dictators Ben Ali and Mubarak and still continues to reverberate in the region. So powerful in fact was Bouazizi's *cri de coeur* regarding basic human dignity that it was able to overcome in the Muslim popular mind the traditional Qur'anic prohibition against-suicide.[38]

Despite the continuing resonance of what I am identifying as a neo-Kantian approach, from abolitionism to Bouazizi, the globalizing mechanisms for which neoliberalism speaks work to change this thoroughly modern equation. As per the Robinson aphorism, we are now in a position to understand how exploitation may not be the worst possibility, even with its dehumanizing aspects. The newer kind of non-recognition involves not merely reducing people to means but simply wishing them away and ignoring them altogether; in this way at the level of concern for the Other, we are transitioning from *abuse* to *neglect*. An increasing proportion of humanity - in the global South but also here at home - grows non-exploitable economically. Their labor is incapable of importing enough value to render them serviceable for traditional capitalist production and so they are economically "out of the loop" - and often geographically as well, as in the case of the restive suburban *banlieues* around Paris. They have become "extra people" and superfluous. At best their relation to the formal economy is occasional and precarious as evidenced by the stunning growth of those living most of their lives in what anthropologist Keith Hart describes as "the informal economy," living, for example, under subsistence conditions of "forced entrepreneurship" such as prostitution or the selling of odds and ends.[39] These are the disposable ones, the "outcasts," from Kinshasa and Dakar to Detroit and Brixton, who increasingly populate our "planet of slums."[40] Furthermore, as anthropologist Jan Breman suggests in his study of the laboring poor in India, "A point of no return is reached when a reserve army waiting to be incorporated into the labor process becomes stigmatized as a permanently redundant mass, an excessive burden that cannot be included now or in the future, in economy and society. This metamorphosis is, in my opinion, the real crisis of world capitalism."[41] Estimates are that about one third of the world's work force presently falls into this category, those more or less permanently ensconced in the "informal" economy without a regular paycheck and beneath the "normal" chain of exploitation (*nb*: they are still of course exploited, but in a modes antedating traditional capitalism such as chattel slavery and patriarchal domination). In Marxian terms they still constitute a vast "reserve army of labor," albeit one that long ago became much more "reserve" than "labor." Their main productive function now is to serve as part of a disciplinary warning to precarious remaining workers that "but for the grace of the (job) Creator, there go I." There is nothing quite so helpful as an economic downturn for reminding workers how grateful they should be for a job, *any* job.

In some areas there is little need for even the pretense of offering these forgotten people an education. Where appearances need to be kept up for political reasons, the new "education" being envisioned for these subaltern populations is no longer that of our grandparents' world of schooling as an extension of economic exploitation. The new educational policy is animated by the simpler and even more chilling logic of eliminationism. Its immediate precursor is not in the dark and satanic mills of eighteenth century Manchester, but rather the literally eliminationist industrial genocides, ethnic "cleansings," and indiscriminate air bombardments of the twentieth century. The shortcomings of current education policy do not equate to the murdering of people in camps. But the moral logic of their situation is structured perilously close to identically: some are no longer exploitable and are beneath even being treated as means to our ends; and if we cannot even use them for our own purposes, we would be better off without them around at all. Chronic un- and under-employment leads ineluctably to disinvestment in universal schooling; austerity becomes an easier pill to swallow when there is a sense that those on the receiving end are no longer needed anyway.

As their surplus labor no longer powers any capitalist's profits, the only schooling that makes sense for them would be in the service of social control: physical surveillance and incarceration, on the one hand, and on the other, the psychological diversion of desire into harmless self-wounding channels of consumerism and/or drugs, the latter providing an expedient way to lock away a huge number of potentially disruptive *lumpen* elements. David Simon, creator of the HBO series *The Wire*, set in what he would surely agree is a post-industrial, eliminationist

Baltimore, writes:

> It's been estimated that nearly half of the adult African-Americans in Baltimore are unemployed or underemployed - a consequence of decades in which the need for an American working class has been minimized and the industrial base has been transferred overseas to improve corporate profit. Meanwhile, we relentlessly pursue a drug prohibition that has quadrupled our prison population over that same period, creating a prison-industrial complex that is the largest in the world. By any measure - in raw numbers, in percentage of population - America now jails more of its people than any country, including all totalitarian states. We pretend to a war [sic] against narcotics, but in truth, *we are simply brutalizing and dehumanizing an urban underclass that we no longer need as a labor supply*. And what drugs have not destroyed in our ghettos, the war against them surely will. [emphasis added][42]

Meanwhile, those (temporarily) outside this growing carceral system are themselves being prepped for a life of perpetual uselessness, where the capacities are cultivated neither for creativity nor production but only for commodity consumption, which presents the only remaining arena of social value and recognition. These are neoliberalism's ideal "democratic" subjects, who political philosopher Wendy Brown describes as "available to political tyranny or authoritarianism precisely because they are absorbed in a province of choice and need-satisfaction that they mistake for freedom."[43] It is no longer so much a matter of fine-tuning schools vocationally to align them with perceived corporate needs (though there is still plenty of that for those temporarily more fortunate). It is ultimately a matter of eliminating education in any meaningful sense as a component of what is expected for a "normal" life for most of the population. To channel Mike Judge's simultaneously horrifying and hilarious film, a near-documentary of "normal" late capitalist everyday life, the planned education-less "idiocracy" awaits.[44]

One does not have to be a Foucauldian adept to suspect that neoliberalism has for some time been redesigning our education systems for failure - just as Foucault's Enlightenment era prisons began a profitable and self-justifying cycle of delinquency and recidivism.[45] These kinds of systems "succeed" as they inevitably fail in a self-perpetuating restructuring of schooling as pre-incarceration. As Simon puts it in the above-quoted interview, what we have created in our urban no-hiring zones, in "places like West and East Baltimore, where the drug economy is now the only factory still hiring," is a situation where the "educational system is so crippled that the vast majority of children are trained only for the corners". On the model of the prison, the one-two punch of accountability and austerity - again, the strategic twins known as *abuse* and *neglect* - are designed to destroy the possibility of meaningful education for large parts of the population, beginning with the poorest segments and colonizing outward. Is it mere coincidence that in the urban US, the school dropout rate for young black males hovers around 50% up to 70% in some areas) and their incarceration rates are not much lower, around 35%?[46] And only *one in four* young black men in New York city aged 16-24 are employed.[47]

Under the *ancien régime* of human capital theory, such a situation would have been thought a waste. Why throw away all that potential labor that could, even if engaged only in menial occupations, add value in the production of commodities and services to help enrich elites? Why leave that money on the table? The current situation leaves one almost nostalgic for that older debate. It says, "Spare me your worries about exploitation! You should be so lucky as to have that problem! At least you get a paycheck." Whereas before in the retrospective "good old days" the struggle was to justify one's economic *usefulness*, the struggle at present is to justify one's very *existence*. This is in many ways far more frightening than before. For their part, elites have not clarified for themselves the question of the defensibility of: *If I can neither convert you nor exploit you why bother to teach you?* There is a need for institutions of surveillance and incarceration, certainly, but *education* is a waste. The shorthand way of saying all of this is found in the newfound battle cry of the global capital: "Austerity!" Or, more precisely, austerity for the 99% while the 1% - *purely because of their class position* - enjoy apparently limitless government backstops and bailouts.

This progression away from education-for-exploitability to educational contingency has given a new urgency to the basic question of the universal distribution of public education; the basic Kantian moral question of what is involved in treating others as ends in themselves rather than mere means takes on a specific new urgency. In recent years we have conceded the argument about universal education almost wholly to a narrow economic instrumentalism about the aims and purposes of the enterprise. Predictably, we now see that those who live by the sword of economic utility die by it too; if educational outlays are to be justified on the basis of their economic utility, when the utility is gone, so is the justification. As recently as a few decades ago, one might still hear in public discourse talk about human rights, democracy, civic and moral education and maybe even the odd murmur about such broader ideals as human creativity and flourishing as such. That is all gone now. Even once politically bedrock Jeffersonian and Deweyan visions of education as the bases of democratic sovereignty and intelligent social policy are few and far between. At best there is a distributive justice argument - a mere shadow of the civil rights movement - that sees education as one consumer good among others that should be distributed more fairly so that those who are disadvantaged can enjoy consumer goods at the same rate as their wealthier compatriots. Implicit in this argument is that education is a *personal* good that is "owned" by the individual as a legitimate vehicle for personal enrichment and that the magic of the invisible hand aggregates these educated individuals and purposes them toward an overall societal good. But it is in no sense a *public* good that creates any wider communal obligation beyond one's personal consumerist horizon. The "good *for everyone*" part we never quite reach; as an alternative "next best" outcome, a certain segment of the population is simply enriched instead.

The victory of this narrow ideology of educational economism is so complete that it is no longer distinguishable from what passes as common sense. These unexamined assumptions grow more powerful as they become less explicit, withdrawing into an *éminence grise* controlling position from amidst the shadows of our collective psyche. *It goes without saying* that the point of education is to enhance personal economic life chances. *It goes without saying* that the reason to expend public funds on schools is because the economy demands it. *It goes without saying* that universities are worth funding because they help "grow" the economy, meaning that they are to be repurposed toward corporate and military interests.

Philosophically all this presents a stark challenge concerning the ideal of universal of public education. The neoliberal educational new order negates the universal aspiration by bifurcating educational subjects into two main categories: the narrowly economically useful "saved" and the narrowly economically superfluous "damned." Not that there once existed some Golden Era of "education for itself" from which we are now fallen. One should remember that industrial capitalism gave rise to the current system of universal public education in the first place. But when Marx famously wrote "all that is solid melts into air" he meant precisely "*all*." Not even one's most cherished institution is safe from the creative/destructive capitalist whirlwind - not even practices and verities that once seemed completely outrageous to alter. We have thus come to a point where the economic base has shaken elements of the educational super-structure such that parts of it once thought impregnable have started to crumble and fall. Those who hitched their education cart to an exclusively economic justification - we should educate all children because of the economic benefits that will accrue to us all collectively - have no answer when automation renders even "educated" labor unprofitable to elites. During times of economic crisis, "education for its own sake" and even "democratic citizenship" become feeble rationales for the vast outlays necessary to maintain a system of universal free public education. Plus, the logic of education-as-commodity comes home to roost precisely here: if school credentials are one's own *personal* ticket toward economic advancement, why should the rest of society have to pay for it? (See Chapter 4.)

It is important to understand further that eliminationism may come in many forms. It is not necessarily that campuses and schools are being physically shut down. There may even be a building boom. It is that these institutions lose any independence and directional autonomy, for example, schools that become little more than a testing factories, military recruitment centers, and in-processing operations for the penal system. (I was reminded of this personally when I observed the three banners decorating my son's rural high school cafeteria: "Go Navy," "Join the Marines," and "Drink Milk!") So it is not necessarily so much a matter of the physical boarding up and shuttering of the buildings. The bricks and mortar can be used for whatever purpose. Consequently, it is a mistake to assume that one is necessarily preserving anything essential by maintaining them.

From a wider lens, what is actually occurring is that monop-olistic neoliberal elites are asserting their grip more strongly by more directly harnessing all social institutions as adjuncts for their ever-more desperate drive to accumulate capital. The Nazis called this cultural harnessing *Gleichschaltung*, by which they meant the airtight alignment of social institutions with Party ideology. This was one of their most distinctive ambitions. In 1930s Germany, *Gleichschaltung* was accomplished by subjugating the population through mechanisms of fear, prejudice, propaganda and legally-sanctioned Party criminality. In the contemporary world it is accomplished through fear, prejudice (against the Undeserving Other), propaganda, and legally-sanctioned banker criminality. In terms of the potential richness and complexity of human life, however, the end-result is structurally similar: a flattening-out and homogenizing of the range of what human beings value, where every activity is to be translated into the language of only *one* would-be totalizing sphere. This in the end is the neoliberal leviathan in all its monomaniacal glory. It seeks only *itself*, a monomaniacal sameness, ultimately offering the existentially terrifying boredom of absolute self-identity.

In making itself its own goal it thereby excludes such extraneous claimants for moral status, such as, say, human beings. This should begin to make us quite suspicious of this neoliberal "ideal." Who are these rugged competitive heroes who live by the global free market alone? Who actually embraces this? It is manifestly not today's capitalist class, who by now by and large enjoy secure monopoly positions from which they can *watch at a distance* the little people tear each other apart as gladiatorial economic sport. As they have utilized government rules to snuff out anything resembling the free markets of yore, the monopolists atop the system are perhaps the least likely actually to believe in neoliberalism. There are segments of the rest of the population who do embrace it, though, in bits and pieces here and there - albeit manifest in sometimes incoherent sentiments such as the pitiful cretins holding signs warning the government away from their medicare (a government program). These are people who have half-internalized the idea that turning against one another and competing for crumbs is somehow more ennobling than collective action against the gluttons at the high table.

Old tricks of divide and conquer such as racism, xenophobia, religious clannishness (which yields a sense of belonging and "metaphysical comfort"), and sometimes purely Madison Avenue-manufactured aesthetic preferences, like the designed distaste for protesting "hippies," further confuse the crumb-seekers. The depressing irony appears to be that the only people who "believe" in neoliberalism - and then only halfway - are the ones who are actively being victimized by it, the ones against whom it is wielded as a propaganda weapon. Neoliberalism thus reveals itself as nothing more than a propaganda campaign, an ideology that corresponds to nothing and has no actual adherents; those who mouth its rhetoric loudest would not dream of actually living by what appear to be its precepts of radical competition and value monomania. In the end it is a *weapon* whose power derives from its not being viewed as such, an empty signifier whose very potency derives from the vacuum at its center. Like a well-placed ellipse, its appeal lies in its ability to become the object of whomever's projections, as is often the case with abstract ideals like "freedom." As Kierkegaard suggests in his wickedly sardonic *Diary of a Seducer*, contextually vague abstractions are always the best for seduction and flattery, as they are indeterminate and open enough to serve as a blank screen for the flattered one's projections.[48] Vain creatures, we always love *our own* projections more than those of others. In this way, an ideology in which nobody believes is potentially the most dangerous of all; in its very vacuousness resides great power. Traditionally, this core of narcissism, flattery and deceit is the telltale modus operandi of none other than Satan himself. "When flatterers meet, the devil goes to dinner. Flattery is so pernicious, so fills the heart with pride and conceit, so perverts the judgment and disturbs the balance of the mind, that Satan himself could do no greater mischief. He may go to dinner and leave the leaven of wickedness to operate its own mischief."[49] *Ye old deluder neoliberalism!*[50]

Am I saying neoliberalism is Satanic? Yes, precisely that. As per the English proverb, it is the perfect demonic possession for a secular age: it is Satanic but without the need for Satan himself. With neoliberalism as the reigning ideology, the 1% can go to dinner; they can relax, enjoy themselves, and allow their favorite ideology to babysit the masses and put them to sleep with all the right stories. It is the Platonic noble lie perfected and made global.

Is this perhaps itself an elitist conception of Althusserian "false consciousness"? Yes. It is. I do not believe there is a deep-rooted, respect-worthy peasant Truth to be found in pickup truck ads, personal ownership of assault weapons and FOX News. On offer in this sloppy neoliberal mix is a colorful collage of self-contradictory and self-congratulatory images: pristine nature to race a car through by oneself, an eternal sunshine of abundant fossil fuel, insatiable consumer appetites, and also, somehow, allegedly "traditional" Christian "family values." It is a simultaneously senile yet also infantile hallucinogenic panorama of illogic and ignorance. It is the ideological expression of the strip mall and the chain restaurant, all simulacra, all nostalgia and every molecule of it geared toward immediate consumption. Bright lights, dim bulbs. Or, I should say, bulbs *made* to be dim.

This is the educational world we fall into when we allow the ideology of neoliberal eliminationism to take hold. Capitalism has run its course. And as per Nietzsche's Zarathustra, it is the capitalist class and not the proletariat who have killed it. But still, zombie-like, the appellation "Capitalism" still roams the earth, gratifying adherents and frightening the children. But the major capitals of the world are no longer in a competitive position vis-à-vis one another; they have become, as Marx foresaw, a more or less fused and generalized capitalist class whose dominion over states is almost total. The alleged existence of a "competitive capitalism" is arguably the greatest illusion of the era, and the greatest credit for the victory of that illusion goes to a neoliberal ideology that softens the targets sighted for monopolist dominion. As argued previously, the sphere of education is one of the juiciest of these targets. It is one of the last bastions where people work for paychecks, yes, but also for something other than a paycheck. This "other than" must of course be eradicated - through austerity, testing, merit pay, public shaming of teachers, in short, by whatever means are at hand. All save the true owners of the world must be disciplined by market forces in order that they too must learn that they are mere tools in another's workshop, mere things to be discarded when no longer of use. And the educators' uses are running out. At present, they are mostly in fact running on the fumes of the historical promises and labor militancies of yesteryear.

Only a shrinking segment of the population is economically useful anymore; they are no longer providing sufficient value to justify themselves economically. They are simply not needed and are now a net drain, just as is their very biological existence (witness the US politics of health care.) From the point of view of neoliberal systems and the monopolists they - and the terrorizing point is that one never knows when that "they" becomes a first person "I" or "we" - are in the most literal sense from a systemic point of view *better off dead*. This, I think, should concern us: that we have come to inhabit economic and educational mechanisms that stand to benefit from our non-presence - our *elimination*.

Chapter 4

Educational eliminationism I: Student debt

The American higher education system succeeds brilliantly at one thing: producing a subservient graduate who has no choice but to join the labor force on terms dictated by her future corporate masters.
Dmitry Orlov[1]

Debts that can't be paid won't be.
Michael Hudson[2]

Education as investment and debt

Contemporary educational debt has unique features that render it especially pernicious. It is also colossal, in the US having recently surpassed both consumer credit card and auto loan debt. This chapter describes student debt as a kind of "existential debt" that may be analogized to previous forms of legal indenture and/or bondage that are morally illegitimate on their face. It is not that student debt is identical to chattel slavery - one needs to maintain some perspective. But it shares structurally similar features sufficient for it to be a legitimate arena of emancipatory struggle. Education as human capital represents productivity augmentation and as such it is just as crucial a part of the internal gearing of capitalism as is technological and financial innovation.

In terms of the larger picture associated with the TRPF, personal financial education debt functions largely as a displacement of the costs of augmenting labor productivity *onto the backs of (future) workers*. These costs are incurred mostly in order for firms to keep pace with technological innovation occurring during the course of intra-sector competition. Both Acme and A-1 manufacturers and also Acme and A-1 service providers need to keep pace with one another within their respective sectors. Capital owners then reap for themselves most of the resulting competitive "victories," though, as we have seen, *ex hypothesi*, those victories are necessarily short-lived and occur within long-wave historical cycles of falling profit rates across the ensemble of all sectors. As part of the productivity equation, education is an indirect tool for enhancing capital owners' profits, a mechanism whose usefulness waxes and wanes according to the needs of production. At a certain level of techno-logical development, namely, the previous two centuries' long wave of industrialization, a moderate level of education for workers (i.e. basic literacy and socialization) was needed in a widespread enough manner for an ideal of universal education to achieve ascendancy.[3] Previous modes of production, where the vast majority were involved in rural agricultural production required correspondingly little or no formal schooling for most people, and even then the motive forces propelling matriculation were mainly ancillary cultural reasons such as religious literacy and/or a nationalistic affiliative "civic education" consonant with the emergent nation-state. The historical scaling up of schooling thus contributes - adds economic value - via produc-tivity enhancement (on the demand side it also lubricates exchange by fabricating consumers' "needs"). As such, mass education has served as one of the crucial counter forces that have perpetually kept the TRPF at bay.

As emphasized earlier, even in its institutional manifestation as schooling, education is of course valued culturally for many reasons other than its ability to enhance profits and, dialectically, the very economic needs that occasion mass schooling often lead to political consequences that elites do not anticipate and sometimes find unwelcome. (For example, the expectation of consumption, say, at a Woolworth's lunch counter in Greensboro, NC in 1960, engenders companionate expectations of universal nondiscriminatory access.) So a simple economic reductionism is not adequate to the phenomenon. Yet the mechanisms of capital accumulation must be recognized in order to curb the excess idealism and uncritical triumphalism that is commonly built-in to standard accounts of the supposedly glorious spread of state-provisioned universal schooling. Despite its inherent complexity, contemplating the origins of mass schooling illuminates how the systemic sustainability of mass education depends on its macro-economic use-value to elites and, secondarily, its *perceived* use-value to the public at large vis-à-vis individuals' perception of their own individual life chances and that of their children. In times of relative stability and prosperity (as during the American post-war period), it is easy to take this economic functionality for granted and in its smooth operation forget it exists, as tools in the flow of their working use tend to "hide" from the consciousness of the tool-user as objects of the tool-user's conscious attention.[4]

Episodes of economic crisis, however, have their own pedagogic function, as they make the economic system a conscious object of attention whereas previously it had been taken for granted *sub rosa*. Perhaps there is widespread collective "discovery" of how expensive, dys-functional and even strange and "unnatural" it is. (This psychological realization process is given huge momentum via the spread of personally-accessible information and communication technologies.) Though formal education is valued for many, many reasons, periods of acute economic crisis reveal its functionality for capital to be at least a *necessary condition* for schooling's intra-systemic stability; once the *economic* costs are perceived to exceed its *economic* benefits, the mass schooling enterprise is much more easily cut loose from the apparatus, an event we are now seeing on a widening scale. This is a large component of the willingness essentially to abandon whole city school districts as components of what Chris Hedges calls capitalism's "sacrifice zones," as well as the platform now given to a growing chorus of doubters questioning whether personal and societal "investment" in higher education is worth it, both for individuals and for society at large.[5] In the cold-eyed context created by economic crisis, the non-economic rationales for education against such powerful economic tides reveal themselves to be laughably weak, quaint anachronisms of a bygone age: education for itself, civic virtue, citizenship, character etc. These rationales are all washed away as official rhetoric grows more crabbed in response to economic exigencies; those promoting non-economically utilitarian justifications are ultimately consigned to the status of mere curiosities, at best reserved for brandy and cigar time at self-congratulatory elite conclaves - after the *real* business is concluded. If it does not directly aid capital accumulation, it is not "serious" and it does not exist.

Viewed through a wider lens, as a large-scale investment in human capital, the educational "improvement" of workers represents an audacious effort by elites to have their cake and eat it too: to enjoy the enormous profit taking opportunity presented by industrialism's efficient scalability of productive labor (qua variable capital) while at the same time *fixing* that labor (qua fixed capital) so that it is *existentially immobile*, no more likely to leave the circuit of production than a bolted-down machine tool would walk out of the factory and start looking for a new job. (I say "existentially" immobile as distinct from *geographical* mobility, which only increases, as workers are expected to render themselves increasingly geographically fluid according to employer needs: moving away from families, commuting wherever etc.) Conveniently, it also aids wage repression by credentialing the surplus army of labor in order to limit the bargaining power of that army's higher-end "labor aristocracy." The "educated" workers are thus shaped in ways more suitable for whatever are the profitable industries of the day and less suitable for vestigial modes of production such as farm labor which, until surprisingly recently, constituted the vast majority of the labor force even in advanced economies such as the US.[6]

The workforce is thus urbanized and, especially in the postwar period, suburbanized into industrial and post-industrial (service) sectors.

Meanwhile, as discussed in the preceding chapters, at the level of the political superstructure, even more audacious is the *upstream externalization* of the costs of all this pre-workplace training, most of which are borne in developed economies by the public at large. This takes place historically first in primary and then, for the last century or so, in secondary education. Concomitant with this process, education becomes a double-barreled universal human right: not only is it extended as an entitlement to the entire population (including, eventually, women, minorities and even the disabled) but it is also rendered *compulsory* for children and adolescents within prescribed age ranges (in the US this occurs sub-nationally at the state constitutional level, wherein resides the formal legal mechanisms of entitlement-compulsion, guarantees of provision and age requirements being examples.)[7] They make one an offer that one cannot refuse; one receives the schooling as a mandatory and thus structurally ambivalent "gift."

Tertiary education presents a mixed picture, as the political forces around it remain diverse and unsettled, analogous to the ferment of forces and counter-forces present in the nineteenth century prior to the near-universal extension of secondary education. Higher education presents a hybrid of relatively direct state subsidy (e.g. university appropriations, scholarships, government student loans and loan guarantees), private philanthropy (especially at elite universities) and, increasingly, personal financial obligation on the part of the students themselves. There is also significant tit-for-tat corporate involvement, especially in university research and co-curricular areas of study such as business and business-relevant technology that are often regarded as comprising, as at my own university, a "pipeline" of relevantly-skilled labor.[8]

As technological development began requiring matching labor productivity enhancements (aka "schooling"), higher education became increasingly seen as a necessary condition for a "decent" middle class life with a modicum of personal economic stability and a tolerable level of dignity. "Don't be a fool, stay in school" - for longer and longer. Yet offloading the costs of worker productivity onto the public proved to be insufficiently cost-effective. The US still provides perhaps the purest example of the "solution" of simply charging students and making them essentially customers of a privatized higher education system that could, ideally, enrich itself while enriching the students who are supposed, in turn, to enrich their future employers with their prodigious university-added productivity. At first, state systems were erected alongside the older elite colleges as so-called land-grant institutions (state supported colleges erected mostly in the nineteenth century and devoted at least rhetorically to the public good), a process that reached its zenith with the G.I. Bill (1944) that extended free higher education and other job training to millions of returning veterans. Since then, however, especially in the last generation, that zenith of public subsidy of higher education has declined precipitously (though not in absolute dollars), to the point where today it accounts for only a small percentage of the funding of even nominally "public" universities.

Public involvement is now present mostly in the form of government-run and government guaranteed college student loans that may be utilized for courses of study at public, private and even private for-profit institutions. For young people in many advanced economies, this is perhaps their first life experience of the crazy quilt of Mészáros's systemic hybridization: government loans to attend private colleges, private bank loans to attend public colleges etc. As with the home mortgage tax deduction and other home ownership encouraging policies, state policies promoting college attendance, increasingly via personal student loans rather than direct institutional subsidy, have contributed to the gigantic private debt bubble that now defines and dispirits the rising generation. As a college degree has become no longer *sufficient* but merely *necessary* for the good life they have been sold, the rising generation has become effectively trapped within walls that are now moving in on them. The education that was supposed to be the ticket *out* of a lifetime of economic difficulty is for more and more now a ticket *into* chronic economic difficulty. Yet it is still necessary as the alternative of not attending college promises even worse prospects for individuals' life chances. As fewer and fewer workers are needed due to capitalism's productivity overshoot, there will be no exit from credentialed penury for the inexorably enlarging and inevitably restive pool of youthful surplus labor. This generation is now destined to *occupy* and otherwise challenge an educational-financial complex regarding which they constitute evidence of failure and against which they begin to appear as a mortal threat.

Student debt as debt bondage

Stadtluft macht frei ("city air makes one free") was a medieval German motto reflecting the legal situation of many serfs.[9] If one fled to the city - dare we say "occupy"? - and survived for a year and a day then one was considered liberated from the feudal bonds that had legally tied one to a lord's estate. Rural serfs were expected to engage in agricultural production, including the customary yielding of a percentage of one's harvest and/or husbandry to one's lord. Increasing sophistication in banking and trade allowed labor-hungry cities to begin asserting themselves against the nobility, in large part because of the latter's chronic thirst for liquidity. This was a key internal contradiction within feudalism: landed nobles' need for cash, causing them to become dependent on urban bankers and their ilk, which helped accumulate the capital that preconditioned modern capitalism itself. Meanwhile, as per the motto, arising from within the interstices of the feudal contradiction was an enlarged set of liberties for the erstwhile tradition-yoked serfs, formal freedoms which in turn generated their own contradictions.

Considering the recent global occupy movement, it is apparent that the city air is still capable of at least allowing us to glimpse what freedom might mean; as the chants suggest, "this is what democracy looks like." Prominent among the concerns of occupiers worldwide is the extent to which educational debt has truncated their possibilities and, in effect, tied them to a certain way of living in a way that is structurally not unlike what faced an eleventh century European serf. The spatio-temporal parameters are of course quite different: student loans do not bind one for life to a particular lord's physical estate. Rather, they bind one for a significant *part* of one's life (and if one is not careful and/or lucky, *most* of it) not to a particular estate but to whatever rent-collecting corporate bank happens to own one's educational debt.

Yet it is clear that the very articulation of this disanalogy reveals important underlying similarities; the comparison of contemporary student loan debtor to medieval serf is more than mere hyperbole.

Indeed, some argue that "neo-feudalism" is a fitting appellation for the debt-driven, "systemically hybridized" corporate monopoly state in which we now find ourselves.[10,11] What we face with this neo-feudalism, according to one blogger's Jeremiad, "is more like serfdom with declining opportunities and increasing debts for all, but especially for the young."[12] More effectively than the Sheriff of Nottingham ever could, the comprehensiveness of our collection grid has rendered it impossible to flee to any safe haven, urban or otherwise. Financial analyst and philosopher Charles Hugh Smith minces few words about the overall situation:

Our dependence on debt has turned America into a neofeudal society, where the financial Elites are the equivalent of the Feudal Lords living in well-protected castles, while the debt-serfs (the rest of us) toil our entire lives playing interest on our own debt and paying taxes that are used to pay interest on the government's debts.[13]

As the idea and practice of "occupy" itself embodies, the only alternative is, literally, to stand one's ground, petitioning one's debt masters and the public at large.

Accordingly, efforts to organize around student debt forgiveness and/or repudiation continue to gain steam, as manifest by newly sprung efforts such as StudentLoanJustice.org, Occupy Student Debt and forgivestudentloandebt.com.[14] There is also a large-scale petition effort aimed at obtaining a million signatures from student borrowers, university faculty and sympathetic others demanding loan forgiveness under the slogan "Can't Pay! Won't Pay! Join Us! Don't Pay!"[15] As might be expected there are different perspectives among activists, from "pragmatic" reformists who merely want easier repayment terms to radicals who argue for complete repudiation - and just about every position in between. And there are practical difficulties faced by individuals that may or may not conform to whatever is the most principled public policy position. Just as it is not inherently hypocritical to advocate for public transportation while owning a car, under actually existing conditions individuals must be given leeway to deal with their own student debt as best fits their situation.

Whatever may be strategically wisest for individuals and the movement(s) as a whole, my purpose here is to argue that educational debt repudiation is *in principle* justified because educational debt is *in principle* illegitimate. Sure, it is legitimate within the context of hyper-financialized capitalism and the monopolist rent collectors who are kings of that particular hill. But why should those at the bottom accede to such an unjust topography? It is time to reject the network of assumptions that make student borrowing seem "normal," "a good investment," in short, as a one-way obligation of borrower to creditor in which the former makes a "free" choice to purchase a commodity for which she must now pay - and pay and pay.

Following traditions of social imbalance-correcting Jubilee practiced in pre-capitalist times, it is necessary to recognize that the debt system can evolve from being an instrument for human use to a tool of domination over the vast majority of humanity, one of those Hegelian master-slave reversals akin to that which Marx identified with regard to accumulated capital itself.[16] Crushing student debt loads have, because of their very nature, begun existentially *enslaving* a significant percentage of our youth, who because of them author less and less of their own lives.

Last year, it was widely reported that US student debt surpassed credit card debt, racing past the $1 trillion mark. Average indebtedness for all college graduates continues to grow, skyrocketing into the many tens of thousands and is in many cases dramatically higher.[17] Moreover, student debt is legally and perniciously special, as since 1998 it has been rendered largely undischargeable in personal bankruptcy proceedings.[18] The Orwellian-titled 2005 "Bankruptcy Abuse Prevention and Consumer Protection Act" (the title of which implies that the "abuse" is on the student-borrower side) further reinforced the non-dischargeability of student debt by including private loan providers in the state-enforced protection racket that will go to almost any length to chase down debt runaways. If the debt is to the federal government, at least it takes several months of missed payments to be considered in default. If, however, it is a private loan, *one single payment* can be sufficient to throw the borrower in default. What happens in default? There are still limits to the amount of money that can be extracted at a given time, but it can and will be taken eventually, along with any federal benefits, tax refunds and wages that can be garnished. In some cases, professional licenses such as those in law, medicine and teaching can even be revoked. Enormous penalties can be levied: in one case reported by the *Wall Street Journal* last year, a family practice physician was charged $53,870 for a *single* late fee when her medical school loans were turned over to a collection agency. One can also be sued. Though such extractive mechanisms still operate within limiting legal parameters (for the time being), the point is that this kind of debt has been specially designed for durability; it is, one might say, practically less "alienable" than, these days especially, one's basic civil rights. In the words of one financial advisor, "Don't think Uncle Sam will drop the matter. The feds can and will stalk you indefinitely."[19]

There is almost no escape from this iron cage that has been carefully refined by our banking overlords and puppet politicians. This inescapability, secured by the coercive power of the monopolists' predatory state, resolves long-term student debt into, essentially, a system of government-backed mass peonage, a kind of debt bondage with copious historical analogs. The most famous of these in American history is probably that endured by ex-slaves in the Reconstruction south, where the newly freed were informed that they must now work off the "debts" they had allegedly incurred to their erstwhile masters.

Common worldwide, this debt peonage form of slavery has been explicitly prohibited by the United Nations Supplemental Convention on the Abolition of Slavery (1956): "Debt bondage, that is to say, the status or condition arising from a pledge by a debtor of his personal services or of those of a person under his control as security for a debt, if the value of those services as reasonably assessed is not applied towards the liquidation of the debt or the length and nature of those services are not respectively limited and defined." (From "Section I. - Institutions and

Practices Similar to Slavery," United Nations, 1956).[20] Given the usurious and predatory nature of today's student loan industry (including colluding universities), as is appropriately decried and documented by English professors Andrew Ross and also Jeffrey Williams (who both label these debts a form of "indenture"), any assessment of the "reasonableness" of those debts - let alone the extent to which their "length and nature" is appropriately "limited and defined" must proceed with grave doubts about their legitimacy.[21] As Ross relates, "the agony of student debt has been a constant refrain. We've heard truly harrowing personal testimony about the suffering and humiliation of people who believe that their debt will be unpayable in their lifetime."[22] In the name of the UN, perhaps it is time for the blue helmets to roll in and to cordon off our universities and their financial aid offices, before they sell off still more unsuspecting 18 year-olds into lives of unremitting debt bondage.

These new student debt slaves are neither bullwhipped nor pressed into chain gangs (yet). Rather, they are far more cost-effectively indentured in a form that allows them the "freedom" to choose the job by which they will repay their creditors. While crude peonage systems tend to prescribe the exact means by which the debt is to be repaid (e.g. "build this," "plant that" etc.), the wise modern financier understands how needless and bothersome it is to assume the old *paterfamilias* kind of responsibility, which has its own associated costs. Rather than housing and feeding the slaves as extensions of one's manorial holdings, "free" them to wander around outside in search of their *own* food and shelter; let *them* worry about it. And outsourcing tracking and enforcement actions against the debtors makes this "freeing" of the peons all the more profitable. From the point of view of the capitalist, it is a perfect synthesis of modern and ancient systems: all the control of medieval serfdom combined with wage slavery's freedom from any responsibility for individual workers' welfare.

Meanwhile, in parallel with housing and health care, as real incomes decline and what remains is rendered more precarious through record un- and under-employment, particularly among youth, this system of neo-peonage is being tested.[23] Unlike housing, where one can in principle walk away when the monthly mortgage payments can no longer be met (or squat until physically removed), with educational debt there is nothing from which to walk away. The education you've received is "in" you and so the creditor's would-be collateral is inaccessible - just as you can't "give back" the post-disease health you now enjoy via the medical realm. Even if, *per impossibile*, one could return the education, it would not be fungible for the creditor, i.e. convertible into anything he could use. Hence the singular importance, for the system of neo-peonage, of the non-dischargeability of this non-collateralized debt: not one of your possessions - car, house, computer etc. - but your very educated *self* is the "property" that is owed back. In a sardonic twist on the American Declaration of Independence, the world ruled by bankers ascribes "inalienability" not to one's basic civil rights - which may be compromised away on the flimsiest of pretexts - but to one's personal financial debts which, ideally, must be given priority over and against all other aspects of one's legal and political status. One's rights are debatable; one's debts are not.

The non-dischargeability/inescapability feature of this kind of debt is very much in line with the monopolist rent-seeking strategy of risk removal, where the goal is to inhabit a site within the system where income streams are guaranteed without contingency. From the rent-seeking perspective, the student loan should not be seen as an investment/gamble on the future prospects of the student, where there is some risk that the borrower may not graduate or make enough money post-graduation. In the Banker State, such contingencies are to be removed by whatever necessary means. With gravity-like reliability, loaned money must simply be returned at as high an interest rate as possible but without any risk. In contrast to the ideological storyline, the competitive part of capitalism must actually be mitigated so those already possessing capital can sleep at night, those ones who *deserve* their money without having actually to earn it in the traditional venture capitalist mode of assuming risk.

As is the case historically, with debt peonage comes a flipside aristocratic mentality about money; creditors should not have to be sullied with unseemly bourgeois *effort*. Their money should just "arise" as divinely ordained rents from below; the ultimate sure thing, an entitlement. The ideal of freedom operates dialectically here. Financial freedom, in the sense of freedom from the contingencies of the market, is purchased by the monopolist - i.e. they gain their own financial security - at the expense of student borrowers' ability to "pursue happiness" over the course of their lives. Given the inescapability and the long-term nature of the debt, the debtors are, as is intended, rendered ever more precarious and subject to the volatilities and downward wage pressures of the globalized labor market; the *first* question is, of course, does the job *pay* rather than whether it is consistent with one's own conception of human flourishing - let alone whether it represents anything morally defensible. The sense of having an open future consistent with one's personal ideals crashes hard against the rocks of the debt repayment imperative. Admittedly, this is partly just life cycle maturation: by definition as one traverses life one chooses some paths at the expense of others; in this sense, possibility foreclosures can be merely artifacts of maturity, an inescapable aspect of the human condition. One grows up and becomes one thing and not another. What is not an inescapable part of the human condition, however, is that one's life choices should be determined by rent-collecting financiers, whose very existence is made possible by the ghoulish existential feast they make of the possibilities of our young. As Dmitry Orlov pointedly describes it,

Along with accepting the burden of educational debt, the graduate makes a number of key concessions: the financial success is more important than doing what you want; that having a career is more important than family life; and, perhaps most importantly, that failure is not an option. The newly graduated dentist cannot afford to realize that rotten teeth really freak her out and that she should perhaps do some volunteer work unrelated to dentistry. The need to repay the guaranteed student loans means that she must drill those teeth, whether she wants to or not, while heavily medicated if necessary.[24]

We have given away so much that it becomes radical to suggest that anyone other than the 1% should be able to exercise any meaningful control over their own lives.

But is this whole comparison of student loan debt to peonage/slavery just hyperbole? Taken a certain way, the analogy is easy to ridicule. The deflationary humor consists in the juxtaposition of vivid images of American style race-based chattel slavery, with its cages, chains and bullwhips, its radical involuntariness and its life span - even intergenerational - comprehensiveness. Its brutal physical aspects spring immediately to mind as well, the prevalence of backbreaking agricultural labor and the physicality of its routinized punishment and torture. That set of images, played off against that of an office-working twenty- or thirty-something making monthly rerepayments, provokes a smug and dismissive laugh. Where's the bullwhip?

What the merriment conceals, however, is how the two systems share an underlying logic; my point is not of course that they are *identical* but that they are structurally similar. Under classical capitalism, wage "slavery" replaces actual slavery (including its equivalencies such as lengthy indentures, the aforesaid debt peonage, feudal serfdom, and the like), as the laborer sells her labor time piecemeal. For Marx, the ideal system for the capitalist is one in which production has been deskilled such that any given worker has nothing at all left to sell but her labor power; all direction and autonomy in the workplace must be given over, ultimately to the capitalist class as a whole, i.e. more or less, the 1%. Though structurally precarious as part of a surplus army of labor, the worker is formally "free" to contract with whichever capitalist in exchange for, it is to be assumed, life-sustaining wages. Though the capitalist owns the labor during the pendency of the contract, it is formally *my* labor to sell because it is something that I yield to the capitalist only temporarily as per the agreed upon conditions. This hazy idealization represents a central component of the ideology of capitalism: workers freely contracting with employers, invisible hands benignly adjusting labor markets, employers competing to secure the best workers and the rest of the sales pitch.

But when I am working to repay a debt that is securitized by my very person, even the pretense of formal freedom is hard to maintain. This is where the analogy with slavery and/or serfdom comes into play. Under traditional slavery there is no exchange of labor for wages. In a sense, the labor is not extractable - alienable - from the slave because the master owns him *in toto*. There is no decision to become employed, no *contract* between parties, no *exchange* of labor for wages etc. Ostensibly, a slave working in his master's workshop might look the same as a day laborer manufacturing the same tool in a capitalist's factory. Yet the internal dynamics of the two processes differ critically. To use Marx's (1867) language, capital is composed of "fixed" (or "constant") and "variable" (or human) capital, the former consisting of things such as factories, plants and equipment - the "stuff" of production - while the latter consists largely of the human component of production, namely, the workers and what it takes to sustain them (as such this kind of capital has an "objective" and "subjective" aspects). Under conditions of full blown slavery, properly speaking there really is no human capital, as the "human" has formally been removed from the equation. The physiological entity doing the work must be fed and housed, "it" may suffer injury, and "it" will need to be attended to in various ways. But such attention is no different in kind from the ongoing attention required in order to maintain the productivity of fixed capital: oiling gears, cleaning, repairing and replacing machines, and so on.

Admittedly, recent forms of slavery and serfdom exist as anomalies to the "normal" arc of history in which they seem destined to be replaced by wage labor. But wherever such situations do still exist they are capable of yielding up profits to the capitalist-owner just as surely as are the more modern arrangements. Marx writes, "The process of production ends in a commodity ... A commodity produced by a capitalist does not differ in itself from that produced by an Independent laborer, or by a laboring commune, or by slaves."[25] Slavery and associated forms tend to lose out in the economic long run because of the greater service provided to the accumulation, concentration and deployment of capital offered by the more fluid surplus army of wage laborers. But in any given isolated instance, the degree of micromanaging control that old time slavery provides still proves tempting for even the most modern of capitalists. Yet ancient slavery, as complete ownership of a person and all he produces is too blatantly a violation of contemporary legal norms (plus the optics are very bad, witness the campaigns against child labor). Feudal serfdom, while more promising as a *partial* ownership of the fruits of the landed laborer, remains overly contingent because it subjects the owner's profit to the vagaries of production on a particular geographical estate or in a particular economic sector such as agriculture (which itself contains contingencies such as weather and input prices like seed and fuel). The new educational debt bondage is an improvement on these more primitive arrangements because it unites, from the financial capitalist's point of view, the best features of old and new: the flexibility and disposability of the wage laborer and the personal ownership and debtor's inability to escape provided by the old. In many ways one can see it as a companion - and even furtherance - of the "race to the bottom" wage repression perpetrated on workers generally by neoliberal globalization. Instead of the bother of opening a plant overseas - or threatening to do so - the financial capitalist can now simply extract wage concessions *directly* through mandatory ongoing payments.

This is why the battle over student debt is also a battle over economic (and moral) self-definition of so-called "human capital": What about those educated (and hence expectantly productive) human workers? Are they part of the fixed capital machinery, tied to their jobs as surely as the machines are bolted to the floor? Or are they, as human beings, better understood as variable capital and hence at least to some extent contingent and self-determining agents who may come and go, demand more for themselves, and ultimately perhaps use their own autonomy to alter their workplaces and what comes out of them?

Student debt as existential debt

Because the education for which one's debt accrues becomes an inextricable part of one, it becomes a chain that is tethered not to a particular commodity but to *oneself*. One cannot leave the keys and walk away from oneself or present oneself to the repo man. Perhaps brain science will one day discover a way to lobotomize away one's college years, but even so such a "return" would be valueless to the creditor, as there would seem little exchange value to a snipped prefrontal cortex. So in a relevant sense, after having acquired it, one is "stuck" with one's educational purchase as decisively as one is stuck with one's own vital organs. This is because, as human capital theorist Gary Becker explains, "you cannot separate a person from his or her knowledge, skills, health, or values the way it is possible to move financial and physical assets while the owner stays put."[26] What this means is that an inseparable and non-isolable part of oneself is the debt generating culprit; in this case one does not owe a debt *for* the car or *for* the goods purchased via credit card, but rather one owes educational debt *against oneself* or, more precisely, against what one has become. One might call this species of debt *existential*, a kind of debt from which it is impossible to separate one's very continued existence. Basic health care and, arguably, at least survival threshold levels of other goods such as food, clothing, and shelter would all fall into this category, the category, one might say, of basic human rights and needs. The only way to escape such existential debts, i.e. those accrued as the raw material of survival and/or such as educational debts that have become an inseparable part of one, is by jubilation, flight, or death.

I would suggest that existential debts in areas such as education and medicine provide a coherent focus for protest. Debts like these that have been accrued against one's very being are *ipso facto* intolerable for any kind of just and democratic society because they attach too comprehensively and exert such excessive control over individuals as they move through life. Distinctions would need to be made, of course, so that "existential debt" does not become an overblown category. I do not think this would be so difficult, really. Maintaining a simple quantitative threshold would head off most criticism, for example, that which might say, "that haircut" or "that movie changed my life and is now an inseparable part of me." The response is that such debts are *de minimus*, a legal category meaning that some things are so trivial that they are beneath the notice of the law. A movie, book or performance may alter one's outlook on life, and so metaphorically speaking become an inextricable "part" of one, but the debt associated with the $10 entrance ticket will not be determinative of one's life chances, in the way that large medical and educational debts commonly are.

Also, as the term implies, existential debts are those that have been attached in the service of maintaining life itself. This is obvious enough in the case of medical bills. (Though even here one needs to distinguish elective from necessary procedures - a fraught but achievable undertaking, perhaps one regulatory aspect of the current health insurance system that could be salvaged and repurposed.) But given our contemporary economic and social context, educational debts would still fit comfortably within the "existential" category as well. For some time now it has been clear that in most cases at least a college degree is needed for any kind of job security and the level of income most Americans would consider a "normal" middle class life. For better or worse, educational credentials have simply become more and more relevant to one's life chances. As the premise for a moral argument such as the one I am making here, this consideration is not at all an ethereal and merely speculative point; it is in fact solidly ensconced in one of the most important moments in all of American legal history, in none other than *Brown v. Board of Education* (1954), the US Supreme Court case that made official racial segregation unconstitutional. A curiously little-discussed aspect of *Brown* is its actual argument for overturning a century of racial apartheid in American schools. As a major premise of their argument, the unanimous *Brown* Court pointedly articulated what I am calling the existential importance of education in American life:

Today, education is perhaps the most important function of state and local governments. Compulsory school attendance laws and the great expenditures for education both demonstrate our recognition of the importance of education to our democratic society. It is required in the performance of our most basic public responsibilities, even service in the armed forces. It is the very foundation of good citizenship. Today it is a principal instrument in awakening the child to cultural values, in preparing him for later professional training, and in helping him to adjust normally to his environment. In these days, it is doubtful that any child may reasonably be expected to succeed in life if he is denied the opportunity of an education. Such an opportunity, where the state has undertaken to provide it, is a right which must be made available to all on equal terms.[27]

In 1954, the basic right to education was understood as extending through secondary education. Nearly sixty years later these same considerations apply full force. The only difference is that, just as changing socio-economic realities in the nineteenth century extended the right to education through primary school, and the early twentieth century extended that right through secondary education, in the 21st Century surely "it is doubtful that any child may reasonably be expected to succeed in life if he is denied the opportunity" for higher education as well. If higher education has truly become a ticket into the American "good life" then it ought to be kept fiscally neutral, i.e. not conditioned by students' economic class or ability to pay. One should not have to sell oneself into decades of debt bondage just to find a decent job - or, increasingly, the mere *opportunity* to try to find one.[28] As Samir Amin explains,

We speak highly of continuing education, which the rapidity of the transformation of productive systems imposes from now on. But this training is not designed to favour social mobility towards the top, with a few unusual exceptions. Additional knowledge and perhaps new knowledge, is necessary to simply retain their place in the hierarchy. This continuing education is conceived, at its best, to reduce the disaster of lost usefulness (and employment), to slow down the social mobility towards a lower level (marginalisation), but no more than that.[29]

The time has long passed when post-secondary education constitutes some kind of exceptional vehicle of social mobility, where four years of college places one on an upward path. This is indeed another feature of existential debt: with an air of desperation in the larger context it tends to involve the borrower's mere maintenance rather than positional socio-economic gain - analogous to situations in which pressed households will turn to credit for necessities.

Overweening banking interests further reinforce the neoliberal drive to commodify education by promoting the credential, ideally a mere token of educational experiences, at the expense of those experiences' actual occurrence. As a first step toward commodification, the credential is given increasing ontological priority over the actual education because the credential is saleable; it sells *ergo* it *is*. In the context of an increasingly precarious and massive student loan system, one can understand the drive toward reducing the educational experience to a credential as an almost desperate attempt to *securitize* educational debt, to turn it into a credential-commodity over which some control could be exercised, such as withholding it or, indeed, repossessing it (maybe by refusing to release the diploma, as is currently common practice among registrar's offices with regard to transcripts for graduates with outstanding debts). This would provide additional leverage to the creditor, so long as there is a social consensus that an education is valueless if it is not fungible, that is, ultimately transformable as a personalized commodity into money for the one educated. In this connection, it helps if the education received actually has little to do with that for which it allegedly "prepares" the student, as we see in many professional programs.

In my field, education, there is a longstanding dilemma in this regard: to the extent that the professional preparation, in this case of teachers, is made relevant to the extant "real world" of public schools it looks more and more like an apprenticeship program and as such begs the question of why such a program is housed within a university at all. Why not simply let school districts develop their own apprenticeship programs for student teachers? The same could be said of business programs and other pre-professional programs that are not overly technically demanding. As it stands, the university in many cases supplies a credential standing in questionable relation to the practice for which it is supposed to be a reliable supplier of initiates. This de-tethering of the credential from the actual practice is part of the commodification drive; *the credential* is one's goal, and the classes, any incidental learning that might take place, etc., are so many streamlinable means to that end. The risk to the universities in playing this short-term game is, of course, that the emperor will be discovered to have few or no clothes, as they allow the "educational" part of the experience to wither away - as, arguably, is currently happening across a higher education system that is failing even by its own terms.[30] One might term this a certain "dilemma of relevance" caused in part by the pressures exerted by students-as-customers who want a proper return on their educational investment: the "education" received must be pursuant to job prospects and future remuneration but to the extent that the university answers this imperative by making its curriculum "relevant" in the requisite manner it undercuts its own *raison d'être*. If what one really wants is an apprenticeship program, why attend anything like a traditional university at all?

What we are learning, I think, is that this financialized drive to commodify education ultimately resolves itself into a commodification of *oneself*. Existential student debt provides a crucial step in this unfortunate alchemy. In another one of those master-slave reversals, college graduates find that the education-commodity that they thought they owned turns out in fact to own *them*, just as surely as does the ensemble of mortgage, car loan and credit card debt that one usually finds out about later. If *ex hypothesi* the education one has received is now an inextricable part of oneself, a component of one's very identity, a great deal is at stake here. In a word, it is one's very *autonomy* that is on the block. Via consumer debt, the capitalist class through their banks own our houses, cars and who knows how much of the "stuff" of our lives. A line is crossed, however, when the owned goods turn out not to be physical stuff but component parts of our very selves, for example, education and health care. When the 1% assert ownership over not only our things but *we ourselves* as well, we have entered - or, I should say re-entered - a neo-feudal space wherein we have become literal peons, doomed, Sisyphus-like, perpetually to be working off our debts so that we can, one day, be free.

Members of the previous generation would dream of the great day when they would at long last make their final mortgage payment and then in old age own their houses free and clear. The current generation dreams the same dream, but with a crucial twist: that elusive final payment pays off the educational debt that is by definition part of their very being. So it is not the house that is to be fully owned (minus taxes!) but it is their *very being* over which they long to take possession. Dreaming of owning houses and cars is one thing. But it is axiomatic that free people do not need to dream of *their own* freedom; when they do so they are obviously no longer free.

Nothing to lose but their chains

The solution is, as always, revolution. In this case the revolutionary act would be to repudiate educational debt as illegitimate. *All* of it. This would at the same time involve seeing at least basic, pre-professional higher education as a human right and a public good that should be free to all who wish to benefit from it; a rollback at one of its most vulnerable points of the neo-enclosure movement that seeks continuing privatization of everything. Cary Nelson, President of the American Association of University Professors (my own union), elaborates:

Now, when we could have everyone's attention, let's promote a basic principle: public higher education should be free. We need an educated citizenry to participate in public debates in an informed way. We need to fund public higher education at a level that makes it accessible to all qualified high school graduates. We need to reform a system that too often extends poor-quality education to the poor and high-quality education only to those whose families can afford it.[31]

The cost would be perhaps $60 billion a year, less than we have invested in corporate bailouts, far less than the federal government spends on unnecessary weapons systems. The struggle to shift our priorities will be neither brief nor easy. Those who have sought for years to decrease access to higher education will certainly attack this proposal or mock it. Nonetheless, it is time for an unambiguous, principled national campaign for free public higher education.

To appreciate the magnitude of this gesture, it is necessary to understand how education, first at the K-12 level and for the past couple of generations in higher education, has become an arena like so many others in which the capitalist class has socialized the costs of their productive processes. Instead of taking it upon themselves to provide basic education and training to workers, enlightened and "progressive" business interests lobbied successfully for the erection and extension of free and compulsory universal public schooling, where the costs of a more educated and hence more productive workforce could be displaced from the profiteers onto the public as a whole. It is one of the earliest and most enduring forms of the neoliberal project (for K-12 *avant la lettre*) of socializing risk while privatizing gain. The children who are placed into them are the only truly innocent aspects of kindergarten. Seen through a historical wide lens, our education system has for generations massively enhanced worker productivity which has in turn massively enhanced elites' profits.

At the very least it is time now for some social payback. We can start by that $60 billion referenced by the AAUP President and throw it *immediately* right onto the backs of the 1%. They can afford it; the rest of us cannot.

As Engels wrote, "The slave frees himself when, of all the relations of private property, he abolishes only the relation of slavery and thereby becomes a proletarian; the proletarian can free himself only by *abolishing private property in general*."[32] Analogized to student debt, this means that the struggle is not to ease *my own* payment terms or, lucky me, have *my own* student debt forgiven. It is, rather, to eradicate the *very idea* of student debt in general by making higher education free. If nineteenth century America saw fit to do this with primary education and early twentieth century America with secondary education, surely twenty-first century America can follow suit with higher education. What, one wonders, is the alternative? Reforms aimed at easing payment terms and/or making college "more affordable" for individuals, while understandably appealing to desperate borrowers, will not alter a system of predation based on two main lies: that education is a commodity possessed by individual students and that those students may in turn have their lives possessed by whomever owns their erstwhile education, i.e. whomever owns *them*. As per Engels, it is the privatized conception of education that must *itself* be abolished.

This radical conception of one's education as something other than one's private possession leads to two further thoughts. First, advocating for free higher education is not equivalent to asking for a commodity (education) to be doled out to acquisitive self-interest maximizers, as neo-classical assumptions about human nature would have it. Just as in K-12, though it may lack a direct price tag, an actual public education system can obviously never be free from cost. Despite the hypocrisy of elites - one remembers George Bush I's quip that "dollar bills don't educate children" - who selectively embrace the need for funding only their own children's expensive schools, quality education always must be paid for. For one thing, however satisfying an occupation it may ultimately be, teaching is unequivocally *work* and it must be compensated. So the point is not to make education "free" in the simple mode of giving away a commodity, any more than we as a society should expect health care magically to appear without prioritizing and paying for it.

Despite its flaws, our current K-12 system offers an instructive case in point. It greatly socializes the costs of public schooling (representing ca. 90% of American school children) and is ideally - through elected school boards and the like - an outcome of relatively direct democratic processes. There are of course radical inequities in our public school system, particularly in our reliance on local property taxes for such a large proportion of school funding, which has the effect of more or less guaranteeing injustices that are reflected in poor kids having much less spent on them than their wealthy counterparts. But the basic structural formula is present in the current school governance setup: recognize the costs through an open budgeting process and make public decisions about how to pay for whatever it is we decide we want. Peering beneath the cynicism about school governance, this is not a laissez-faire model of individuals out there "on their own" choosing their individualized education-commodities. (This is one reason why neoliberalism takes direct aim at a public school system that it sees, perhaps rightly, as a latent outpost of an American socialism.) As an artifact of a historical decision to think of education as something other than an individualized commodity, the basic - and currently underutilized - governance structure of the US public school system illustrates how one can understand that public goods have costs but they are not *reducible* to those costs. Going further, in a society in which education (including higher education) is no longer regarded as a privately disposable commodity belonging solely to the student - dare we say a post-capitalist society? - student debts would still exist, but they would be transmogrified into *social* debts that are to be repaid not to bankers but directly to the public itself through a wide variety of service arenas that would, I'm sure, be providedby a society better ordered than our own present one.

But first we have a great deal of financial and conceptual detritus to sweep away. And there will be nothing easy about it. "Jubilee" may sound happy and fun but the vein of debt represented by student loans runs deeply and complicatedly throughout the whole of our financial and higher education systems and it will be a fraught and complicated enterprise to root it out comprehensively. Perfect fairness in this enterprise will be elusive and as always when real progress is to be made, we all will have dirt on our hands. However difficult it may prove to be, though, the elimination of higher education debt is necessary and just.

Education as human capital represents productivity augmentation and as such it is just as crucial a part of the internal gearing of capitalism as is technological and financial innovation. The economic imperatives that drive so many students into college and thus into debt are the very same imperatives that drive the system generally. Lying as it does close to the heart of that system, that part of accumulated capital that is accumulated student debt is as good a place as any to strike a blow. One wonders if the *human* in human capital can assert itself.

Chapter 5

Educational eliminationism II: Student voice

"Argue as much as you like, and about what you like, but obey!"
-Frederick II of Prussia[1]

Student speech

Though Americans tend to ignore it, there is an interestingly unlikely (though fragile) potential for resistance that lies coiled directly within its public educational institutions at all levels, kindergarten through higher education. The First Amendment of the Bill of Rights of the US Constitution prohibits the government from "abridging the freedom of speech." This Free Speech Clause anchors two centuries of jurisprudence where this laconic formal phrase has interpretively evolved and been given content.. Relevant for present purposes is that, since the late 1960s, free speech guarantees have been extended by US courts into the (mostly) new territory of school children *in* schools. Contrary to much of the world and most of human history, children in the US have an explicit right to speak out against the state-as-educator, or to speak their minds on whatever topic, even as their very presence in school is legally compelled. Like every other legal right, students' free speech rights are not absolute. Far from it, as I explain below, they are qualified in many ways. To the occasional astonishment of foreign observers, though, they very palpably exist. For now.

The existence of such rights provides a wonderful case study for Marxist dialectics of how a systemic internal tension can develop in unforeseen ways. In this case we have a bourgeois Enlightenment era formal freedom, i.e. speech, about which volumes can be said, including that it is associated with the augmented standing of the individual, conceived as an autonomous agent, who is required by the still-new (in the eighteenth century) mode of wealth creation that is capitalism. Production and consumption via these agents requires a much higher degree of flexibility along a host of axes such as personal mobility, assembly, ideas, contractual capabilities among employer, worker and business associates, property and, yes, communicative capabilities such as speech. It becomes much more widely recognized how, despite its annoyances, the free flow of ideas is good for business in the sense that it facilitates exchange and innovation regarding productive assemblages. It also contributes to system stability by helping safely to channel nascent social restiveness in the manner of a release valve on a pressure cooker. In the language of Nassim Nicholas Taleb, it helps guard against dangerous levels of systemic "fragility" by building in a greater degree of elasticity; in this case, potentially "revolutionary" instances of political volatility are safely internalized, and instead of becoming external forces that can shatter the power structure, they are channeled internally in ways that allow for more adaptive "antifragile" responses.[2] Dissent is thereby domesticated, which should not be understood in the facile sneering manner of the would-be anarchist, but appreciated as the ingenious and largely salutary innovation that it is. Keyboard leftists tend to underappreciate it, but situations of actual revolutionary violence are not to be romanticized, as they are just as likely (if not more) to serve dark atavisms of reaction than anything civilized reformers of whatever orientation would recognize as desirable.

As it is designed to do, then, the systemic requirements for augmenting individual autonomy create ongoing internal tensions (remembering, as per the above, that the key innovation here is that these tensions are *internal* and thus minimize the generation of *external* threats), many of which are managed via the rule of law generally and in particular constitutional systems such as those anchored in the Bill of Rights. Inevitably, though, these adaptive mechanisms cause a cascade of unforeseen consequences - a process otherwise known as *history*. And so comes to pass the unlikely contemporary situation wherein a local community's power structure may need to give way to 14 year-old's contrary views about the latest war or her elders' religious convictions. Again, world historically speaking this is counter-intuitive in the extreme. But this is how the internal dialectics have spun: medieval burghers' needs for reliable business contracts (to pick a random thread) weaves itself down the centuries into an American high school sophomore being able to wear a t-shirt about how "Jesus was not a homophobe."[3]

One must guard against some kind of progressive triumphalist picture, though; understanding history dialectically, that is, as an unfolding of internal tensions, carries no guarantee of anything. Dialectics do not function as a happy-ending machine where, by some external measure (the very idea of which is incoherent) things always get "better." Yes, the "new thing" might be wonderful. And the "new new thing" even better. But that third generation "new thing X3" might just wreck it all, in a currently unimaginably horrible and unanticipated manner. The only guarantee in dialectics is that things will keep moving in *some* direction, the axiological coordinates of which are not internally determinable. Nobody can say whether the ultimate direction will be "good" or "bad" because such judgments are necessarily a function of diverse desiderata that are not necessarily internal to the developments being judged. Murder and genocide are "good" from some perspectives.

By the laws of probability, such reversals should be expected, the recognition of which is central to wisdom traditions such as Taoism. Consider the Taoist story of a farmer who lost his horse:

That evening the neighbors gathered to commiserate with him since this was such bad luck. He said, "May be." The next day the horse returned, but brought with it six wild horses, and the neighbors came exclaiming at his good fortune. He said, "May be." And then, the following day, his son tried to saddle and ride one of the wild horses, was thrown and broke his leg. Again the neighbors came to offer their sympathy for the misfortune. He said, "May be." The day after that, conscription officers came to the village to seize young men for the army, but because of the broken leg the farmer's son was rejected. When the neighbors came in to say how fortunately everything had turned out, he said, "May be."[4]

The expectation that change - let alone large-scale change - should proceed in some sort of linear normatively "upward" manner is a rather obviously indefensible bias and should be discarded. Contexts and perspectives alter and, as the story of the farmer illustrates, maintaining equanimity through such shifts of fortune is a rare accomplishment for individuals.

This multi-layered historical contingency means that key components of an era, such as historical liberalism's commitment to the progress of rights, including students' rights, should not be understood as either guaranteed or guaranteed always to advance in either a predictable or desirable manner. This is true because it is true of everything. Thus it is wise to examine the phenomenon of student voice and the legal framework surrounding it as a highly ambivalent phenomenon, as likely to harm as it is to help. Or at the very least proceed on the assumption that a student's right to speak, however innocuous it seems, may be capable of generating darker forces than one might imagine. This indeed is the thesis of this chapter: a certain type of legal eliminationism (a very close cousin to moral and existential eliminationism) is currently cutting its teeth on this relatively new framework of rights and its alleged "excesses," biding its time and waiting for the right time to display itself with full force. As it happens, the eliminationist mentality has now shown itself, singularly but rather brashly, in this particular area. One does not know whether to laugh or to cry. It is a curious story, with the oddest "heroes" and "villains."

It is not that the forces of light are all on the side of students' rights whereas the forces of darkness are arrayed in opposition. In fact, it is hardly unreasonable to argue that the notion of constitutional rights is misapplied within a school setting or that we overdo it with the "rights talk" that has become our almost default mode for framing whatever grievances. Any number of philosophical perspectives might be marshaled in support of such a perspective. Perhaps, on balance, recognizing students' rights does more harm than good. Perhaps young students are not developmentally equipped, that is, they are not (yet) sufficiently rational to be legitimate bearers of rights. Perhaps the identity "rights bearer" is inimical to more important identity or character sorts of virtues that we the people have decided should reign preeminent in our schools. Whether such views are ultimately defensible or not, there is nothing *a priori* unreasonable about them.

There exists, however, one recent and very prominent argument against students' rights that I wish to argue is *a priori* unreasonable. This is to be found in the conservative activist Justice Clarence Thomas's widely noted concurring opinion in the recent US Supreme Court student speech case, *Morse v. Frederick*, 551 US 393 (2007), perhaps better known as the "Bong Hits 4 Jesus" case.

I contend here that the central argument of Thomas's concurrence should be rejected as unreasonable by all sides in the legal debate, even by those who may by whatever alternative means arrive at a conclusion congenial to his. This is because Thomas arrives at his conclusion via an eliminationist turn, which in the context of legal hermeneutics involves a refusal to engage with the relevant area of jurisprudence and instead betrays a desire for the simple elimination of opposing voices and the traditions that animate them. It is a power play in that it seeks to gets its way by brute force rather than developmentally through the internal norms of the sphere of activity that it seeks to reform. There is nothing magical about the legal sphere in this regard: judicial independence is a contingent achievement and can be extinguished, just as surely as can the autonomy of universities or any other social sphere ideally guided by unique internal norms.

Within legal hermeneutics, Thomas's eliminationism represents a fundamentally *unreasonable* move in that it violates the typical developmental patterns by which legal reasoning makes sense and enjoys its very legitimacy. It is unlike "pure" and relatively untethered philosophical argumentation, which, *pace* the dreams of Plato's Republic, is sufficiently lacking in immediate concrete consequences such that it can be happily irresponsible - or at least relatively freewheeling vis-à-vis its own master thinkers. While philosophical discourse may be said to be in some indirect sense answerable to its enabling historical tradition, legal reasoning is more directly and more powerfully answerable. Most notably, it contains the foundational imperative of *stare decisis* (Lat. "to stand by things decided"), where there is a strong sense that precedent, the sheer fact of its existence, carries its own weight and commands an allegiance that is separable from the abstract "quality" of whatever argument a judge is considering. It is commonplace in law, for example, and there are many famous examples, of a judge bowing before *stare decisis* against her own best judgment, were she simply free to decide the case singularly on its merits. There is nothing like this in philosophy, where the idea that one might be bound by what, say, Kant said, simply because Kant said it is anathema and would be recognized by philosophers as an "unphilosophical" obeisance (and certainly by Kant himself!). By contrast, legal history is replete with this gesture, which is even typically admired in the abstract. A notorious example of this is found by the "lone dissenter" US Supreme Court Justice John Marshall Harlan, so-named because he was the sole dissent in the 8-1 opinion in the *Plessy v. Ferguson* (1896) case that held racial segregation to be compatible with the Fourteenth Amendment's Equal Protection Clause, and was overturned generations later in *Brown v. Board of Education* (1954), which outlawed *de jure* racial segregation in American public schools. Harlan's *Plessy* dissent reads in pertinent part:

> Our constitution is colorblind, and neither knows nor tolerates classes among citizens. In respect of civil rights, all citizens are equal before the law. The humblest is the peer of the most powerful ... The arbitrary separation of citizens on the basis of race, while they are on a public highway, is a badge of servitude wholly inconsistent with the civil freedom and the equality before the law established by the Constitution. It cannot be justified upon any legal grounds.[5]

This is a forceful moral, philosophical *and* legal judgment that builds its argument by reference to the, at the time, recently passed post-Civil War Amendments (Thirteenth, Fourteenth, Fifteenth) that freed the slaves and formally guaranteed their equal legal status. What is noteworthy for present purposes, however, is how in subsequent cases dealing with racial segregation, Harlan, despite is obvious personal predilections as stated above in his *Plessy* dissent, sided with segregationist majorities - and even wrote for them - on grounds of *stare decisis*.[6] Although the practical stakes were extremely high, Harlan understood himself above all to be ensconced in a *legal* hermeneutical tradition that was distinguishable from whatever merely philosophical wiles might be brought to bear. It sounds strange to appreciate someone towing a segregationist line, but in context - literally *because of legal context* - Harlan provides an example of avoiding the eliminationist temptation, even at great cost.

To be sure, it is not that he is necessarily a hero for avoiding it, only that Harlan is a *jurisprudential* hero, which is far less exciting. Thomas, on the other hand, reveals himself to be indeed far more exciting than Harlan, because he shows a reckless indifference to the preconditions of his own profession's legitimacy, like a professional gambler who throws away the charts and statistics and risks it all on one throw of the dice. Legally foolish. But exciting.

To illustrate Thomas's recklessness, I will provide, first, an account of what is reasonable and unreasonable in the legal context of the students' rights debate and, second, an explanation of how Thomas's argument is, within that legal context, "unreasonable." The first is relatively easy. As I will show, however, given the nature of its argument, the first line of discussion necessitates that the second be accomplished with careful attention to relevant detail; there are pertinent legal data to bring to bear. The quantitative bulk of this section will therefore be occupied with the second point, after which I will conclude in a more speculative vein, briefly sketching what I see as a source of Thomas's eliminationism.

Unreasonableness and legal hermeneutics

So what counts as "unreasonable"? As stated previously, I do not hold there to be any *a priori* unreasonable position on the desirability of students' rights in general. The meta-problem here is when the anti-students' rights argument is mounted from *within* the legal tradition and in a certain manner. It must be remembered that the argument under consideration takes places as part of a US Supreme Court opinion where Thomas writes as *Justice* Thomas. Consequently, he is not simply expressing a view, say, a philosophical or historical one that he might defend (however well or poorly) when he does not wear his judicial robe. I am not arguing against Thomas in the guise of after-dinner speaker, breakfast table conversationalist, blogger, philosophy journal article author, or the like. The situational ad hominem argument is directed specifically at Thomas *in his capacity as a Supreme Court justice*. The subject position from which he speaks is relevant because it is firmly and ineluctably ensconced within the determinate institutional context of the federal judiciary that is its sine qua non. If Thomas were not writing from within that institutional role, no "concurring opinion" from him would exist.

This gets us close to the crux of the matter, the above mentioned principle of *stare decisis* - namely, the existence and persuasive weight of precedent - is the golden norm upon which all jurisprudential interpretive legitimacy is ultimately based. If one wishes to advance a meaningful interpretation within a particular hermeneutical context, one must, so to speak, play by the local rules; in hermeneutics one by definition makes meaning with reference to understandings that have built and thus make up that particular hermeneutical context. This is as true for "conservative" views as it is for "progressive" views as it is for any meaningful view. Even putatively "radical" views that seek a sharp new direction, even an overthrowing of precursor views and the assumptions upon which those views are based, must do so with reference to - or, if you like, in conversation with - the extant context that is "always already" there. Otherwise, one is not overthrowing those views, changing that tradition; the truly "clean break" would, according to the assumptions made here, be involved in something else, perhaps expanding on or, if this is possible, founding a new hermeneutical context *de novo*. Owing to the indispensability of *stare decisis* in legal hermeutics, and especially in the context of the US judicial system, this imperative to play by the rules is doubly pronounced. For *stare decisis* marries this hermeneutical imperative toward meaning-making with the practical imperative of exercise of judicial authority. The two imperatives are inextricably intertwined. A Supreme Court ruling is just that: a ruling. At the High Court level, what is important is not so much whether Party A or Party B wins, though this is certainly important to A and B themselves. Rather, the wider import, that is, why the rest of us who are not direct parties to the dispute should care, consists in the precise nature of the precedent that is advanced, the rule by which future relevantly similar cases will be adjudicated. To deny this would be to deny such a basic rule for how this particular game is played that one would be playing a different game. An analogy would be with a mathematics word problem, the point of which is to extract the math from it, perhaps a rule or formula by which to solve it. If one started overly to appreciate it for, say, its literary qualities, if one got too wrapped up in what is going to happen to Johnny after he has given out all his apples, then we would say that one has missed the point, at least the mathematical one, or that one has started to play a different hermeneutical game, in this instance perhaps that of literary criticism.

The problem with Thomas's concurrence is that he does not play the game in a way that is appropriate for a Supreme Court justice writing for posterity as part of the official case record. To be sure, a concurring opinion is considered formally to be *obiter dicta* (Lat. "said by the way"), that is, it is not part of the majority opinion and thus lacks the force of law; it is, formally, so much legal chatter. And in this precise sense Thomas is admittedly a bit freer in all relevant senses than if he had been writing for the majority. Yet our legal history is filled with examples of concurrences becoming influential in the context of the unforeseen jurisprudential future, becoming influential rallying points for the like-minded. A fairly recent example in education would be Justice Sandra Day O'Connor's concurrence in *Wallace v. Jaffree* (1986).[7] This First Amendment Establishment Clause case had to do with religious exercises in an Alabama school, and it has come to be associated in particular with the question of the constitutionality of the so-called "moment of silence" (that is, a moment of "silent meditation or voluntary prayer") in public schools. While agreeing with the majority ruling going against the school in question, Justice O'Connor wrote a separate concurrence arguing that while the moment of silent prayer was unconstitutional in that particular case, a better-crafted moment of silence law would be able to withstand constitutional challenge and so be perfectly acceptable. And indeed subsequently states received the hint and O'Connor's scenario has come to pass. To date, following O'Connor's "instructions," several states now have moment of silence laws that have effectively withstood constitutional challenge. This illustrates one of the many ways in which a concurrence can be highly significant. In fact, these days, in an inversion of the usual situation, *Wallace v. Jaffree* is legally noteworthy much more for O'Connor's concurrence than for the majority opinion that, in the end, breaks very little new constitutional ground. So Supreme Court concurrences can be quite important legally and should not be ignored, particularly from a long-term viewpoint. Though qua concurrence it is not legally dispositive, what Thomas is writing here still matters within "the game."

Thomas's views are also significant because he has come to exercise considerable influence both outside and, by most reports, inside the Court. Politically, since his ascension to the Court, Thomas has become beloved by political conservatives, from popular radio talk show hosts such as Rush Limbaugh to the more upscale end of the ideological spectrum, where he is regularly a featured speaker at major think tanks such as the Claremont Institute, the Heritage Foundation, and the Council for National Policy among many others. He has also become a highly sought-after commencement speaker by universities and law schools. Even more significantly for present purposes, it seems that within the Court, far from being the mere follower of Justice Antonin Scalia that he was initially and mistakenly assumed to be, Thomas represents a crucially important and distinctive voice on a range of key issues and is frequently a rallying point for conservatives on the Court. He also demonstrably possesses, as in the *Morse* case, the courage of his convictions and has developed a track record of standing by himself among his colleagues (in conference, concurrence, and dissent), and he has in several instances brought others to his side. In discussing the dynamics of one such situation early in Thomas's tenure, journalist Jan Greenberg argues that it "foreshadowed how Thomas, willing to be the lone dissenter from the outset, would reshape the Court."[8] Though essentially a far right activist, Thomas is a formidable intellect who not only enjoys the inherently powerful platform of the Supreme Court but also gives influential voice on relevant matters to important opinion and policy making segments of the American right. Like it or not, he is part of the policy landscape and as such even his loneliest *dicta* are significant.

So, again, the point is not that Thomas's views on students' rights are uninteresting philosophically or politically. On the contrary. It is that in the actual legal context in which they are voiced they are unreasonable. So what does he do that is so clearly against the rules? My view is that Thomas sins largely by omission in that he simply ignores all the relevant legal precedents. In fact, he simply wishes away an entire precedential area by saying that the 1969 *Tinker* ruling (more about which later), the main precedent establishing the existence of students' rights, should simply not exist; *Tinker* was "wrongly decided." This is all well and good for the breakfast table, the philosophy seminar, even the constitutional law class. But rejecting *Tinker* at this late date requires also abandoning the nearly forty years of students' rights jurisprudence that is premised on it, not only in the area of student free speech but also in adjacent areas, such as students' rights that have developed concerning Fourth Amendment search and seizure (for example, searches of students' persons and drug testing[9]), Fifth and Fourteenth Amendment due process (for example, procedures for student suspension and expulsion[10]), and even in some situations marrying free speech issues with church-state separation (for example, the impermissibility of discriminating against student groups on the basis of the content of their beliefs).[11] In the final analysis, the hermeneutical problem with Thomas's eliminationism lies not with the substance of the view he ends up with, but rather with his refusal, as a Supreme Court justice, to engage the relevant legal precedents. He seeks instead simply to eliminate them. It is as if a philosopher, convinced of the falsity of Plato's doctrine of Forms, were to "argue" her case by suggesting that the way to overcome Plato's view is to avoid reading it or, perhaps, to pretend that Plato and his writings did not exist in the first place. One can imagine conditions under which that ostrich-like strategy might "work" (hyper-efficient censors and book burnings, for instance), but of course it would not exactly be philosophy. So it is with Thomas in relation to the law. In the end, his eliminationism is based not on legal considerations (despite a thin rhetorical veneer of "originalism"), but on extralegal ones, namely, a highly selective reading of the history of school discipline. In sum, Thomas's concurring opinion is unreasonable because it does not engage and, indeed, in a sort of performative self-contradiction, seeks to eliminate its own hermeneutical context, without which it is merely "someone's view" rather than a legitimate matter of judicial record.

Student speech's constitutional framework

In *Morse v. Frederick* (2007), Juneau, Alaska high school student Joseph Frederick was suspended by his school principal (Morse) for unfurling a large banner reading "Bong Hits 4 Jesus." The unfurling took place across the street from the Juneau-Douglas High School, while school was in session, in the context of a "school approved class trip" in which students were allowed to watch the procession of the Olympic Torch Relay as it passed along the street in front of the school. The banner was visible to everyone in its vicinity and Frederick succeeded in his stated goal of getting on the local TV news. From all the available facts, it appears that the purpose of the banner in Frederick's mind was really just to get laughs. As *Time* magazine reported, "As TV cameras rolled, senior Joseph Frederick and several friends unfurled the infamous banner, thinking it was, according to Frederick, 'meaningless and funny,' just a way 'to get on television.'"[12] And indeed, maybe everyone was still having a good laugh when Principal Morse handed Frederick a ten-day suspension (later commuted to five), upon which Frederick sued, claiming that the school had violated his free-speech rights under the First Amendment. Winding its way ultimately to the Supreme Court, the case takes its place alongside a long legacy of offbeat exercises of speech that nonetheless raise serious and potentially far-reaching constitutional questions.

So what is at stake in *Morse*? And what then is the precise nature of Thomas's hermeneutical error as outlined previously? Answering these questions requires an explication of the existing constitutional framework for assessing students' free-speech claims as it has evolved over recent decades. Toward that heuristic end, it is helpful to represent this framework as composed of a series of questions to be answered upon the basis of the facts a given case presents. I have also constructed a heuristic as a companion to the narrative description of the framework.

The first question to ask is basic but deceptively simple: Is the student expression in the given instance actually speech? Or is it, let's say, conduct? This distinction is legally crucial because, based on its literal wording, the First Amendment's Freedom of Speech Clause explicitly protects "speech" and not necessarily the broader and more act-like category "expression." This point is often overlooked by casual observers, for there is a persistent assumption that the Constitution protects "freedom of expression." But it does not, necessarily; the explicit protection is for speech. The reason for this terminological austerity is easy enough to fathom. "Expression" adds an element of action or conduct to "speech." This is to be sure an area where philosophy and law do not coexist very easily, as the latter rests much easier distinguishing "pure" speech and conduct. While philosophers may (rightly) balk at overly facile terminological distinctions, it is quite clear why those involved in designing and enacting laws must not. Freedoms of speech and conduct may and do admit of varying degrees, but overly robust notions of freedom of conduct are inimical to any imaginable legal code. "Do what you like!" in an unqualified sense would be a patent anathema to the rule of law itself; it would be less a legal maxim than a recipe for unmitigated lawlessness, a Hobbesian *bellum omnium contra omnes* ("war of all against all"). Accordingly, free-speech jurisprudence, even as it has expanded and evolved, has maintained a principled aversion toward the protection of anything roughly and readily interpretable as conduct rather than speech. So, for example, in the original 1969 student speech case, *Tinker v. Des Moines*, the Court carefully establishes that the black armbands worn by the Tinker children (to protest what they viewed as an immoral escalation of the Vietnam War) were in fact "symbolic speech" rather than conduct. This is why *Tinker* ends up as a constitutionally relevant free-speech case and not a simple complaint about an obscure Iowa school's dress code. Though the armbands are nonverbal, the *Tinker* majority rules that they are in fact "symbolic speech" because in context they possess a clear communicative intent and so contain a determinate and specific enough meaning to count as "speech" under the First Amendment.[13] This is as opposed to, say, what we might call a mere "fashion statement" or some such more generalized or vague expression. The full story here is outside my present scope, but this is, roughly, why students almost always lose the very common sorts of complaints centering around school dress codes. The wearing of miniskirts, big earrings, low-riding pants and the like may be expressive of something, but whatever that is would tend to lack the specificity of message required to count constitutionally as speech. Absent contextual factors that might confer the requisite level of specificity, they therefore tend to count as conduct, and as such they are outside the First Amendment's ambit.

The upshot of *Tinker* is this: expression that is in fact determined to be student speech, whether symbolic or the ordinary verbal kind, is eligible for constitutional protection, provided it ultimately passes what has come to be known as the *Tinker* test.[14] That test asks whether or not the speech in question causes a "material or substantial disruption" of the educational process at the school. The qualifiers "material" and "substantial" are present in the formula in order to emphasize that the disruption must be a serious one, rather than merely a brief annoyance or distraction. This insistence is also meant to guard against possible and easily imaginable abuses of the *Tinker* test where a school official may be tempted to shut down student speech for fear of generating controversy or, as everyone says these days, because someone might be "offended." That sort of thing is not supposed to be good enough as a rationale for stifling speech. There are rare circumstances where one can utilize the *Tinker* test proactively - for example, where a climate of, say, racial tensions has resulted in fights and student walkouts, a school principal could ban a provocative speaker on racial issues for fear of continued serious disruption. But on the whole, and outside such extraordinary circumstances, the *Tinker* test is designed to be used reactively, in response to actual serious disruptions. This reactivity is a safeguard against school administrators following a time-honored instinct to contain controversy, not to ruffle feathers, and so on.[15] *Tinker* recognizes that the "marketplace of ideas" demanded by a free and democratic society will occasion a bit of turbulence now and again and that students, as emerging citizens, need to be able to experience some of this.[16]

In a larger frame, the *Tinker* test is but one example of how basic constitutional rights, as restraints on government, are to be weighed against the varying intensity of the government interest at stake. Legal scholar James Ryan persuasively argues that, as a rule, in this weighing process the basic rights and governmental interests are adjudicated in a sort of inverse proportion to one another. That is to say, in weighing the competing interests, the more prominent the governmental interest appears to be, the basic right at stake will tend to be regarded as less decisive. So, according to Ryan, to reach a reasonable balance between educational goals and student rights, therefore, one must distinguish between the true 'business' of the public schools from the goals that fall outside of that sphere.[17] To look at it in another way, the closer one gets to the core of the governmental sphere at issue - for example, health care, tax collection, education, the military - the more likely it is that the "thicker" sphere-specific concerns will trump the "thinner" constitutional norms. To illustrate with an extreme example, even active duty soldiers enjoy a degree of free-speech protection, but those diminish to near a vanishing point on the battlefield. In all but the most extreme examples (such as the Nuremberg war crimes), soldiers' speech involving, say, questioning or protesting superiors' orders is not protected. Refusing battlefield orders could even be grounds for the death penalty.[18] In an analogy with education, the classroom is like the battlefield, the central site wherein the government's compelling interest is transacted. If the military's essential function is to fight and win wars, schooling's essential function is to engender learning in students, which is presumed to take place most importantly in the arenas where instruction is deliberately attempted.

Given current institutional arrangements, this will be thought to be classrooms along with, perhaps, a few other sites (such as assemblies, athletic competition, meetings with administrators and school counselors and suchlike). Given this dynamic, the *Tinker* test will tend to be most strongly weighted toward the school where the venue is, so to speak, on the front lines of instruction. If instead of her silent black armband, Mary Beth Tinker had chosen to jump atop her desk with a megaphone in the middle of math class, by causing the requisite disruption she would have lost her case. So, once the presence of a bona fide instance of student speech is established, how that speech claim stands with the *Tinker* test will be a primary consideration. Yet it is by no means the only one. In fact, prior to any application of the *Tinker* test, it must first be determined whether or not the content of the speech in question is determined to be "vulgar" or otherwise "uncivil" or age inappropriate.

The matter of vulgar and otherwise age-inappropriate speech was addressed in *Bethel v. Fraser* (1986), which involved a student council election speech laden with "sexual innuendo."[19] In *Fraser* the Court hands a double victory to schools' *in loco parentis* by allowing them both to define vulgar speech and ban it. This gives the school wide latitude to act in such cases, especially in the absence of any reliable legal definition of obscenity; one must simply "trust" school officials not to abuse their discretion here.[20] The *Fraser* ruling means, then, that for all practical purposes any speech that can reasonably be categorized as vulgar is off the table constitutionally and will not be protected. The verbal expletive and the t-shirt bearing an obscene message can by and large unproblematically be punished.

Especially pertinent to the bong hits case, examples of the wider category of "age inappropriate" would be speech that could reasonably be seen to be advocating illegal activity (more on this later), including activity that would be illegal for school-age children, for example, tobacco and alcohol; the school can fairly unproblematically ban depictions of pot leaves (or, yes, bongs), along with Jack Daniels, Joe Camel, and the like.[21] The school could probably also ban something like an anti-abortion demonstrator's graphic depiction of an aborted fetus, on the movie ratings-like grounds that the images are too disturbing for young children. What most would regard as the "commonsense" norms of adult society hereby hold sway; the unmistakable tone of the *Fraser* opinion has the air of "the grown-ups are talking now, kid." Despite its aura of obviousness (to most people), the ruling is legally necessary as a complement to *Tinker* because not all (or even most) instances of pornography, vulgarity, obscenity and so on are materially or substantially disruptive. Much of it, in other words, would pass the *Tinker* test and so would have to be permitted but for the discretionary range *Fraser* authorizes.

Interestingly, in reaching beyond the realm of formal instruction in order to chase down vulgar speech wherever it may exist on campus, the Court formally recognizes a broader role for schools than the formal curriculum, a role that includes larger educational aims having to do with schooling's socializing mission, such as moral and citizenship education: "The process of educating our youth for citizenship in public schools is not confined to books, the curriculum, and the civics class; schools must teach by example the shared values of a civilized social order."[22] In this era of obsessive standardized testing of a narrow range of competencies, it is instructive that the United States' highest court has recognized that there is more in heaven and earth than the formal curriculum. The constitutional permissibility of this broader role should be kept firmly in mind. As we shall see in the final *Morse* ruling, it allows for a certain interpretive elasticity at crucial points.

The school may also restrict speech occurring in the context of a "school-sponsored activity." In a case involving prior-restraint censorship of a school newspaper, the Court ruled that because the newspaper was part of a journalism class and was otherwise directly underwritten by the school, the school had the right to control its content, so long as it could produce an educational reason for the restriction.[23] This last consideration is tantamount to "anything goes" because it is almost always easy for school officials to come up with some educational reason or other. In the newspaper case the educational reason was that of teaching the norms appropriate to good journalism, in this instance securing a balance of viewpoints and going to greater lengths to preserve informants' anonymity. Because the principal alleged violations of these norms in students' feature-length stories about divorce and pregnancy, he was armed with the needed educational rationale for censoring the school-sponsored activity that was the paper. Even though *Kuhlmeier* is famous as "the student newspaper case," it is important to remember that the precedential category is the broader "school-sponsored activities" and so would include venues such as sports teams' practices and games, a high school spring play, the yearbook and others. Most anything students are doing under the school's official imprimatur would count. An example would be, let's say, at a football game the sideline cheerleaders were chanting disrespectful cheers directed toward the opposing team. Were they punished for it, they would likely lose any free-speech claim because the cheerleading squad is a school-sponsored activity and for this reason the school has discretion to restrict the speech so long as they act with an educational purpose, not hard to grasp in this example, of something like moral education, teaching proper sportsmanship, or the like. Anticipating considerations relevant to *Morse*, a school field trip, to a museum or wherever else, would almost certainly count as school-sponsored.

The one important exception is where the school-sponsored activity has created what is known as a "public" or "open forum," where a heterogeneity of views is invited or otherwise solicited. This could be either a physical place, such as a campus quad or a community bulletin board, or it could be a less tangible state of affairs, such as the situation, obtaining in most US public high schools, where a large range of student groups and clubs are allowed to exist, draw members, use school facilities and so on. (In legal terminology, making this determination is known as a "forum analysis.") More precisely, these would be considered limited open forums in that, for reasons outlined previously, schools can restrict speech and, *a fortiori*, expressive activities that are age-inappropriate, violent, or the like. For instance, the school does not have to allow the "Beat Up Little Kids and Steal Their Lunch Money Club," the "Pornography Viewers' Club" or the "Cuban Cigar Aficionados Club." (Much of this would in any event be taken care of by the *Fraser* decision.) Apart from beyond-the-pale exotica like these, however, when the school creates an open forum, it is obliged to depart from the easier *Kuhlmeier* standard of "censor so long as one gives an educational reason" and must instead revert back to the old standby of the *Tinker* test. So if the forum analysis yields the determination that the student speech occurring in a school-sponsored activity also takes place in a (limited) open forum, the speech would be protected so long as it does not cause a material or substantial disruption of the educational process. The forum analysis is an important item in the *Morse* case because if the Torch Relay event were to be considered a (limited) open forum, then, even though it may be a school-sponsored activity or trip, so long as it did not violate anything pertaining to the "limited" qualification of "limited open forum," it would be subject only to the *Tinker* test of disruption. Given the absence from the case record of any evidence of an actual disruption, such a consideration could well be decisive.

One last significant consideration is that schools may always enforce reasonable "time, place, and manner" restrictions on any type of student speech. They just have to be "reasonable," which here means having a rational relationship to some clear educational purpose, not merely serving as a pretext for shutting down the speech altogether. So it would not be reasonable to say to the anti- or pro-war group, "You may pass out your leaflets from 6:50–6:55 AM on the southwest corner of the baseball field." However, it would be reasonable to say to them, "You may not pass out your leaflets from 3:00–3:30 when school buses are being called because it causes logistical problems like hallway bottlenecks, students being distracted from hearing their bus numbers, and so on." The *Tinker* decision emphasizes this point:

> Freedom of expression would not truly exist if the right could be exercised only in an area that a benevolent government has provided as a safe haven for crackpots. The Constitution says that Congress (and the States) may not abridge the right to free speech. This provision means what it says. We properly read it to permit reasonable regulation of speech-connected activities in carefully restricted circumstances. But we do not confine the permissible exercise of First Amendment rights to a telephone booth or the four corners of a pamphlet, or to supervised and ordained discussion in a school classroom (393 US 513).

As usual, there is a great deal of fluidity in the preceding usage of the term "reasonable," but its proper usage here is usually clear enough.

The bong hits case

Now back to the bong hits case, this time suitably armed with a working knowledge of the student free-speech framework. How to assess the case? There are certainly several interpretive pressure points whose resolution could steer the analysis one way or another. And while this essay is not the place for a detailed defense of a particular analysis, I will suggest that there is at least a range of reasonable responses to the case, including, for the most part (save, I would argue, for one area), Chief Justice Roberts's majority opinion siding with the school principal. I mean "reasonable" here in the most minimal hermeneutical sense: a reasonable interpretation is one that takes into account the extant free-speech framework by justifying whatever resultant decision with reference to it. So I am defining "reasonable" simply as playing by the legal rules that have been established over the last half-century.

My own view would be, first, that the "Bong Hits 4 Jesus" banner was unfurled in the context of a school sponsored activity (this is agreed to by just about everyone), despite the rather bold claim by Frederick that since he was late to school that day, did not check in with the school office, and went straight to the torch-bearing parade event, he therefore was not officially in attendance at school on the day in question. No one seems to accept Frederick's argument on this particular point. Joining classmates in what amounts essentially to a school field trip, whether or not one's attendance box was checked off by the front office, seems pretty clearly to be equivalent to coming to school. So far so good. Note that this establishes that Frederick is at once placed in a different category from the Tinker kids, in that the latter's armbands were not being worn in the context of their partici-pation in a school-sponsored activity, but rather were their own individual expression during the course of a regular school day. (Perhaps if they had worn their armbands on a school field trip, we would have had a different ruling.) In line with the student speech framework, so long as the forum analysis does not indicate the presence of a public forum, the school has the ability within the "school-sponsored activities" category to censor so long as an educational reason can be produced for doing so. There is surely room for reasonable disagreement here, but I think it is highly unlikely that a school field trip that is taking place for a specific educational purpose would count as a public forum.[24]

There are two possibilities here that seem to me equally viable. First, following *Kuhlmeier*, would be to argue that Morse was within her rights to halt the expression because of its perceived incivility. I think it could be seen as plain goofing off, really (the students never claimed any agenda other than getting laughs and trying to get on television), and, as such, boorish behavior that was neither welcoming nor polite to the Olympics people passing by their school. It is simply disrespectful. It should therefore be punishable along the same lines as one might punish members of an athletic team for a display of bad sportsmanship. I think this would be the right judgment to make, and it could be differentiated from some nonfrivolous message such as, say, some political statement about the International Olympic Committee. This "moral education" argument would reference that part of Fraser that recognizes the legitimacy of the school's socializing mission. A second possibility would be to circumnavigate *Kuhlmeier* altogether by recognizing that "Bong Hits 4 Jesus" seems reasonably to be construed as advocating illegal activity. I agree with the majority opinion on this point. I think it is clear that the phrase "bong hits," understood within our particular cultural context, clearly means marijuana smoking and only with a wink and a nod and a chuckle might one say that "oh, it can be used for tobacco, too." That is true. One could smoke shredded cardboard in a bong, too, I suppose. But even tobacco is now illegal for minors (in Alaska the age limit is 19), so even the purported tobacco use would still be illegal. So, since the students are in school - even though across the street, since they are participants in a school-sponsored activity, they are in school, just as surely as is a sports team on an away game - the "Bong Hits" banner has no greater claim to constitutional protection than would a Jim Beam T-shirt or a soccer jersey sporting a beer logo. Either or both paths of analysis would seem sufficient for a more-than-reasonable ruling on the case.

The majority opinion agrees in part but then takes a rather dodgier tack. Capitalizing on the previously noted elasticity of *Fraser's* conception of the school's socializing mission, it places great (and in my view undue) weight on the idea that the "Bong Hits" banner does not accord with the antidrug message that the school perceives to be an important part of their "educational mission." The very substantial worry here, as Justice Alito wisely cautions in his own separate concurrence (joined by Justice

Kennedy), is that this educational mission argument "can easily be manipulated in dangerous ways."[25] For the majority opinion could be read to endorse the view that students lack free-speech rights concerning any areas that the school has designated as "part of its educational mission."

Consider how badly this could go. For example, schools these days commonly take students' achieving "excellence," usually defined in large part by their doing well on standardized state tests, to be fundamental to their educational mission. This would seem to mean that under *Morse*, students would be punishable for criticizing standardized testing. The main problem here is that what is or is not a school's educational mission is in large part a moral, social, and political matter and, as such, under just about any theory of democracy, a paradigmatically protected free speech zone where citizens must be allowed - if not encouraged - openly to debate important matters of public concern. As Alito warns, "the 'educational mission' argument would give public school authorities a license to suppress speech on political and social issues based on disagreement with the viewpoint expressed."[26] This would cut directly against *Tinker's* core argument about the centrality to democracy of a marketplace of ideas, even in a public school setting. Contrary to the opinion of Justice Breyer's interesting *Morse* dissent, which centers around both the potential ambiguity of Frederick's banner and his (rightful) concern that the majority opinion could be construed as prohibiting students from protesting matters of public concern, such as whether or not, say, tobacco or marijuana ought to be legal. So could a student advocate a change in drug laws? This is a difficult issue, not fully addressed anywhere in the opinion, including in Breyer's dissent. On the one hand, one can share Breyer's concern for the need for robust debate about what our laws should be even - and perhaps especially - in controversial areas. Yet the special setting of schools gives rise to singular problems, where psychological and civic immaturity could enhance an implied threat of violence. What if a student wanted to express the view that, say, rape or anti-lynching laws ought to be eliminated? In such a case, we might not be so confident about the distinction between advocating illegal activity itself and advocating for a change in the law. Perhaps some laws are so basic to civil order and personal security that advocating overturning them can implicitly contain a threat against a defined group. Of course context could be all-determining here. One can very easily imagine a reasoned discussion about some aspect of rape laws as opposed to, say, an in-your-face and sloganeering "rape should be legal!" statement directed by a male student specifically at female classmates. Though formally advocating a change in laws rather than the illegal behavior itself, such an alarming situation might even be appropriately considered to be "disruptive" under the *Tinker* test.

This quasi-totalitarian insistence on kids not being allowed openly to question whatever school officials say is their educational mission must be abandoned. Fortunately, the majority opinion gives no indication that it aims to overturn the entire student speech framework that has *Tinker* at its core, and so one hopes and assumes, along with Alito, that in time the hyperbole that occasions this incongruity will be rectified. Still, with this priority placed on educational mission, they may well have planted the seeds for something unforeseen to develop.

This brings us to Thomas's concurrence, which is another sort of creature altogether. Though I see the majority opinion as ultimately wrongheaded, I recognize it as a basically reasonable view in that it builds upon the relevant legal precedents. (Even where one might argue it misconstrues them, as I have just done, it has the appearance of an honest enough effort.) In other words, the majority opinion respects its hermeneutical context. Alito's aforementioned concurrence along with Justice Breyer's dissent quite clearly and elaborately do so as well. By contrast, what Thomas seeks to do is write his own preference into law regardless of precedent, candidly asserting his argument that the *Tinker* test "is without basis in the Constitution."[27] Thomas's argument is not complex. It is simply this, elaborated piecemeal using selected quotes from educational historians concerning school discipline: "the history of public education suggests that the First Amendment, as originally understood, does not protect student speech in public schools."[28] Let us overlook, for starters, that there were no public schools in colonial times (at least not by any definition recognizable today). Let us overlook also that the Constitution, "as originally understood," allowed many things that would today be regarded as unconscionable and at this point wholly alien to now well established moral and political traditions, such as - to name but a couple of examples - slavery and the permissibility of one of the states of the union establishing an official religion.[29] Most salient for present purposes is Thomas's sheer willingness simply to cut out a whole well-established area of legal precedent on the basis of a wishful "order and discipline" view of the way things once allegedly were, a longing for the days when, supposedly, "Teachers commanded, and students obeyed."[30] His alleged "originalism" is inconsistent even on its own terms. He acknowledges that "colonial schools were exclusively private" and that public schools did not flourish until well into the 1800s, generations after the Constitution was written (1790). But somehow the fact that the nineteenth century did not recognize students' rights seals the deal for the "originalist" rejection of them.

This is at the very least a strange originalism, one that does not start at the 1790 origin, but arbitrarily establishes its "origin" at a later point where legal norms happened to agree with the view currently on offer. Originalism, I would suggest, becomes something else when one is free idiosyncratically to pick and choose one's preferred "origin." It seems an unfair move simply to locate a period in history where one's view appears to be agreed with and fix that period as one's "origin." While this may function well as a debate tactic, from a hermeneutical point of view it is a highly suspect argumentative move, as it neatly circumnavigates the body of legal precedent upon which it in general is allegedly built, while at the same time aggressively donning that endeavor's aura of legitimacy and prestige. It is like merely pretending to give to a charity and then basking in the resultant warm glow of public opinion.

And what of the history Thomas brings to bear? Perhaps Thomas's hermeneutical context has simply been misconstrued. Maybe what has happened is that he has decided to enter into the hermeneutical context of the history of education and is merely recounting the facts. While the final judgment about Thomas's historical accuracy best rests with the historians, it seems rather obvious, even to this untrained eye, that Thomas's history-quoting defense of his position is so cursory and selective as to be patently deficient. Such suspicions are corroborated by at least one respected historian of education, Jonathan Zimmerman, who rejects Thomas's picture out of hand. On the question of Thomas's reliability as a historian, then, I will provisionally lean on Zimmerman's authority. Regarding early efforts to instill school discipline, Zimmerman comments:

Here's the part of Thomas' opinion that would be relevant - if it were true. But it's not. Yes, teachers tried to establish strict order and discipline in early American schools. As often as not, however, they failed.

Consider the 1833 memoir of Warren Burton, a New Hampshire minister. When faced with a particularly cruel teacher, Burton writes, his classmates revolted. They tackled the teacher, carried him outside and threw him down an icy hillside.

The theme appears in other memoirs and especially in fiction from the 19th century, which depicts unruly students - usually boys - challenging or mocking teacher authority.

Think of Tom Sawyer lowering a cat by a string to snatch his bald teacher's wig. Such stories resonated with Americans because they understood - in ways Thomas does not - the chaos and violence that pervaded so many public schools.

So Thomas can spare us the nostalgia. Our schools were never the paragons of discipline he imagines.[31]

Thomas's view does not seem promising, then, as a rendition of straight historical truth. And as shown in the preceding analysis, neither is it a real engagement with legal precedent; for Thomas, if something ought to have existed (history), it therefore does exist, and if it ought not to have existed (legal precedent), it therefore does not exist. One highly sympathetic legal scholar, Henry Mark Holzer, lauds Thomas's approach to jurisprudence as "utopian originalism," and perhaps Thomas's wishful stance in relation to the historical and legal past is a hallmark of that approach.[32] Whatever it is called, though, it seems to be neither legal nor historical analysis in any straightforward sense. There is something else going on. So if neither history nor law can by themselves account for Thomas's convictions regarding this case, what else might?

Elimination and restoration: Thomas's nostalgia

There is no sure way to answer this question. I will however follow the hints laid by both the admirer Holzer's "utopian originalism" and the critic Zimmerman's "nostalgia." For convenience, I will use the latter as a catchall term and so examine nostalgia as at least part of the explanation for Thomas's view. In contrast to Zimmerman, though, I suspect that the phenomenon of nostalgia, as possibly here evidenced, may be more interesting - and possibly more disturbing - than what is conveyed by his dismissive rebuke "spare us the nostalgia." To say that Thomas suffers from nostalgia may be more a beginning than an end to explanation.

Let us enter Thomas's extra-legal and (on Zimmerman's authority) extra-historical dreamscape and consider a few telling lines from his opinion:

> Teachers instilled [a core of common] values not only by presenting ideas but also through strict discipline. Schools punished students for behavior the school considered disrespectful or wrong. Rules of etiquette were enforced, and courteous behavior was demanded. To meet their educational objectives, schools required absolute obedience... [I]n the earliest public schools, teachers taught, and students listened. Teachers commanded, and students obeyed. Teachers did not rely solely on the power of ideas to persuade; they relied on discipline to maintain order.[33]

Hallmarks of at least three relevant kinds of nostalgia are borne by these excerpts. First, there is a quasi-historical originalist type that seeks, by means of an implied narrative of decline, the emotional (or perhaps aesthetic) satisfaction in an allegedly simpler past in which order and discipline were overriding and unquestioned principles in the governance of schools. In this blessed lost world, "Teachers commanded, and students obeyed." Second, and relatedly, there is a more specifically legalistic nostalgia, again for a simpler world, wherein the doctrine of *in loco parentis* obviates the need for rights, and the whole messy set of questions about democracy and schooling are safely put away, out of sight, in favor of an "absolute obedience." Insofar as it would actually land us anywhere, Thomas's legal time travel would land us pre-*Tinker*, when *in loco parentis* needed to make almost no concessions to students' rights.[34]

To punctuate this point, note the sharp and substantive contrast between Thomas's sentiments and those expressed by the *Tinker* majority in articulating why students should have speech rights:

In our system, state-operated schools may not be enclaves of totalitarianism. School officials do not possess absolute authority over their students. Students in school as well as out of school are "persons" under our Constitution. They are possessed of fundamental rights which the State must respect, just as they themselves must respect their obligations to the State. In our system, students may not be regarded as closed-circuit recipients of only that which the State chooses to communicate. They may not be confined to the expression of those sentiments that are officially approved. In the absence of a specific showing of constitutionally valid reasons to regulate their speech, students are entitled to freedom of expression of their views.[35]

This sort of thing just does not enter into it for Thomas; on his view, "closed circuit recipient" is unambiguously the proper role for a school student. Third, there is a more intimate, gut-level form of nostalgia as a lived experience, in the present instance implied in Thomas's concurrence as representing the "in my day" sort of mentality that, while it is never made explicit, seems like an *éminence grise* that drives much of the discussion. One guesses this by subtraction, as both law and history have been removed as explanations for the vehemence and selectivity of his anti-students' rights view. Indeed, in a recent talk to high school students, Thomas wondered, "how can you not reminisce about a childhood where you began each day with the Pledge of Allegiance as little kids lined up in the schoolyard and then marched two by two with a flag and a crucifix in each classroom?"[36]

Putting it all together, Thomas seems to provide a prime example of what Svetlana Boym terms "restorative nostalgia," a tendency that "attempts a transhistorical reconstruction of the lost home," a form of nostalgia that is "at the core of recent national and religious revivals."[37] In words that could not more perfectly apply to the present case, Boym further elaborates how restorative nostalgia signifies a "return to the original stasis, to the prelapsarian moment. The past for the restorative nostalgic is a value for the present: the past is not a duration but a perfect snapshot."[38] Time itself stands still. Were it only illustrated, Thomas's concurrence surely would feature etchings and photos of straight rows, good postures, firm teachers, and the like. This would all be taken as further documentary evidence of "how things were." This points to a telltale feature of restorative nostalgia according to Boym, namely, that it "takes itself dead seriously."[39] It is not an ironic or humorous stance. There is little self-consciousness here, for the restorative nostalgic does not see himself as a nostalgic, as an imaginer of an "imagined community."[40] Rather, "their project is about truth."[41] Like a contemporary nationalist resurrecting archaic symbols, Thomas's selective marshaling of history - or, more properly, carefully-selected elements of history-related mythos - is meant to be taken as the truth of that history, the real lesson for us all to learn. To take an extreme example from recent history, pursuant to the Serbian nationalist's agenda, it is not so much necessary for one to learn "the facts" of the Battle of Kosovo (1389) so much as it is that one learn, by whatever curricular means, the prede-fined real lesson that has, one supposes, something to do with the indomitable, Turk-defying spirit of the Serbian people.

This in its most extreme form is the project of the restorative nostalgic, the quite clearly pedagogical one of offering "a comforting collective script for individual longing." The dissatis-factions of the all too ugly present (Unruly students! Behavior problems! Disrespectful youth!) are refracted through the retro-spective looking glass into a happily inverted past containing all the desired and opposing qualities.[42] In a phrase, this is the mentality of "the good old days" where the actual level of "goodness" is irrelevant.

Further, as Boym points out, the more intense the restorative project, the more selective the history must be (or law, as in the present circumstance). This makes logical sense. And it helps calibrate more precisely where Thomas is as a would-be restorer. His project here is unhidden (and, in its own way, admirably transparent): he wants to eradicate an area of rights, so the history supporting his alleged originalism is just selective enough, but no more so than it has to be. So despite its potential legal dangers, particularly its corrosive potential for other students' rights and for rights in general, it is necessary to understand that Thomas clearly does not go over the cliff and into the most intense and feverish renderings characteristic of modern fascists and contemporary ethnic cleansers. Those peoples' kind of "history" tends to be out-and-out fabulist, for example, blood and soil, Teutonic heroes, Protocols of the Elders of Zion and other cartoon-ugly ethnic villains undertaking conspiracies. As it happens, Boym does mention the adoption of conspiracy theories as another hallmark of restorative nostalgia; Thomas does not explicitly do this, although it would seem that for him, albeit obliquely, "liberals," "left-wing activists," and the like are the ones responsible for the students' rights calamity of recent decades.[43] Yet, via his skewed and selective reading of history, Thomas merely takes baby steps into the eliminationist realm, the psychotic dreams of mass erasure out of which have sprung so many of our age's waking nightmares. His history is merely a bit selectively skewed. So it is important to maintain a sense of proportion about Thomas and not overstate things. At the same time, the experience of the last century has shown that as a collective phenomenon restorative nostalgia can be culturally and politically explosive, and its precise conditions of combustion are not always predictable. Thomas represents a *symptom*, in the legal realm, of the eliminationist death dream that neoliberalism has for some time been carrying forward in the socio-political realm. Just as neoliberalism takes us beyond erstwhile workers' exploitation and into an eliminationist posture toward them, Thomas's restorative nostalgia does not *engage* its immediate hermeneutical context and so alter it in the "normal" jurisprudential mode. Rather, it seeks to circumnavigate its context altogether by locating an allegedly congenial point *in illo tempore* - in this case the little red schoolhouse of "the good old days" - and, as if channeling Scotty on Star Trek, beaming himself down into it, the inconvenient intervening centuries be damned. Like the neoliberal true believer who glories in a fantastical Ayn Randian self-made *Übermensch* who can sneer down at the rest of humanity from his icy moral perch, Thomas's originalism-cum-nostalgia creates a fantastical authoritative Schoolmaster who "in the olden days" once upon a time heroically guarded the virtue of our youth. Until the Fall, at least, when both *Übermensch* and Schoolmaster were crucified due to the machinations of The Enemy, that is, the rest of us.

It is not that it is illegitimate to decry excessive proceduralism as "rights talk" in schools and elsewhere.[44] This is well-traveled territory and understandably so, as there is much to critique in our myopically rights-obsessed vocabulary and the culture of whining litigiousness with which that vocabulary can become associated. Particularly in education, so often the trump-like assertion of a right functions as a substitute for thinking and as an end to conversation. Neither is it unreasonable in itself to raise the question, as Thomas does, of whether *Tinker* was rightly decided in the first place, along with the larger question of whether and to what extent constitutional rights ought to extend to students in public schools; it is not philosophically irresponsible to oppose students' rights. (I would not think it *a priori* philosophically irresponsible to defend *any* view.) There are perfectly reasonable arguments against them, in fact. The problem with Thomas's concurrence does not lie in the realm of nuanced argumentation, but with his (putatively) restoratively nostalgic approach that, not just accidentally but positively, requires him to "rebuild the ideal home" by means of emotive rhetoric and historical distortion.[45] This problem is magnified because of the temptation to use the position as a bully pulpit to which even a lone concurring or dissenting Supreme Court justice is subject at all times. Even a Supreme Court justice's most idiosyncratic views are printed up in the official case record as concurrences or dissents to be widely discussed and debated, and they are fated to be part of that official record for posterity. For this reason alone, and also for the reasons mentioned at the outset concerning his political prominence and high degree of internal influence on the Court, no matter how "lone" may be some of Thomas's *dicta*, his view unfortunately but inescapably matters and so must be addressed.

I reemphasize that his concurrence is not the majority opinion and as such it does not have the direct force of law. Yet the bully pulpit has laws of its own, and it is clear that Thomas's wholesale rejection of students' rights as a historical and legal "truth" has become the most noteworthy, or at least newsworthy, aspect of the public discussion of the *Morse* ruling (as a quick Google search will readily confirm). Thomas succumbs to the ample temptation available to present himself authoritatively as a legal and historical truth-teller.

Even so, at that late point, the basic legitimacy of his presentation might have been saved, but for the eliminationist nostalgia. What the nostalgia does is cause him to engage in a legally indefensible temporal elision, a setting back of the clock. It is one thing to take on a relevant section of the tradition as it has evolved, in this case the established framework for assessing student speech claims, and show why it ought to be unraveled, explain where the wrong moves were made, and otherwise argue for and justify one's position. This would describe a responsible hermeneutical behavior that requires too much careful attention to detail to allow for the more fleeting and otiose emotional pleasure of a cathartic release of the "damn it all to hell" variety.

If the choice is for truth over emotive release and what

Friedrich Nietzsche calls "metaphysical comfort," one must seek to engage rather than eliminate that with which one disagrees, in scholarship as in life.[46]

The student speech bubble

As the gearing of neoliberal capitalism proceeds apace, we are presented by good-hearted activists with a can-do optimism regarding how "the people," that is, humanity at large, can push back against the system, against those at the helm of the encompassing machine. One constant thought is that we can *educate* ourselves out of the predicament, the more the better, primarily via an augmented and more equitable distribution of higher education. If they know the truth then the truth shall set them free, to paraphrase the Platonic motto. Yet as we have seen with the existential trap represented by student debt, the current institutional mechanisms for offering this higher education seem almost irrevocably intertwined with the institutional mechanisms that are, allegedly, to be overthrown. Would that going off to college were akin to going off to join the resistance! At present it is more like signing one's life away to debt servitude. Alternatively, one might posit, there is for the moment, at least in the US, a window of opportunity, which opened during the Vietnam era which, despite the best wishes of those such as Clarence Thomas, has not yet closed. Here it is possible to imagine the voices of students *themselves* being heard through the exercise of their free speech rights. And indeed there are many examples of conscience in the form of individuals - including children - and small groups not allowing themselves to be cowed by bullying authorities and narrow minded local communities: from the atheist teenager who stands up alone against state-sponsored proselytizers to the grade schooler who refuses to parrot what to his mind are the hollow promises of the Pledge of Allegiance's commitment to "liberty and justice for all."[47] These are the kinds of people who have always made things better, in the long run, even for those who myopically style them their enemies. It is an all-too rare occasion to have pride in a system that enables such gestures and those voices should be cherished and supported whenever they appear amidst the darkness.

But from a systems point of view, it is easy to see the trap laid by *Morse* - and not just by Thomas but, even more importantly, by the majority. What are to be allowed are students' *individual* expressions of preference, in the Brand A over Brand B sense. The moment an item of student speech challenges that which may be judged to be outside the inherently *elastic* parameters of the school's "educational mission," which is to say, anything that actually might substantively threaten systemic aims and purposes, all bets are off and students are to be *managed* as the long-term problems most of them are doomed to be in the jobless future of the neoliberal train wreck. As it always has at key points, the US Supreme Court seems willing in this area to throw everything away the moment privilege is actually challenged. On a larger scale, in the 1970s when racial desegregation and school finance equity began to be taken from an elite point of view *too* seriously, that is, to the point that such efforts threatened wealthy white suburbanites, the Court was quick to find a rationale for halting racial mixing at the gates of the suburbs (*Milliken v. Bradley* [1974]), and tax monies from reaching poor urban and rural kids (*San Antonio v. Rodriguez* [1973]). Rhetorical gestures toward "helping" minorities and the poor are welcome, but *actual* challenges: not so much. Vis-à-vis students' rights, the *Morse* decision fits firmly within that status quo-preserving mode; any *actual* exercise of student voice must be legally hemmed in, the majority playing, as it were, the "good cop" who simply wants to help schools cohere around their "educational missions," and Thomas playing the "bad cop" who wants to disenfranchise students altogether in service of a proto-fascist "days of yore" in which roles were clear and The Father ruled.

On the ground, as the "educational mission" of schools moves ineluctably even further toward warehousing and surveillance - pre-jail - then remaining intra-institutional speech rights will easily be quashed. Especially post-Dunblane, Columbine and Sandy Hook (and, I'm sadly sure, further disasters), "safety" will easily trump all and that which is "disruptive" will undergo a magical metamorphosis into childhood and adolescence themselves (both of which are, after all, inherently disruptive.). Just as the exploiting of workers will be looked back upon with fondness as symptomatic of better times, so too will today's students' rights controversies seem like "problems" we would love once again to have. Perhaps years hence they will be studied for their exoticism. It is strange, in fact, how the overflowing of civil liberties onto students maps chronologically onto the period of post-war growth and prosperity, that period (until the 1970s) when competitive capitalism was still turning profits, before the fated arising of the financialized bubble machine. As the *Morse* majority illustrates, following closely in the wake of the falling rate of profits seems to be a falling rate of personal freedom, the kind of thing that gets noticed largely only as it is taken away. This should perhaps not be surprising, after all, to students of the political economy of the twentieth century, for example, the hyperinflated Germany economy of the 1920s that did not, in retrospect, turn out so well for anyone.

And so once again, as always, we look backward to see forward.

Once Upon a Time there was a world in which blue collar parents had stable jobs and raised their kids in decent schools where they could do things like protest against the nation's wars. *In Illo Tempore.*

Chapter 6

Educational eliminationism III: Universal schooling disassembled

The idea that a system of education of an appropriate and suitable quality could by itself transform the world is a naïve idea.
Samir Amin[1]

The first lesson [a youthful, student-led revolutionary movement] must learn is that an ethical, non-exploitative and socially just capitalism that redounds to the benefit of all is impossible. It contradicts the very nature of what capital is about.
David Harvey[2]

Of course...but *maybe*...

The American comedian Louis CK has a bit he calls "of course... but maybe." It takes the form of stating an initial proposition that seems to be the very embodiment of what is good and right, that concerning which *"of course"* everyone agrees. He then goes on to question that piety by prefacing his doubts with, amidst nervous anticipatory laughter, a well-paced *"but maybe..."* Louis says, "I always have other competing thoughts. And I don't believe them but they're there. There's the thing I believe. And then there's the *other* thing. It's there. There's the thing I believe and then that *other* thing. It's become this category of thought for me. I call it "of course...but *maybe*."[3] As the routine proceeds, experimenting with the edge of propriety, Louis goes after one sacred cow after another, including: wounded soldiers, the evil of slavery, kids with severe allergies, racial equality and even the untouchably sacrosanct Make-a-Wish Foundation that satisfies a last wish for dying children.

Comedically, this is a risky hit or miss. Even with a sympathetic audience, he does not always hit the mark. But still he pushes forward and is sometimes able to achieve serious insight, in this instance exposing hidden psychological undercurrents not often brought to light. It is almost rapturous when this occurs and it elicits a swirl of emotions not normally juxtaposed, like guilt and hilarity. Louis makes us uncomfortably complicit in our laughter. It is *so* bad; one should *not* laugh at such things. But we do.

I will not attempt to scale the comic heights of Louis CK. But I am inspired to try my own less-funny version with some inherited certainties from the world of education reform.

Teaching. *Of course* pedagogy matters. Kids need good teachers. They make a huge difference in children's lives. We can all think of wonderful teachers who helped us along the way and to whom we will be forever grateful. We can all also remember the bad ones, who may just as powerfully have harmed us. A great teacher can change a child's life, just as a bad one at the wrong time can ruin it. Through their unending influence, teachers may even be said to be immortal in a way.[4] Given the vocational needs of today's economy, in fact, having a good teacher - especially in crucial areas like math and science - matters more than ever. *Of course*. If we could just ensure that every student has a great teacher, we could radically change schools for the better and consequently decisively enhance the educational opportunities open to all. *Of course* this would be a good thing. *Of course* it is morally right and even a matter of social justice for everyone involved. If you have good teachers, *anything* is possible. Teachers matter - and they are professionals who should be respected. *Of course!*

But maybe…

Maybe the importance of individual teachers is over-emphasized. *Maybe* it's even okay, and *maybe* even in a way desirable, for a kid to have a few bad teachers along the way, having to encounter and adjust to some difficult adult personalities that do not automatically "care" for them like Mom and Dad. *Maybe* even encountering injustice is not the worst thing in the world. *Maybe* it is not bad in the long run for a kid from time to time to have to take learning more into her own hands because a teacher here and there is not very helpful. *Maybe* it's the *overall* panorama of experiences that's important, the good *and* the bad. *Maybe* there are a lot of vested interests served by thinking that the key to educational progress has to do with "teacher quality," in fact a strangely unholy alliance of market-oriented corporate school reformers (who want to "free" teachers by busting up public schools and their unions) and education schools (who want everyone to feel dependent on their product, the credentialed teacher, to whom they have added *so much* value that they (the education schools among others) should be considered indispensable - not to mention the "education research" dollars flowing toward these universities that are allegedly a matter of ongoing national urgency. *Maybe* parents and politicians also find it suspiciously convenient to focus teacher-ward: a Madonna/whore complex where the objects of their affection/disaffection, teachers, are either doing "the world's toughest job" and should be maudlinly lauded or they are thunderously blamed for a child's individual failure or the failure of children generally. *But maybe* good as well as bad societies throughout history and across cultures have *all* had their share of good and bad teachers - and the goodness or badness of their societies was not a function of those teachers' pedagogical competence. *Maybe* teachers as individuals are who they are and will continue to be so, representing, more or less, a slightly-more-benign-than-average cross section of adult society (those able to hold a steady job, have a moderately higher level of education, and some affinity or at least tolerance for children of the relevant age group). *Maybe* it's not even really possible deliberately to "manufacture" good teachers and to improve them by technical - and expensive - formative processes having to do with their curriculum and pedagogical training at the hands of university-based "experts" in teacher preparation. *Maybe* not much would be lost to society as a whole without all this "professionalization" and bureaucratic hoop-jumping.

School reform. *Of course* good schools are vital to the nation and moreover are a matter of social justice, both in the sense of the equitable distribution of educational resources and also the sense of making more progressive school governance policies and internal practices. As with teachers, *of course* every child needs one, has a right to one, and the quality of kids' futures depends on access to one. Nothing is more important than getting this right. Everyone understands that, *of course*, these are the larval sites for future generations, and therefore the quality of our collective future is a direct function of *their* quality, how much we attend to and invest in them. Major battles have been fought over schools, like the decades-long fight over racial segregation in the 1950s and 60s, and *of course* these battles were over something significant, just as individual parents striving to get their children into the best schools are making efforts that are surely worthwhile. *Of course* schools matter and reforming them should be among our highest priorities. *Of course* we should fight hard for them and doing so is the same thing as fighting for our kids themselves. Everyone knows this. *Of course.*

But maybe...

Maybe the focus on school reform is a kind of diversion, a large-scale attention feint. Following John Marsh's argument in *Class Dismissed*, maybe the focus on schools is all too convenient, in that it lets the primary structures and perpetrators - i.e. capitalism and capitalists - off the hook too easily.[5] As Marsh puts it, education fulfills an important ideological role in that it is what "lets us sleep at night" vis-à-vis inequality because, owing to the existence of our school system, we can assure ourselves that we really do believe in equality of opportunity and therefore do not have to worry about equality of outcome.

As long as schools are there as arenas of voluntaristic striving and documentable achievement, our socio-economic losers may be told "you had your chance," and what, *loser*, did you do with it? Maybe school reform is in this sense the last refuge of elite scoundrels (the venture philanthropists discussed earlier) who want to maintain the *appearance* of meritocracy while economic structures are the near-exclusive determinants of their own and others' kids' life chances. As the late capitalist monopolies have consolidated themselves, as journalist Chris Hayes documents in his searing indictment *Twilight of the Elites*, they are able both to perpetuate their own often mediocre progeny and simultaneously systematically shrink the "talent pool" from which the competition, in theory, should come.[6] Taking a step back, *maybe just maybe*, beneath the rhetorical fog, schools can be expected roughly to correspond to the societies within which they are ensconced; as argued previously, under communism we have communist schools, fascism generates fascist schools and - surprise, surprise - capitalism yields schools that also reflect and perpetuate the socio-economic system of which they are a part.

Even more so, as I have argued in this book, despite the illusions of the moment - perhaps adjusted for some lag time and isolated counter-trends - schools can be expected eventually to reflect the dialectical mutations that are always - inevitably - occurring within the economic base of society. It is so *boring* to have to remind everyone of this, but as much as we love to pretend otherwise, schools are still an integral organ within capitalism's respiratory system, rising and falling in rhythm with their encompassing chest cavity. In and out. Up and down. During the past two centuries' expansive era of capitalism, where capitals were on the whole starved for labor and, eventually, accelerating individual laborers' productivity gains, support for an all-inclusive and comprehensive school system swelled to new heights. Our recent ancestors now saw the importance of mass schools! Huzzah! Toss your hats! With almost all the productive forces aligned toward it, the nineteenth century was a blessed time to champion universal education. But now, at the dawn of the twenty-first century, the great machine is contracting. And so therefore is the need for all these well-schooled types. No more huzzahs. Instead, hold onto your hats. The forces of production have altered and just when you thought the relations of production might be out of their age-old harness, to channel Michael Corleone, *they pull them back in*.

Base and superstructure: boring but true.

And now, because of automation, the global labor arbitrage and other phenomena associated with the TRPF, capitalism has, as long prophesied, entered a terminal phase. Only, as if with a cosmic and very dark sense of humor, it is not *capitalism* per se that is necessarily terminal. (As always, nobody knows where things ultimately stand with regard to *that*.) Whatever capitalism's longevity, what is now revealed as terminal is - wait for it - most all of *us*. Like a firearm that is lethal for some and not others depending where it's pointed, capitalism is terminal for the vast majority of human beings on the planet. Ironically, it now seeks to cut back on its own population overshoot, through the twin internal and external crises of: (1) the diminution of human labor needs via technology, and (2) the destruction of the human-habitable planet via the same, from the externalities associated with resource depletion and climate change. It never loved us, you see. But now it no longer even *needs* most of us anymore; the old slaves have outlived their usefulness and now they're just *takers*, merely costs to be deducted from the great balance sheet. Accordingly, capitalism seems headed toward a kind of quasi-"singularity," to adapt Ray Kurzweil's famous term, where it fuses itself onto a small and exclusive subsection of humanity - the 1% or whatever tiny proportion - and creates a new and far more monstrous entity than Marx's gentlemanly Victorian Vampire Herr *Kapital*.[7] Drinking blood is quite inconvenient and passé when one no longer needs blood to survive.

This new techno-financial elite entity seems to want little to do with the rest of us, seeing us, perhaps rightfully from within its own lenses, as walking dead. It is not accidental the zombie has become a pop cultural icon. We love to kill them on Xbox and, vicariously, in countless recent shows and movies.[8] We can even obtain kitsch "zombie hunting licenses" and buy actual zombie bullets for our actual firearms. As the American magazine *Guns & Ammo* reports: "*Be PREPARED – supply yourself for the Zombie Apocalypse with Zombie Max ammunition from Hornady Loaded with PROVEN Z-Max™ bullets…yes, PROVEN Z-Max™ bullets. This stuff is live ammo, it's no toy or Halloween gimmick.*"[9] In the ironic post-modern spirit of trendy viral marketing, the sales pitch surrounding the zombie ammo is tongue in cheek, but the rounds are real. In fact, sales are reported to have spiked after a reported "cannibalism" incident last year in Maryland.[10] There is a persistent undercurrent in modern culture that is fascinated by horror, the occult, and like categories. I only note how suggestively zombies, somehow, "fit" the cultural moment. They are our opponents and yet also, simultaneously, *we ourselves*. Extrapolating from present labor and environmental trends, it is unfortunate but "walking dead" seems all-too apt: a cinematic representation of our fears of others' and our own placelessness, of the moral numbness of humanity conceived as *surplus* and reduced to the status of sickening objects, what Sartre identified, through his protagonist Roquentin, as an experience of nausea directed at ourselves and existence itself as "*de trop*" (literally, "too much" or "in excess"): "I dreamed vaguely of killing myself to wipe out at least one of these superfluous lives. But even my death would have been *de trop*. *De trop*, my corpse, my blood on these stones, between these plants, at the back of the smiling garden. And the decomposed flesh would have been *de trop* in the earth which would receive my bones, at least, cleaned, stripped, peeled, proper and clean as teeth, it would have been *de trop*: I was *de trop* for eternity."[11]

Roquentin is remembering what we tend to forget in our busy everydayness: we were never anything other than walking dead because we are mortal. Our demi-monsters obliquely remind us that the question of elimination is nothing new for anyone; from the perspective of the individual, dead is dead, whether it is from starvation, disease or climate disaster. Through horror we come to grips, as philosopher Eugene Thacker postulates, with the normally unthinkable possibility of a *"world-without-us."*[12] As the threat of nuclear apocalypse forced the post-war generation to contemplate (ducking and covering under their grade school desks), the novelty consists not in the simple prospect of elimination (aka the human condition), but rather in its unprecedented scale and timing. We are all on the clock; and so the timing is everything.

Universal education's downcycle

Downcycling is the process of converting waste materials or useless products into new materials or products of lesser quality and reduced functionality.[13]

Back to education and the tremors of elimination explored earlier with student debt and the precariousness of students' rights. A more fundamental issue even than these has to do with the ideal of universal education itself, education for all, which should be counted among the most significant progeny of the marriage of historical liberalism and maturing capitalism. Here we once again learn concerning Marx's phrase "all that is solid melts into air" that "all" indeed means "all." What has for generations been taken for granted as a "solid" foundation for everyday life in the industrial world, viz., the public provision of education, contoured only by an apparent trajectory of expansion and inclusivity (religion, gender, race, disability), is now open to question in a way that it has not been for generations. As is raised in the student debt discussion, the question of whether education is "worth it" - from the perspective both of individuals and the allocation of ever-scarcer state resources - is once again with us. At this point, with the eager and shortsighted collaboration of education officialdom, the rationale has been stripped down to the bare-bones quantitative analysis of the cash returns of various degrees over a students's lifetime. This rhetorical economism is typically featured on school marketing brochures and in fact is more present than ever in students' minds as the primary reason they are in school at all.[14] (As discussed in the student debt chapter, this is only understandable; as the debt mounts, most not only desire but *require* a return on their personal investment.) Live by the sword, die by the sword.

Educational institutions have profited in public esteem by hitching their stars to the wagons of "the business community," to use the common brain-dead euphemism. This was a nice short-term strategy. But as the TRPF grinds down our grandparents' capitalism and replaces it with automation, global labor precarity and financialized looting by the few, that rationale for educating *everyone* grows weaker and weaker. Here too, in this most sacred precinct of historical liberalism, a child's right to an education, educational eliminationism stalks the land. Culturally, this is where the endgame really begins.

A more detailed look at this development is in order. The ideal of universal education is a composite of two conjoined impera-tives: a right of *access* to education via government provision and also *compulsory* education secured by police power. It is thus double-barreled, in the sense of possessing twin imperatives to:

1 *extend* the right to the whole of the age-appropriate population;[15] while, at the same time,
2 *require* members of that same population to avail themselves of it.

This double nature distinguishes "education for all" from other basic civil rights such as speech, religion and even political participation, where there is rarely any officially coercive element regarding the *exercise* of the right in question. However strongly a state guarantees freedom of speech, for example, it would be altogether exceptional to *require* citizens to utilize it. Even the most basic democratic right to the franchise has seldom been exercised under formal compulsion in the global North (though there are a few exceptions). There are perhaps elements of "forcible exercise" legal compulsion to be identified in what many would regard as basic rights, such as participation in health care provision or, perhaps, aspects of military service and taxation (though speaking of a "right to be taxed" might be a rhetorical stretch). Such considerations only underscore how uniquely robust has become education's double guarantee.

This strong pairing of the right to education and compulsion is experienced as *force majeure* exercised against the family unit by the political and economic needs of the capitalist state; with the advent of industrialism this assertion of state power vis-à-vis children blows in as a powerful storm front against the set of previously existing domestic arrangements. The state now asserts its right to a decisively timely and sustained forming of the young and a concomitant further disciplining of the old. The compulsion is formally directed at parents qua guardians, whose failure to comply with state attendance laws provokes legal sanction and even, ultimately, the loss of parental rights and/or incarceration. Though at this point not often thought of as such among the "civilized," the police power of the state lies behind it all, make no mistake. Liberal triumphalism represents this network of coercion as one of its greatest achievements: children removed from mine, field and factory are brought into a more "proper" setting and positioned for greater human flourishing. Their growth as human beings is no longer to be retarded by their family's myopic need for extra income or hands around the farm. Parents would simply have to delay this potential income stream or do without it altogether. No more five year-olds in coal mines or at harvest (though this latter takes some doing, historically speaking).

Compulsory education and child labor protections were (and are) championed along Kantian lines by idealists as patently morally defensible causes. And so they may be: children are allegedly being conceived by parents and employers as economic instruments rather than as (potentially) flourishing ends in themselves. But calibrating the supply of child labor has always been a functional aspect of the "normal" workings of capitalism, part of its "respiration," one might say, one among a panoply of fail-safe mechanisms ready to be adopted during periods of economic volatility and high unemployment to adjust the labor supply and maintain social stability. Keeping certain segments of the population out of the workforce helps solve crises of unemployment, including the absorption of new wage-earners such as women and minority breadwinners. A degree of social unrest and disruption is thereby avoided until capacity "catches up." It is a costly and elaborate but clever mechanism for helping ameliorate the "bust" part of capitalism's perpetual boom-bust cycles. The universal matriculation thus enabled by compulsory education's legal framework also helps secure a range of cultural "enablers," that is, legitimations, of capitalist production such as the instilling of such industrial work habits as punctuality and efficiency, the acquiescence to managerial authority and standardized measures of output, a strict division between work and leisure ("holiday"), an augmented acceptance and psychological dependence on abstract and fungible markers of social worth such as grades, money, and suchlike.[16] All these factors of educational production *add value*, ultimately, to the processes of capitalist production. The school graduate, now a credentialed worker, has gained the skills and dispositions necessary in order to increase the future employer's efficiency at capturing and monetizing the higher level of surplus labor of which the more productive educated laborer is capable. Especially as production undergoes automation (as in most any competitive environment), the toil of *schooled* workers is so much more *exploitable*. To the martial strains of Elgar's *Pomp and Circumstance*, they and their cohort march off for hire under a promise of augmented service toward ever-expandable profits.

This golden era of universal education is thus also the golden era of elasticated worker exploitability. As per the classical Marxist thesis concerning the extraction of profit from workers' surplus labor value, under moderately advanced conditions of production (e.g. moderately advanced industrialization), the educated workers - the "symbolic workers" - simply present more to exploit, the "low hanging fruit" of near-universal basic literacy (now 99%-plus in Europe and the US) having provided by far the biggest educational augmentation of labor productivity;[17] a once-in-an-age great leap forward that, despite its collective cost, massively increased the capacity of labor to generate surplus for owners, that is to say, their profits, in the form of personal takings and also further capital accumulation. Premised on compulsory education laws, universal schooling has on the whole been immensely profitable. Again, this is not the *only* reason to value universal schooling, and neither is it the only reason it has been championed historically. Profitability is the necessary condition and driving force, though; durability is secured only by those institutions that serve the needs of capital.

Yet as Job comes to recognize about God, what capitalism gave, capitalism also hath taken away.[18] Just as the era of universal schooling began with massive changes in the plate tectonics of capitalism, it is now beginning to recede in accord with further changes within those same tectonics. Extending the geological metaphor, from a wide historical perspective, one might see universal schooling as a temporary ontogenetic phenomenon, one that is essentially a by-product of larger substructural alterations, in the same way the outcropping represented by a mountain is generated from subterranean pressures. Over the historical long run, social institutions are always dynamic as they respond to the push and pull of a range of forces; they come, they change, they go. And even what "they" appear to be is to some extent a temporal mirage, as they - like all other matter - neither appear nor disappear *ex nihilo*. Rather, they are always created out of existing materials and become in turn the materials for *what comes next* - "dialectically" as would say the Hegelian-Marxist tradition. As with the river, one does not step into the same school twice.

The mutability and finitude of all human arrangements are important to keep firmly in mind here. For one thing it is never "all-or-nothing" with large-scale social institutions. They are never completely destroyed nor are they ever completely created out of thin air. One may destroy all physical trace of them, in fact, but they will live on, somewhere, somehow, *in mente*, as a cultural antecedent to whatever comes next.

This insight entails that one should not expect "compulsory education" to end *full stop* in the sense that school buildings and those designated as "teachers," "students," "administrators," and so on will necessarily vanish. What is overwhelmingly likely - and is in fact already occurring - is that we will have sites populated by youth that are "compulsory" and sites populated by youth where "education" occurs. But we will no longer be seeing as many sites where youth are subject to "compulsory education." Certainly compulsion will remain for the vast majority as they are warehoused and surveilled in a vestigial educational apparatus that becomes increasingly punitive and carceral in orientation, sites devoted most obviously to social control of "disposable" youth than anything recognizable as "education."[19] They will probably even still be called "schools." There will also certainly be "education" occurring at different sites, where a certain, ever-smaller percentage of managerial and technical sub-elites are "educated" to service the apparatus of the tiny fraction of the population represented by the owners of capital, these latter no doubt continuing to populate their glorious and personally fulfilling "voluntary" private preparatory schools and elite universities. So there will still be plenty of "compulsion" and a certain amount of "education," but these two phenomena will be occurring at sites increasingly distant from one another. Compulsory education as a *mass* phenomenon will, if present trends continue, be eliminated. Again: this elimination may not occur in name or regarding its physical infrastructure - in fact, one can anticipate that more sites labeled "schools" will continue to be expanded and built. Rather, the elimination of compulsory education will consist in large part of the alteration of what "compulsory education" had previously meant, at least as a component of a larger ideal, namely, an equipping of all citizens with productive capacities and hence a social *place*.

Instead of exploiting them - an exploitation that in retrospect seems desirable compared to mass youth unemployment, currently nearing 60% in such countries as Greece and Spain - the telos of the eroding institutions of compulsory education must now be the efficient managing, not of laborers but of the labor-less and the population overshoot they represent. Vast segments of the population, especially the rising generation, are simply "extra" people who are no longer needed as exploitable material by capitalist enterprise. The situation with production has changed due to its automation and globalization such that proportionately far fewer of the individuals once comprising the working classes of the global North are needed *as workers*. These people are being cut out of the economic loop altogether through a variety of proximal means: outsourcing, attrition, layoffs etc. They are being "casualized," which is to say rendered ever-more precarious as forced participants in an increasingly stressful, dangerous, less stable and less remunerative subsistence "informal" economy. The autoworker becomes a service attendant who becomes a street vendor or worse (and I mean "worse" in terms of economic stability). How much education do these latter really need? How much will elites tax themselves for such "waste"?

Why is this happening? As described in earlier chapters, what has happened is that capitalism has happened or, more precisely, has continued to happen. The dynamics of "normal" capitalist production includes a tendency for firms' profits *in the long-run and in the ensemble* to diminish if their processes remain static. The TRPF's profit-sinking tendency generates powerful counter forces as capitalist enterprises continually remake themselves in order to keep profits up, as an aircraft must overcome the force of gravity in order to fly. The most important of these counter forces have been present with capitalism since its inception and are inseparable from it: technological advances that provide firms with (temporary) comparative advantages and the need to discipline labor to conform to inevitably changing economic conditions. These processes have always caused mass upheaval and social disruption. History has not halted in this regard.

What is new is that technological change has reached a sort of tipping point in which the advancements have outmoded the need for mass labor, skilled and unskilled. Domestically, first manufacturing and then service work are automated to an increasing extent while technological efficiencies in areas such as communications and transport allow for the exporting of the remaining human labor needs. The factory in Detroit or Leeds closes and the jobs end up in Mexico, China, or Vietnam; the insurance agency or customer support service relocate call centers to Ireland or India. Technological efficiencies thus create a powerful one-two punch aimed against the working class life that has heretofore been taken as "normal" for generations of Americans and Europeans: first an outright replacement of positions made redundant, from the assembly line to the secretarial suite, and second a brutal global labor arbitrage that places global North workers for the first time in full competition with those from the global South. Thus the technologies that make possible automation and globalization together provide the ultimate disciplining of labor: the credible threat of *eliminating* it. The most elegant solution is simply to *remove* the jobs by whatever means.

It is a happy short-term situation for the capitalist as labor gets cheaper and cheaper while there is still vestigial systemic demand being propped up by elaborate mechanisms of consumer and sovereign credit and debt. It is a curious situation in which every serious person knows how it will end in the long run (viz., with the bursting of the various demand-aiding debt bubbles), yet there seems no non-ruinous short-term option. So we are fully strapped into a situation that education policy analyst Kenneth Saltman describes as "smash and grab" capitalism, where hyper-financialized enterprises are competing to extract what they can *avant le déluge*.[20] Part of that increasingly desperate extraction has to do with "taking and breaking" traditionally public provisions of health care, schooling, policing etc., through mechanisms enjoying anodyne public-relations department labels such as "private equity" or 'public-private partnerships."[21] As they say, "get them while they're hot": MOVE IN - TAKE OVER - PRIVATIZE - EXTRACT - LOCATE NEXT VICTIM - REPEAT.

This process comprises its own one-two punch vis-à-vis institutions such as public education:

1 as schools' underlying economic rationale of creating workers for capital-accumulating enterprises diminishes,
2 expenditures for those operations start to seem less justifiable and more "wasteful," rendering them fit only for profit-taking raids by corporate privatizers, consulting firms, and the like.

Schools simply become a *target*. No longer needed for the production of long term exploitable "human capital," they are "restructured," "reformed" and "privatized," that is, oriented toward short-term profit extraction by capitalist enterprises that no longer *make* but simply *take*. In this they are no more "capitalist" in the traditional mode than are the "too-big-to-fail" banks who survive purely by sovereign financial manipulations in their favor, as in central bank bailouts.

As we have seen, all of this creates the conditions for the elimination of public education as we have known it, an *educational eliminationism* that now sets its sights on the set of vestigial commitments represented in the very idea of universal education, one of modernity's core utopian promises.

The temporal and spatial *consignment* of young persons will certainly continue and intensify qua incarceration. Features of those consignments resembling what was once taken as "educative" will, however, continue to cycle down and, if present trends continue, eventually phase out altogether for the vast majority of the population, the extra people who really are no longer needed.

As argued in earlier chapters, because of changes in capitalist production occurring over the last several generations, we have moved roughly from an era in which the predominant *telos* of worker subordination involved *exploitation*, i.e. as per Marx, the extraction of surplus labor value pursuant to capital accumulation and capitalist profit. From the capitalist's point of view, in the best case there existed a "surplus army" of workers whose existence would help ensure that labor market competition was kept internecine among the workers (i.e. worker vs. worker) rather than amongst the capitalists themselves *for* workers' labor (capitalist vs. capitalist). In the former scenario, wages tend to fall and in the latter they tend to rise. The traditional capitalist, of course, wants wages to fall in order to maximize workers' exploitation and hence, ultimately, profits. It is in short all about worker exploitation.

Amidst these powerful and increasingly rapacious economic interests, public schooling, in its twentieth century "universal education" form of expansive inclusivity and government provision, is structurally doomed. It is, literally, carrion for the thus aptly named "vulture capitalists" who have now come to view it as a carcass-like amalgam of both waste and prey. After a century-plus of uneasy but creative mutualism, capitalism and public education are now parting ways. What remains to be seen is whether the public will part ways with capitalism before it drives the entire project of universal education - and the public itself soon thereafter - into history's dustbin. This prognosis does not really require any fancy theoretical machinery or super-natural clairvoyance. On the contrary, all it requires is the simple credulity of taking the elite's favored ideologues at their word. In this connection, there is no better historical example than Margaret Thatcher's presciently apocalyptic 1987 remark that "There is no such thing as society... There are individual men and women and there are families and no government can do anything except through people and people look to themselves first... and people have got the entitlements too much in mind without the obligations, because there is no such thing as an entitlement unless someone has first met an obligation "[22] More recently, US presidential candidate Mitt Romney also said as much when he was behind closed doors speaking privately (so he thought) to a group of wealthy donor-supporters in his notorious 2012 "47 percent" speech about those allegedly "dependent upon government, who believe that they are victims, who believe that government has a responsibility to care for them, who believe that they are entitled to health care, to food, to housing, to you name it. That that's an entitlement. And the government should give it to them... And so my job is not to worry about those people - I'll never convince them that they should take personal responsibility and care for their lives."[23] If there is no such thing as society and no such thing as entitlement then there certainly is no such thing as a social entitlement, a universal right to government provision of *any* kind for *those people*, the ones who are unwilling to "take personal responsibility and care for their lives." This willingness to abandon huge segments of the population - "those people" - is as chilling as it is explicit. History shows all too well that when those controlling the levers of power begin to wish people away rhetorically, "those people" are often, in fact, eventually eliminated.

What is stunningly novel here is how large a percentage of the population is to be written off, how many of us are simply *absent* from what appears to be the guiding vision of our self-perpetuating elites. Once upon a time, as per the US Declaration of Independence, the people at large declared their independence from distant elite rule. Now elites, secure in their social (and increasingly geographical) distance, are the ones to declare *their own* independence from their compatriots and the mass of humanity in general: a declaration of independence from humanity. This is the mad dream of the gated community, a fantasy of ridding oneself of dependence upon undesirables ("those people"), a kind of zombie apocalypse from which elites escape and establish an unsullied paradise where reside only the heroic individuals and their families (presumably also heroic). There they lead shining lives of entrepreneurial virtue, *per impossibile*, with only one another and wholly within their peaceable gated domain. Safely within the gates, there is education aplenty for the well-connected, perhaps even histories of what the world used to be like when the useless and menacing zombies outside used to be trained in what were called "schools." As for the idea of venturing beyond the gates, perhaps on some dangerous and quixotic altruistic campaign "for the children" ("some of them *are* cute, it just tugs one's heartstrings") dreamed up by the beautiful souls at the Oxbridges and the Ivies, one can only predict: *not bloody likely*.

Determined resistance

It is customary to offer a ritualized gesture of activism and to make "recommendations." My recommendation is to prepare for catastrophe, within education and generally. Capitalism will not halt and will not stop mutating into newer and ever more deadly forms due to anyone's cleverness or idealism. Social hope lies in the direction of the generation of opposition thrown up by the system's own operation, as discussed previously, both endogenously having to do with the TRPF and associated phenomena, and exogenously having to do with resource depletion and climate change. The masses of people who are no longer exploited or exploitable, in the global South and increasingly in the global North, especially youth, as the ones who are unaccounted for in the neoliberal vision justifying the present world system, are the populations from whom change will arise, as they have necessarily been positioned this way, with their backs against the wall. They must either revolt or die. Urban riots, occupy movements, Arab Springs and similar events are the tremors presaging this apparently inevitable existential fight. In whatever form, this resistance will only grow stronger and more intense. One does not need to be Nostradamus to see this. There is no alternative: the current economic system simply has no place for "those people" and so their restiveness is fated. Unfortunately, much of this will be, as always, self-destructive in the manner of recent urban riots in Los Angeles, Paris and London. Arrayed against this social instability (less clinically, "cry of humanity") is the horrifyingly comprehensive carceral and surveillance state along with its vast military and policing forces. As in many areas already, these will become the true new educators. "Compulsion" is a euphemism for the manner and techniques of social control these armed teachers will exercise.

The question remains, though: In the face of these large-scale economic and political cataclysms, what kinds of responses are rational for individuals on the ground, those living their lives, as most of us do, within these ill-fated educational institutions? As mentioned at the outset of this chapter, there is what might be termed the "heroic assertion" model championed by the humanists, probably the most common oppositional vision on the left - and to some extent the right - that wants us to get up and act, to "be the change we want to see in the world," and that sort of thing.[24] Both the existentialism of the left, historically associated with such figures as the early Sartre and the Ayn Randian-inflected libertarianism of today's right share this view that the all-defining human being is always capable of existentially bootstrapping itself into an active, co-creating position vis-à-vis the world at large. We always have at least some ontological elbow room, some clear space of freedom to define and make ourselves - and in fact that is what it is to be human in the end; our humanity is located in this ability to "negate," to use Sartre's language.[25] This kind of view is widespread and implicit in many models of activism. It is not the product of any particular philosophical argument and is quite understandable and commonsensical. It is also to an extent scripted because a belief in personal efficacy, qua "agency" or "free will," is a keystone conviction in our inherited Judeo-Christian voluntarism that, among other things, makes it possible to hold others accountable for sin, criminality and other malefactions. *We could choose to do otherwise. We can make a difference. People are responsible for their actions - and lacks thereof.* Such statements pass for moral common sense; any view that does not pay proper respects to this folk moral inheritance is considered *ipso facto* "problematic."

For example, one of those things that "everyone knows" - including many learned types - is that one of the great flaws in Marx is how "deterministic" his views are. As Terry Eagleton explains in his very effective send up of this lazy myth, the allegation is that Marx sees us as mere "tools of history" subject to "iron laws," and so advances a set of deterministic beliefs that are "offensive to human freedom and dignity, just as Marxist states are."[26] Marx, it turns out, actually made but one or two remarks about the inevitability of socialism, most famously in the *Communist Manifesto*, which is a deliberately hyperbolic pamphlet of political rhetoric composed, according to historian Eric Hobsbawm, at "a relatively immature phase in the development of Marxist thought."[27] Reflective of this undeveloped state, Marx, I think, presents no clear view on the question of determinism in this document. At best there is ambivalence. On the one hand there is the quote that everybody knows: "What the bourgeoisie therefore produces, above all, are its own gravediggers. Its fall and the victory of the proletariat are equally *inevitable* [emphasis added]."[28] Score one for the proponents of Marx being a determinist. Yet on the other hand, also in the *Manifesto*, there is this: "Freeman and slave, patrician and plebeian, lord and serf, guild-master and journeyman, in a word, oppressor and oppressed, stood in constant opposition to one another, carried on an uninterrupted, now hidden, now open fight, a fight that each time ended, *either in a revolutionary reconstitution of society at large, or in the common ruin of the contending classes* [emphasis added]."[29] The "either ... or" in this latter passage quite clearly represents something other than the inevitability of a particular outcome to the class "fight." On the contrary, as Hobsbawm concludes, the *Manifesto* "envisaged failure ... It is hoped that the outcome of capitalist development would be 'a revolutionary reconstruction of society at large' but, as we have already seen, it did not exclude the alternative: 'common ruin.'"[30]

Given that there is very little else in Marx's corpus that directly suggests "inevitability," the thesis that Marx is a determinist is terribly overblown. It seems that Marx simply did not have a nuanced philosophical position on the question of historical inevitability. In fact, it appears he has a rather unremarkable, even conventional, middle-of-the-spectrum position into which he did not care to delve too deeply: although we inherit circumstances not of our choosing we can through our actions exercise influence on how those circumstances run their course. Fully consistent with his conventional common sense view of historical determinism, Marx's position here is perhaps best characterized, along with Étienne Balibar, as "evolutionary," as "there is in his writing a progressive *line of evolution* of modes of production."[31] The analogy with evolutionary biology is a perfect way to capture the middle of the road position: species evolve in ways that are physically hard-wired, that is, in a sense, determined, but the ultimate direction of that evolution is in no way fated in any metaphysical sense due to the existence of circumstance (environment) and chance in the form of random mutation. This is neither hard causal determinism nor pre-destination. With the analog to evolution in mind, Marx is not theoretically really even obliged to produce a position on the fraught question of "free will" - as if anyone in the history of philosophy has "solved" that antinomy anyway.

My point is raising all this is not simply to defend Marx against straw arguments (Eagleton's effort here is sufficient), but to point out the *structure* of this perennial accusation: it is in effect a *reductio ad absurdum*, where the *absurdum* lies in the alleged determinism. If one is committed to believing something as crazy as *that* then *for that very reason* one is wrong. The horror of determinism is thought to be so psychologically (and perhaps morally) unbearable that the accuser's emotive *experience* of repugnance is itself taken as sufficient reason to abandon whatever view is associated with it (analogous to how some analytic philosophers style themselves as science-like because they trade in the "evidence" allegedly provided by their "intuitions" about real and imagined thought experiments).[32] This seems almost a simple "appeal to emotion" kind of logical fallacy, where the auditor's emotional response is used as persuasion (e.g., 'you love cute puppies, don't you?' or the omnipresent '... just like Hitler'). It would cause you to feel mental distress if you were not an "agent" unproblematically in charge of your life; therefore, the thesis that you are not such an agent *must* for that reason be wrong. Q.E.D. Let me provide you with something less mentally taxing instead.

It is not so strange, on reflection, for us to proceed as if wired by nature against repugnant beliefs, or at least those beliefs that do not cohere with the ensemble of our extant beliefs. It is not hard to imagine an aversion to overly drastic belief-alteration to be a survival positive trait in the main, such as eschewing the strange looking berry that doesn't look like the other berries that our group has been eating. That berry might kill you! But it is possible the berry might turn out to be okay. Fortunately the world of ideas allows us to try out the possibilities without the immediate risk. The difficulty with armchair Darwinism (my kind, admittedly), is that a clever mind can come up with a putatively survival positive provenance for just about anything not obviously acutely lethal (e.g. a propensity to want to wander around alone at night or kiss rattlesnakes). So maybe it could be just as survival positive from time to time to be disposed to drop the can-do mentality and adopt a stance of "such is the way it is."

Such a quasi-fatalistic mentality is now very much out of favor, though, in what Michael and Joyce Huesemann term our "techno-optimist" society, because it seeks to *adapt to* pre-existing realities, many of them natural realities, rather than devise strategies for altering them.[33] Instead, our current default setting is to assume that the problem with any given technology is of course that it requires *more* technology: better, faster, stronger, cleaner; if the new iPhone gives you problems, the solution lies in the *next* iPhone (and repeat *ad infinitum*). It feels decidedly odd - vaguely creepy and mysterious, like donning a robe and heading to a sacred grove in the woods, to question whether solutions to any human problems might lie outside of even the best laid techno-fixes. One is immediately accused of Luddism for not eagerly agreeing that "they" will always think of something, from resource depletion to climate change to obscene and rising levels of material inequality. And the thing that "they" will think of will involve technical cleverness such that it will do us all ancestrally proud as *Homo faber*, aka, Mighty Human Problem Solver, whether this is represented by a team of scientists at Bell Labs or what has become the great can-do icon of our culture: the mythic Whiz Kid operating out of his parents' garage. (I am amazed by many conversations I have had with grown up scientists whose ultimate source of techno-optimism is, literally, said Whiz Kid.) The techno-optimist is almost impossible to argue against because, well, maybe there *will* be technical solutions to the big problems. There have been technical solutions to small problems and medium problems so who is to say not the big ones? For example, to mention one cutting-edge enthusiasm, maybe thorium will solve our fossil fuel problems.[34] One cannot deny the possibility.

Yet at the same time there are other possibilities. *First,* as the Huesemanns and others have argued, our technicist propensities may *themselves* be the source of some of our problems, some of the worst of them in fact. And *second*, even if there exists no knock-down argument against the fix-it mentality for a wide range of problems, it might be that some problems - even some entire problem fields - for whatever reason, perhaps due to environmental or historical deterioration, are *not* amenable to the "normal" technical fixes given their potential knock-on effects regarding the range of things we also care about. We may at times be better off abandoning the means-ends matrix of the techno-fix and looking for solutions *outside* what was originally presented as the problem field, thinking outside the box (please forgive the cliché). When the rust reaches a certain point, it's time to abandon that old truck. Yes, the undercarriage and body *could* be replaced, piece by piece, but then under normal circumstances one will need to ask whether the replacement value is *worth it*. Such is the situation, I think, with the school system of late capitalism. It is the rusted truck. The primary causes of its demise are outside itself and it may have been a good truck once. But at this point it's time to stop the losses, finish with the repairs and look toward alternative modes of transportation.

Very few want to hear this, though. It sounds like defeatism. I think it is not, actually; I will try to make this clear as I attempt to make the case for a kind of fatalism vis-à-vis our education system. This message is still - for now - a tough sell to American education activists, a group whose three component parts (i.e. "American, "education" and "activist") represent a veritable trinity of implicit can-do ontology and plucky free will assertiveness. While I do not wish to demoralize anyone (can a philosophical argument really do that anyway?), I do have the agenda of advancing a very specific line of argument that I will call "compartmentalized fatalism" or "pessimism" with regard to the possibility of today's educational institutions being amenable toward social justice - or really, whatever social desiderata one might have. As complex assemblages locked in sociological place by larger and vastly more powerful forces, those within educational institutions have very little choice but to strap themselves in (hopefully there are some straps for individuals to grab hold) for a continuation of a very scary and uncertain ride that probably ends in death. In this it has some resemblance to life itself. So it could be worse.

In the preceding pages I have assessed what are in effect three main educational strategies toward social change:

1 providing *more* education (i.e. higher education) and making it more widely available to aspiring individuals via financial means such as student loans;

2 providing *wider* education by continuing the trajectory of the legal promise of inclusivity inherent in the ideal of education for all (via the child "protections" built into the mechanisms of free and compulsory schooling); and,

3 formally empowering students *themselves* via the largely historically unprecedented American legal mechanism of students' rights, where students may substantively assert themselves - come what may - against the paternalistic ideological ambitions of the state's pedagogical institutions.

A generation or two ago, these three strategies, taken together, would have formed an almost unstoppable progressive agenda: affordability, inclusion, student voice. It is sobering to consider, however, as I hope to have shown, that each of these three strategies meets a "natural" dead end in the context of contemporary capitalist production and the way it is currently cycling down. This should not be in itself surprising, given that the habitable planet *itself* seems to be reaching a dead end via Hansen's earlier-discussed planetary boundaries.

For those with a sunnier outlook, there are two possible lines of response.

First, the efforts thus far made along the above lines may simply not have been good enough; we should simply do them better, more energetically, more creatively. So, for example, as "critical pedagogues" have long argued along Freireian lines, students' rights and other forms of empowerment should be expanded still further, qua democratization, and into more substantive areas like education policy itself, say, areas of curriculum and classroom management. Or, taking a global perspective, sustained efforts aimed at augmenting the inclusion of especially women and girls in the developing world is a vast yet urgent task that obviously seems both morally and practically necessary.[35] Or, on the affordability and access front, making higher education free, or at least much freer, by reforming college loan and/or student debt repayment policies, is an obvious way to help mitigate the crushing existential burden currently afflicting an entire generation.[36] Study and activism in each of these three areas is vital and commendable - "the good fight" if ever there was one.

A second line of response might be to point out sins of omission: there are additional promising areas of reform beyond my chosen three that I have neglected to explore. I would concede this point straight away. While the three areas I have explored seem to me to be huge and, taken together, perhaps even decisive, they are meant to be suggestive illustrations only; there are always more things in heaven and earth. However, it seems to me that the broad areas of non-discrimination/inclusion, student empowerment and affordability/access (which in a way could be considered a form of non-discrimination along class lines), more or less describe the arenas within which progressive education reform aspires to be conducted. Still, there may be others. For example, as indicated above, many across the political spectrum are enamored of the idea that heightening educator competence, so-called "teacher quality," and commensurate status and pay, are key. Despite its obviously self-serving nature, one hears a lot of this kind of talk from university-based teacher preparers. Physician, heal thyself: just as we might educate ourselves out of economic difficulty, we can educate the educators out of educational difficulty. If only they were better, faster, stronger - or, better yet, there were technologies such as online learning and exciting new assistive devices to replace them altogether. There is a very long history of this kind of move in education, for example the utopian hopes unleashed by various waves of educational technology such as radio in the 1920s, video in the 1970s, "teacher-proof" instructional design in the 1990s and now online learning in its many forms.[37] Who knows? As always, this time may be different; history suggests otherwise, but it is possible. Nonetheless, I would predict that a fuller analysis of such phenomena and their education reform potential will eventually run up against the same neoliberal capitalist brick wall as have the others. It would also seem that the basic, and I think fated, endgame reduction in commitment to universal education stands easily to undermine any technical reform schemes, however progressive and well-intentioned. The reforms that are likely to "work" are those that accord with increasingly desperate and rapacious elite capital accumulation needs, for example, the above mentioned public-private "partnerships" and other cost-saving devices that funnel money into elite hands and do little for the average student. Still, there may be strategies as yet unknown (or unknown to me). This is too vast an area. It's not possible for anyone really to get it "right."

I am confident, however, that it is *probable* that any school reform scheme will fail actually to reform mass education in any fundamental way. Contemporary capitalism, in its neoliberal phase, because of inherent internal tensions (ultimately associated with the TRPF and associated counter forces) places hard limits on what even the best and most defensible educational reform can achieve in whatever area. This does not mean that all education activism and reform efforts are worthless and completely *futile* (more on this below). It just means that one needs to discard utopian aspirations while working *within* the institution and recognize that one's good efforts are taking place within a *structurally constrained environment*.

To borrow a term from Gilles Deleuze and Felix Guattari, as utilized in the actor-network theory (ANT) of Bruno Latour and others, educational institutions are "assemblages" composed of many components and are *themselves*, component parts in a network of still larger assemblages.[38] Indeed, as organic substances, our meat-bodies are themselves biological assemblages tied into ecological and then ultimately cosmological assemblages of infinite size and complexity. (We place such an unjustified ontological priority on the membranes that allegedly strictly separate the body assemblage from the environmental assemblages surrounding it, when all such boundaries are necessarily permeable and make possible whatever integrity the assemblage has in the first place, e.g. via respiration.) Such meta-questions, including at the social level, the question of the wholesale "reassembly" (Latour) of such assemblages, are beyond my present scope and competence. (Sorry.) Yet there is one claim that can be made with confidence, laying aside the larger issues associated with systemic change and ANT, which is that no single assemblage in the network, like education, is going to reassemble (i.e. change) itself in isolation from the rest of its environing network - let alone anomalously in isolation from the whole. This would be as difficult to imagine as one of one's vital organs, let's say one's liver, suddenly becoming a fundamentally different organ, and this not having drastic effects on related organs and consequently the whole of the bodily system qua a network of organ assemblages. In this sense, the new liver, $liver_2$, is impossible even coherently to imagine without reference to an overall body reassembly. Sure, the old liver could be altered, say, with drugs to help with some deficiency or new function, but such a measure does not make it into $liver_2$.

Likewise, $education_2$ is not going to occur without corresponding reassembly of what surrounds it. Any over-ambitious attempt to alter such a vital organ-assemblage as education will run up against hard limits placed on it by the existence of its neighboring socio-cultural organs and, ultimately, the even larger network of assemblages (economic and otherwise) comprising the social body that I am labeling with the convenient shorthand term "capitalism" (or "neoliberal capitalism" or whatever). So, for example, unwinding student debt would involve addressing the financialized bubble whose logic necessitated it in the first place which, in turn, involves addressing the financialization of the economy which in turn involves addressing capitalism, the TRPF and all the rest of it. (And as indicated in Chapter 1, a parallel story may be told of the push for universal higher education as a push for credentials qua certifications of productivity, these being in turn necessitated by the augmentation of technologies of production, which are in turn necessitated by the dynamic of the TRPF and all the rest of it.) The leg bone is connected to the thigh bone which is connected to... etc. While these social assemblage-entities are *not* nothing, they *are* nothing apart from the crisscrossing networks of assemblages that shape and define them from the point of view of X, Y, or Z set of assemblages (e.g. the "economics of education," "the legal framework of education," "the politics of education," "educational psychology.") It's all connected, enough said. But the connections are *everything*; there is no "there" there apart from their interstices (any of which may constitute, mind you, a "there," just not one that exists apart from whatever metabolic processes are engaged with alongside the other interstitial "theres.") All of this by way of saying that education qua assemblage (an assemblage among assemblages) cannot "move" beyond certain limits *on its own*. Like we ourselves as "individual" human beings, it is not a wholly independent agent and any institutional autonomy it may possess is a relative autonomy arising from its interdependencies, like a manufacturing firm that grows wealthy and powerful because everyone depends on its product.[39]

So: assemblages within networks comprised of further assemblages and further networks. It is a veritable Russian matryoshka doll-within-a-doll social ontology, where there are "real" objects, yes, but these objects must be seen as so many temporary equilibria that are, every one of them, in principle, under some perhaps as-yet unspecified conditions, breakable into further objects whose very fragmentation reveals, retrospectively, the assemblage nature of the "original" object (on the model of the sub-molecular, the sub-atomic, and so on *ad infinitum*). And *all* of this, *all* of the time, in *all* directions. The error is to take our projected hypostatizations too seriously, especially when dealing with social phenomena, for example, overly comfortably regarding "education" as a social "substance" that can be easily delineated over and against adjacent (and, really, interpenetrating) phenomena. Latour describes this implausibility of settling on a safely demarcated phenomenon as a kind of "overflow" with which our explanations must contend:

> [A]ny given interaction seems to *overflow* with elements which are already in the situation coming from some other *time*, some other *place*, and generated by some other *agency* ... action is always dislocated, articulated, delegated, translated. Thus, if any observer is faithful to the direction suggested by this overflow, she will be led *away* from any given interaction to some *other places, other times,* and *other agencies* that appear to have molded them into shape. It is as if a strong wind forbade anyone to stick to the local site and blew bystanders away; as if a strong current was always forcing us to abandon the local scene.[40]

This "strong current" is, in a sense, the kernel of the Marxist critique of education, viz., that the latter is at bottom something *other* than itself; that it is "molded into shape," in my view inescapably, by the far more comprehensive general processes of production represented by "capitalism." Capitalism is an assemblage of assemblages, an ordering principle - no more and no less - which itself resides within larger and greater assemblages, most prominently, those involving ecological processes. Historian and political economist Jason W. Moore puts it this way:

> Capitalism is the gravitational field within which the "big picture" historical movements of the past five centuries have unfolded. Financialization, shifts in family structure, the emergence of new racial orders, colonialism and imperialism, industrialization, social revolutions and workers' movements - these are all world-ecological processes and projects, all with

powerful visions for re-ordering human- and extra-human natures. Capitalism, in other words, does not have an ecological regime; it is an ecological regime.[41]

As Moore exposes, if there is a flaw in traditional Marxist social ontology it may reside here, with due respect to the rehabilitation efforts of environmentalist Marxists such as John Bellamy Foster et al., in the tendency to halt at the level of the economy and grant it not only explanatory but *ontological* privilege over and against, say, something called "the environment." There is simply no warrant for this.

With thinkers such as Moore and Latour, I would contend that even the assemblage-of-assemblages known as "capitalism" or "the economy" is not ultimately to be reified on some special ontological plane but is better understood as *itself* a contingent node of intersection among processes as varied and basic as the chemical, biological, geological, climatological - even unto the realm of the cosmological and the farthest reaches of conceptions of reality in physics.[42] A unifying example would be energy, and how, say, fossil fuel burning HVAC systems (oil, natural gas, coal-fired electricity generation) make possible the nine-month factory-style school campuses that have been deemed efficient for modern schooling's (erstwhile) mass-scale productivity enhancements. The temporary historic fossil fuel windfall our culture has been experiencing has premised our style of schooling.

Not only do the means of production (including energy inputs) tend to shape the relations of production, but the ensemble of those two in turn shapes the means of re-production in families and school, just as surely as the stirrup, via horsemen and cavalry, made feudalism possible, we might say that the oil drum (with an assist from the coal mine), via modern HVAC and transport, gave us the factory-style school.[43]

Chapter 7

Fatalism, pessimism and other reasons for hope

I think the system will collapse, but not through our agency.
Alexander Cockburn[1]

Pessimism of the intellect, optimism of the will.
Antonio Gramsci[2]

Fatalism Marxist style

If you don't like any of this, but you know you can't stop it, where does it leave you?
Paul Kingsnorth[3]

A bedeviling psychological problem ensues with the understanding that education is an assemblage among assemblages and is itself comprised of lesser assemblages (all the way down) at the same time it also exists as a mere component part of greater assemblages (all the way up).[4] Let's say, *per impossibile*, that one were to gain a complete understanding of all of the relevant assemblages and their interactions, becoming a veritable Laplacean demon of assemblages. Such omniscience would win one a complete mapping of assemblages. Who can guess what this cartographic competence would enable? Like the original Laplace's demon, one could predict the future, for starters, charting the trajectory of assemblage interactions involved in, say, how the stock market will react to rumors of war or how schools will devolve as fossil fuels become scarcer. Whatever one wants to know: just map it and trace a certain future.

The motivational problem, though, is what Frederic Jameson

calls a "winner loses logic," where the theorist "wins" by constructing as total and air-tight a theory as possible.[5] Yet by doing so he simultaneously "loses" in that the point of having such a complete theory is lost owing to the very fact that he has accounted for *everything*; that is, since all has been determined beforehand in the theoretical model, including all causal interactions, there remains no place for intervention because everything has already been accounted for. So why bother with the cartography in the first place? As Jameson explains, "Insofar as the theorist wins, therefore, by constructing an increasingly closed and terrifying machine, to that very degree he loses, since the critical capacity of his work is thereby paralysed, and the impulses of negation and revolt, not to speak of those of social transformation, are increasingly perceived as vain and trivial in the face of the model itself."[6] If a particular assemblage, in this case the educational assemblage, seems so tightly locked into its surrounding network of assemblages and, even more, is wholly in the orbit of some gravitationally denser, solar assemblage such as "the economy/capitalism," it would seem to lose any meaningful institutional autonomy. Its marionette status may explain a great deal (Jameson's theorist winning) but at the expense of not being able to envision let alone act toward any way "out" (Jameson's theorist losing).

If such a situation obtained, it would be rational for those on education's "inside" to feel as if their efforts toward substantially *moving* education's institutional assemblage in a chosen direction would be *futile*. Without movement from neighboring assemblages, which itself may not be possible without movement on the part of the ordering assemblage (*ex hypothesi* the economy/capitalism); things are just too *hemmed in*. Whatever the internal rearrangements, the borders are too well patrolled and the overall shape of the assemblage's perimeter is too well maintained. This in my view is precisely the situation in which would-be education reformers and education activists find themselves. Their failure is fated: the gears and pulleys are simply arranged too tightly for any one of them to "give" without accommodating external movements. They are straight-jacketed and unable to escape, no matter how hard they struggle. So insofar as they are *inside* the assemblage they might as well relax. And try to find some other way.

When I say "relax," I mean it and I mean something specific. I have no strategy (spoiler alert!) for slaying the capitalist dragon that time-honored narrative archetype has led us to expect as a rousing finale a la St. George and Bilbo Baggins: the plucky hero cleverly finding *that one weakness* in the monster's underbelly. However tempting and psychically gratifying this reverie may be, one must refuse the story time impulse and its short-term aesthetic satisfactions. (Even as I write these words I can still feel the archetype's ancestral pull: 'maybe peak oil will do it, exposing unsustainable high net energy requirements as the beast's soft underbelly, bringing it all down ... and *soon* ... Collapse! Apocalypse!' Be still my heart...)[7] History shows that this kind of utopian/dystopian impulse, which may be the same in this case, is to be distrusted. It is always a possibility, of course, and there is no argument against it as such, probability suggests one should move on. But to where?

Again, I have no general argument for 'what we should do.' That is too large a question for me here, one that may not even admit of an answer, as there is no guarantee that agency vis-à-vis the entire capitalist system will accomplish anything at all, or is even a relevant construct. What I do have is an argument for something *not* to do, at least perhaps to help better distribute activist energies where they might possibly be useful. Flying in the face of what most critics of whatever politics believe, and taking everything into consideration, it seems to me that, at least for those opposed to capitalism as inherently unjust and environ-mentally destructive, *education activism does not matter and is a waste of time.*

As the critics' knives sharpen, let me clarify at once exactly what I mean. I *do not* mean that education does not matter. (I have no doubt about this.) I *do not* mean that activism does not matter. (No doubt about this either). I mean specifically that, *insofar as it aims at "social justice,"* as most left visions of education activism do (and right visions too, the difference being in how social justice is conceived), education activism is not only: a) futile (the 'does not matter' part) but b) also misallocates attention and energy (the 'waste of time' part). We should not be fooled into thinking that reforming schools will generate serious social and political reforms. To the famous (in progressive education circles) old question asked by George S. Counts, "Dare the school build a new social order?" I answer, "no, it shouldn't."[8] As I hope to have illustrated somewhat already, even with the little bit of relative autonomy they enjoy, the major educational institutions are far too constrained and are growing more so. At the level of individual instructors, "radicals" in academia achieve very little except for furthering their own careers (myself included) in a consumerist environment that rewards novelty, and educators market themselves accordingly for publication and tenure (where the latter still exists). It almost goes without saying that K-12 school teachers are yoked to an ever-more oppressive assessment-driven curriculum (and even pedagogy) just about everywhere in the industrialized world.

At best, what one develops by leaving the large scale institutions is developing one's own little island of harmony, creating one's own little "point of light," to paraphrase George Bush I. And there are wonderful examples of this sort of thing that are more than mere objects of cynicism and should not be sneered at, though these off-the-reservation efforts are by definition a Pandora's Box. For example, there is the growing legion of home schoolers - a million or two strong in the US - most but not all of whom are doing so for religious reasons. By definition, these situations are heterogeneous and so are hit-and-miss as far as their worthwhileness (from any perspective). There are also ongoing quasi-utopian educational communities that seem to cut against the grain of their surrounding culture, the child-centeredness and romanticism of Waldorf education supplying an example popular in some areas.[9] There are even some inspiring anomalies that seem nicely integrated into their local social and environmental surroundings, like the famous Reggio Emilia schools in Italy.[10] And many others.

A venerable example would be A.S. Neill's Summerhill School in Suffolk (UK), now run by his daughter Zoe Redhead. Summerhill's philosophy is to teach children to be free people - "where kids have freedom to be themselves" - to as large an extent as possible.[11] Having visited there as an initial skeptic, I can say that Summerhill is an extremely charming place and one cannot help but root for its continuing survival against the government inspectors (a battle they seem to have won for the time being).[12] However, these little utopian experiments have never proven to be *scalable* and so they remain, in effect, isolated outposts of privilege, often literally so (Summerhill, for example, is small and very expensive.) And there are of course elite schools of many types that are far out of reach financially to most, like the lavish private schools of the US East Coast. Though invaluable as examples of alternative possibilities, this grab bag of home schoolers, utopian "progressive" educational communities and elite prep schools, what these "alternatives" share in common is precisely that they are *not* real alternatives for the vast majority of the population. They have never proven scalable (and home schooling is not scalable by definition) and they are simply out of reach financially for almost everybody. As a matter of general education policy, what goes on in these isolated peaceable kingdoms is largely irrelevant.

So this leaves the vast majority to the tender mercies of *public* education. In the US this is where some 90% of children still attend, the bulk of the remaining 10% being enrolled in parochial or other larger systems that are, in the end, really not *so* different in their essentials from the public systems alongside which they operate. This means that nearly *all* schoolchildren, except for the happy few in their designer lifeboats, are fully subject to the larger forces I have been discussing throughout this book. No matter how groovy or "progressive" their teachers, their futures are still determined by the same iron realities that I have been discussing here: First, their future possibilities are subject to harsh logic dictated by the TRPF, which by now has become a kind of *falling rate of learning.* Second, the possibilities for expressing their own voice in their schools, while still real and valuable, is hanging by an increasingly thin thread. And third, their continuing on and attempting to beat the economic tide through higher education - and at least save *themselves* - is now caught in a future of relative joblessness (even for the moderately credentialed) with the added insult of crushing and increasingly unpayable debt. What are those involved in such dead-end institutions to do? The heroic gesture is pointless. And everyone seems stuck in place, strapped in and unable to leave even if they wanted to (in part because they are subject to the great lesson in labor discipline so helpfully provided during economic recessions/depressions, which is that *one is lucky to have a job - any job*). My suggestion is that a certain kind of pessimism is wholly rational in this situation; it is ethically warranted and even survival positive.

Consider the familiar school-prison analogy. Both are massive institutions involving scores of millions of individuals. The main employees are teachers and guards. I take it as obvious that prison guards are unlikely through their activism to do much to change the basic role and nature of US prisons (if they wanted to). They may improve their own working conditions (more power to them) and they may in an ancillary fashion help improve the general lot of prisoners with some humane reforms (more exercise time, say). Such efforts are nothing to sneer at. Yet it seems clear in this case that the prison guards are not going to alter the prison's basic place, qua carceral assemblage, within the totality of social institutions that it serves. As prison guards, they are unlikely to obtain legal reforms to the criminal justice system that underwrites the prison's basic metabolism. As prison guards, they are not going to get the drug laws changed. They are very unlikely to change gang culture, save families, alter racism and patriarchy or increase job opportunities. As prison guards, they are not really within social reach of the main and chronic factors that populate, structure and perpetuate the carceral system within which they function. Though for some reason we don't when discussing education policy put them in the same category (perhaps partly because most educators would find the comparison unflattering), teachers and professors are, *vis-à-vis their activist potentialities*, in roughly the same position. (Please understand I am not claiming these are the *same* jobs and that they are comparable in all respects.) With respect to *structural* issues pertaining to social justice, the educators are functionally similar to the prison guards in that they are the rather hapless marionettes of the larger forces that by and large write their occupational script. *As* prison guards and *as* teachers, their movements are similarly restricted.

What I am not saying. I am *not* therefore saying that it is not worthwhile to be a prison guard or a teacher, that these are not potentially dignified vocations worthy of respect and remuneration. Neither am I saying that it does not matter whether individuals in these occupations are kind, conscientious and competent. Teachers can obviously make huge positive differences for their pupils, to the extent that we might even say they can achieve a kind of immortality.[13] My argument for pessimism in formal education is not an argument for the cessation of teachers' conscientiousness and caring. On the contrary. At the level of interpersonal ethics, it is optimal for individual young people to have wise and caring adults around them. Plus, it is independently valuable (I mean independent of economics and politics) to bring students into their cultural inheritance, turn them on to a particular subject, and help them develop communicative and other mental skills with a wide range of potential applications. These achievements are worthy of apolitical celebration whenever they occur. But it would be easier on everyone if we dropped the political shtick. Not to say, of course, that the politics is irrelevant. There are many examples of actually existing real change from which leftists can draw inspiration. Chávez's Venezuela comes to mind.[14] Yet such examples reinforce the present point, as it is quite obvious that the precondition for the substantive education reforms in a place like Venezuela is precisely the Bolivarian Revolution itself, as per my thesis; it is the *revolution* that is building the schools. *Pace* Counts, it does not seem to work the other way around. Is there an historical example of schools pushing real societal change from within?

Educators should however be as concerned - *and as politically active* - as anyone else. But at this point that political energy is best directed *outside* the education system; *not* inside toward education reforms that are supposedly going to make the prison, er, school, more tolerable, but *outside* the education assemblage in search of more promising activist sites. Even though the politics are a dead end, teaching is a worthwhile profession on its own terms and has nothing for which to apologize. The same might be said of nurses and physicians, social workers, psychologists, therapists, EMTs and many others in the so-called "helping" professions. (One cannot quite say the same about most lawyers and corporate types, as their fortunes are almost completely proportional to their ability to help elites rob labor and sequester capital.) My argument here is for a *compartmentalized* and *political* pessimism that is directed intra-institutionally. I am not arguing for a *global* pessimism or a wholesale abandonment of political activism in spaces outside doomed institutions, only that a *targeted* pessimism is more rational. In that vein, generally speaking, better an unofficial blog or an occupy protest than a speech at a faculty meeting or a petition to an administrator. Interestingly, this is wholly consistent with Kant's original enlightenment-defining distinction between the "public" and "private" uses of reason, where the former denotes speaking in one's universal capacity as a citizen, to the world, as it were, and the latter consists of the voice one adopts when one is constrained by the duties inhering in one's job or office. In the "private" realm of one's job, one does what one must; in the "public" realm of the citizen or, we might say, the activist, one does what one *oneself* thinks must be done. Exercising one's public use of reason in Kant's sense, which in the US still enjoys legal protections not guaranteed to the private use, may be the best posture for those employed within especially supine capital-subordinate institutions, such as schools and universities, whose character is, *ex hypothesi, fated.*

Note that I am not considering the "beautiful soul" approach of the quitter or the hermit. The heroic gesture is available only to a very and usually quite privileged few; curiously akin to the utopian miniaturist, it is not scalable. On the inside, *you simply do your job*, which you have to do because you need the income and you care about the people around you (and you care about *yourself*, like all sane people). In his research on dissidents in the former Soviet Union, anthropologist James Wertsch terms this attitude "internal emigration" and considers it "a form of resistance to a totalitarian state."[15] The wisdom of the ages counsels in such situations: just try your best to be kind and at least to *not be an asshole.* As philosopher William B. Irvine puts it, often "we must learn to adapt ourselves to the environment in which fate has placed us and do our best to love the people with whom fate has surrounded us."[16] One could dress that insight up with fine phrases from Aristotle about *phronesis* and "virtue" or perhaps Kantian moral imperatives toward human dignity and respect, but in the end the philosophically-pedigreed synonyms wouldn't add a great deal; it's just that simple and every decent person knows it.

John Holloway identifies these moments of decency, which become more difficult to enact as things grow grimmer, as a potential "dialectic of misfitting" that has the potential to enlarge, one by one, the "cracks" in the capitalist edifice.[17] For him, resistance should be conceived as an "interstitial" process, whereby the small cracks we encounter in our everyday lives can be widened into fissures that can in turn be widened ultimately into real breaks: "Break it in as many ways as we can and try to expand and multiply the cracks and promote their confluence."[18] Holloway's is an inspiring and optimistic vision. It gives people something to work toward and to place their small acts of kindness and decency into a larger revolutionary frame. It appealingly avoids grandiosity. And I think it is largely consistent with what I am suggesting here, with one important exception: I think his "crack capitalism" may underestimate the temporal urgency of the mutually exacerbating economic, climate and energy crises and the extent to which they may not be able to be "turned around." There may not be time to work through all these cracks and the environmental damage may already be done. Holloway does clearly appreciate the larger point about contingency, though: "The old revolutionary certainty can no longer stand. There is no guarantee of a happy ending."[19] It is, I think, an unpopular thing to say but what is missing is that authentically pre-capitalist notion that will not quite concede the anarchist point that we can be the authors of everything we choose, that we noble human beings are sovereign over our own and each other's lives. What is missing from even this most inspired activist vision is, in a word, *fate*.

"Character is fate"
Heraclitus[20]

It is a maxim, then, of conservation of energy, a "know when to hold 'em, know when to fold 'em" sensibility, with the added dimension that the implication that the notion that changing *schools* is the solution is misleading and therefore likely to be deleterious.[21] Regarding political aspirations for keystone institutions like education (usually distinguishable from one's personal everyday ethical conduct), my suggestion is that those positioned inside those institutions ought to fold 'em and direct their political energies outside those systems. Since these institutions are so tightly wired as to respond primarily from directives from the outside, one is best positioned on the outside, closer to the sources of the directives. Owing to its essential attachment to capitalist production, education institutions are on a very-short-to-nonexistent leash; there is almost no institutional autonomy, and more, no significant future prospects of achieving it (contra my own previous hopes).[22] I make no claim here about the dependent status of every social institution, because there are still degrees of relative autonomy. This question must be decided ad hoc, based on the best judgment of those with the best information (including of course those actually working within) the institution in question. What can nurses achieve? Librarians? Sanitation workers? Police officers? Analyses of the prospects for movement within these particular arenas should constitute an urgent research priority. My suspicion is that the closer one gets to core productive and reproductive functions, those that a triage of capitalist production would assign a position of priority (e.g. energy, business and financial regulation, education, policing, taxation), the constituent institutions coalescing around those areas will be the hardest to move and will best be moved via outside leverage; in other words, it is largely beyond the capabilities of those on the inside. But these are empirical matters and as such they may yield surprising and counterintuitive results on a case-by-case basis. My only claim here is that education under advanced capitalism is too far gone, maybe not for little islands of "critical pedagogy" here and there, but for substantive and scalable resistance. As the ensemble of the examples discussed in this book indicate, things seem to be getting worse.

This picture admittedly implies a somewhat deterministic outlook, at least for certain institutions like education. And unfortunately, yes, that is the picture I'm advancing. *Ex hypothesi* the larger picture is that capitalism itself is *fated* to move in certain ways and by tight association, those institutions most tightly bolted into the sinking ship are going to go down with it - while conversely the ones that are less bolted in have a chance (though not a guarantee) of escaping. I am therefore arguing for a species of Marxist *fatalism*, though one that is not necessarily psychologically "depressing" in the sense that it necessarily leads to quietism, or in any way conflates with *futilism*, the idea that nothing we do matters. In connection with the false equation of fatalism and futilism, there are important historical lessons to keep in mind. Certain types of fatalistic outlooks demonstrably *do not* result in futilism, quietism, "giving up," conventionalism - or anything like that. There have never been two more fatalistic worldviews than that of the Roman elite and the Calvinists (predestination).[23] Yet, for their own internal reasons, there have also obviously never been two more *activist* worldviews than these as well. The assertion of any necessary link between fatalism and futilism is simply not tenable.

It is complicated, though, to grasp exactly what might be meant by "fatalism." There is an almost infinite variety of positions available in this neck of the philosophical woods, as the discussion now skirts perilously close to the perennial - and 100% irresolvable - set of debates often to be found under the heading of "free will v. determinism." This includes the contemporary rage for "compatibilism" (the more common philosophical view there is no conflict between the two) and "incompatibilism" (the more common popular view that free will and determinism *do* conflict). I will not be bogged down in this quagmire from which there really is no exit. Fortunately, the conception of fatalism that I mean to employ here circumnavigates most of the difficulties.

One last preliminary. There are different relevant senses to the terms "fate" and "fatalism." The first and most archaic of these, and one I am *not* meaning to employ, has a more supernatural connotation and is most often employed against some sort of religious backdrop. So for example in the ancient Greek tradition, fate is an autonomous extraterrestrial force against which rebellion is impossible, even by the gods (usually). In the classical story, the fates, the Moirai, are typically conceived as autonomous personages: Clotho (who spins the thread), Lachesis (who measures it) and Atropos (who cuts it).

'Three other women were also sitting on thrones which were evenly spaced around the spindle. They were the Fates, the daughters of Necessity, robed in white, with garlands on their heads; they were Lachesis, Clotho, and Atropos, accompanying the Sirens' song, with Lachesis singing of the past, Clotho of the present, and Atropos of the future.'[24]

Though de-personified, there is an ontologically allied conception in the Judeo-Christian tradition in certain understandings of divine providence and predestination, as discussed earlier, the latter's Calvinist-Puritan form famously being the object of Max Weber's *The Protestant Ethic and the Spirit of Capitalism*.[25] As with the Greeks, here there is a sense of fate (predestination) as occupying an altogether extra-human metaphysical plane; it is very much written into the fabric of the cosmos (literally for the Fates) and is in no way yielding to the sublunary machinations of ordinary human beings. Though influential and probably the most popular conception of fate, I must dismiss it on Occam's razor grounds (i.e. theoretical parsimony), as it would seem to require an elaborate theological edifice for coherence.

Also avoiding the philosophers' quagmire, I take no position on a contending conception sometimes called "hard determinism," that is scientific-causal determinism, the assessment of which is beyond my scope. I will note, though, that this is perhaps the strongest of the determinisms. Neither am I tempted in this context by Marxist philosopher G. A. Cohen's interesting weak deterministic notion of the "imperatively inevitable," which holds that where X and Y are the live options, and X is so morally repugnant or otherwise odious as to be morally unconscionable, then Y may be said to be inevitable.[26] Regarding the alleged historical inevitability of socialism, a prime example of imperative inevitability is captured in Rosa Luxemburg's famous disjunction "socialism or barbarism," where the former is to be taken as inevitable because the alternative is so unthinkably unacceptable.[27] One might even say that Marx utilizes this form of inevitability in the above-cited passages of the *Manifesto* where he states both that socialism is inevitable *and* that it could all end instead in the "ruin of the contending classes." In the case of the former, he may be using "inevitability" in Cohen's imperative sense. Whatever it is, and though appealing on its own terms, it seems to me that imperative inevitability is *not* really a conception of inevitability, as its disjunctive form logically implies; it seems more of a rhetorical device employed as emphasis rather than an actual commitment to inevitability or fate as those terms have been commonly understood.

So in what defensible sense might we understand an institution's trajectory to be fated? By way of answer, I appeal to another ancient conception of fate, though one not so old as the Moirai: what philosopher Robert C. Solomon terms "narrative necessity."[28] This conception finds antecedents in the Heraclitus fragment that reads "character is fate" and also the tragic plays of

Sophocles and others.[29] This kind of fatalism focuses on the *significance* of events rather than their causal provenance and it has the advantage that it "can be understood without acknowledging any mysterious agency."[30] In a sense bracketing the causal question, narrative necessity represents a recognition that objects and beings can have an inherent *teleology*, that is, they can be directed or oriented in a certain way that seals their fate. If it grows, an acorn will become an oak and not some other thing.

Note that there is an *element* of contingency here that clearly distinguishes this kind of teleological necessity from the cosmic Moiric or Calvinist kind: the telos "oak" is to be understood as conditional, in this case contingent upon the presence of proper environmental conditions for growth. Given those conditions, though, the oak *will*, to paraphrase Nietzsche, become what it is.[31] Applied to human beings this teleological conception typically becomes wrapped in narrative form because it reflects how, apart from some psychopathology, we tend to understand ourselves: as protagonists of our own story. What Solomon means to capture by narrative necessity is that, again bracketing the metaphysical question of causal antecedents (nature or nurture?), our internal makeup can be such that it can be said that, given normal environmental conditions, we are fated in a certain direction, to become some particular thing and not another thing.

There can be biological (e.g. gender), sociological (e.g. class) or characterological aspects to this "fating." Say I'm a junkie who's found himself perpetually fallen into the hopeless Sisyphean mania of "chasing the dragon" such that objective observers would say that that *this is who I am* at this point in my life: an addict headed toward oblivion. In such a sad situation, there comes a time when even the most sympathetic loved one must see the trajectory for what it is, that because of the present constitution of the addict (physiological, psychological, moral, whatever), the trajectory is *bound* to play out in a certain direction absent the intervention of outside and/or unforeseen forces. Note that this is neither a causal-scientific nor a Nostradamus-like prediction about a future state of affairs at time T: that, say, I will die by June of next year. It is rather an appreciation that the narrative that has evolved (with me as the junkie-protagonist) *must resolve itself* in a certain way that is not other ways (again, absent some unforeseen and/or outside force). As Solomon writes, "Fatalism is just concerned with the significance of the outcome rather than the causal path that brought it about."[32] As such, narrative fatalism is, I think, properly agnostic about the question of individual free will. In philosophical parlance, it is "compatibilist," i.e. it is among the species of views wherein free will and determinism are thought compatible, in this case because narrative necessity can allow for the idea that our own character is "set" by choice or by necessity - or by some admixture of the two. The fatalist wants an explanation of the situation but not necessarily a causal account. What is significant is the distilling of *meaning* out of the sequence of events, "and that means fitting it into a narrative that makes sense of our lives."[33]

This kind of thinking, I should note, is anathema to more individualist philosophies such as existentialism and libertarianism that labor under the conceit that there is always an element of "freedom" or choice even in the direst and seemingly most constrained of circumstances. For Sartre there is always the possibility of at least a brief moment of refusal where, to use his famous example, "the militant in the resistance who was caught and tortured" and could perhaps always have held out for *just one more second*.[34] So the dragon-chasing junkie always has a choice to get high again, and there could in principle be a heroic refusal at every step of the way, even if it *did* mean death. This may be. Narrative fatalism, I think, deftly sidesteps this challenge because it has no need to deny that stories evolve, alter direction, throw up surprises and otherwise may change in ways that are presently unanticipated. It is more of a probabilistic notion, where one would recognize that, at the very least, there is always the possibility of incomplete information (maybe there was something "in" that junkie that nobody knew about). The Laplacean demon does not actually exist, after all, but not because of the existence of a supernatural "will" standing over and against the natural world outside of causation. Shopenhauer, arguing against a facile conception of free will and for a conception of "the innate character of the human being," allows that, "every deed could be predicted with assurance, indeed, calculated, were it not that, in part, character is very difficult to discover, and in part, too, that the motive is often obscured and always exposed to the countering effects of other motives that lie solely in the person's sphere of thought and are inaccessible to others."[35] He then adds that one must also consider as variables "external circumstances" and the person's "apprehension of these, the accuracy of which depends on his understanding and its education."[36] However set is the "innateness," of the character, then, there are bound to be external and internal factors capable of altering any course of direction. Yet at the same time the mere occurrence of such an alteration does not cast retrospective doubt on the "character is fate" thesis. Your fate sends you on your way, but how that way turns out depends in part on factors other than the fatedness itself.

One's conception should not fall into the other extreme, though. The absence of omniscience does not entail that human self-understanding can surrender *completely* to chaos and surprise. While a person's "understanding and its education" may supply wild card variables in this context, they also always provide to human experience a degree of the narrative order that preconditions the possibility of any self-awareness at all. A person experiencing sensory qualia as a purely random succession of mental states would not be an "I" in any recognizable sense; such an entity would be trapped in a whirring eternal "now," with neither retrospective nor prospective capabilities, lacking a first-person sense of being a *self* who is moving through time. A total breakdown of narrative order is the very definition of madness. Even small and moderate break-downs can be psychologically extremely wrenching, shocks to the system from which it may take a lifetime to recover. So the narrative order we project onto ourselves and the world simply cannot wholly disintegrate into hyper-fluidity while still retaining functionality, that is, *life*. While alteration is always possible, at the same time we are narratively restorative and reparative creatures; a change in the narrative is always possible, but for this to happen the extant narrative must somehow actually - not hypothetically - change into the *next* extant narrative. And when it comes to the structuring narratives that order our lives generally, it can take a great deal to turn the ship around. It seems almost impossible for adults. Even with children, the shaping of a master narrative requires sustained education, the very area that, *ex hypothesi*, seems so tightly deter-mined by systemic imperatives. It is no accident that control of primary education is always an essential goal for every political regime, everywhere. While there are predictable patterns, exactly how an individual responds to upbringing has never fully been answered by *anyone*. We are very little farther in answering this question than was Plato's Socrates over two millennia ago, whose conclusion in the dialogue *Meno* about the teachability of virtue, is merely that "it appears to be present in those of us who may possess it as a gift from the gods."[37]

So does that mean one gives up on the project of narrative alteration at both individual and communal levels? Or, we might say, the project of education itself? Not quite.

I have argued that, due to its identifiable internal tendencies, eliminationist capitalism can be described as having a certain character in the requisite narrative sense. As per Heraclitus, this character can thus be said to be dispositive for its systemic trajectory, in a word, its *fate*. The timing is likely impossible to predict, but the *telos* of this apparatus arcs toward the elimination of most human beings as superfluous (their disposability resolved through warehousing or, in the worst case, the war and genocide of "human smoke"[38]) and the destruction of the environment. It is in a morbid "race" between these two interrelated phenomena for which gets there first. We are locked into these internal and external dynamics. No one - left, right or center - has presented any plausible picture for how to defuse this bomb-laden capitalist suicide vest. In the ancient narrative sense of fatalism, I believe, *our demise is fated and our doom sealed.* That is the "end" in "endgame."

I'm sorry it is bad news. The good news, though, is that there is no reason to receive this news with the mentality of the written-into-the-fabric-of-the-cosmos conception of fate. The Moirai are wonderful characters but they do not, as suggested earlier, really help to make the case for fate as an external, autonomous force over and against us and inaccessible on some separate metaphysical plane. As per Heraclitus, character *is* fate, though. And the narrative conception leaves room for the possibility that the fate-trajectory could be altered. Against the odds, there could be an intervention in which the heroin junkie detoxes and heals. *Ex hypothesi* it may not be because of his own exertion of will, but for any number of external reasons: the heroin supply is eradicated, he is whisked off against his will to a detox center, there was something about his internal makeup not previously apparent that impelled him, an asteroid hits the planet and along with much else destroys the heroin, and so on. In short, *something unexpected could happen* through internal or external circumstances that could alter the fated trajectory.

So external to the assemblage, whether that assemblage is an individual human being or a vastly-scaled social, cultural and economic apparatus, there could be a relevant chance occurrence and/or and external environmental change significant enough to change our fate. This may sound a bit like the forlorn Heideggerian cry that "only a god can save us now."[39] Not really, though. It is actually the template for the well-established biological model of how organisms change, for life itself: *natural selection through random mutation*. Organisms survive to reproduce by achieving a threshold level of adaptation to their environment, that is, one that allows for their reproduction. Through random mutation during DNA replication, the resultant mutated organism may alter its adaptive and hence reproductive success ("success" defined as continuance, "failure" as discontinuance). The internal nature of the offspring is thus altered in a way that *may*, in conjunction with their environment, in turn alter the creature's trajectory, its fate. So character is fate, yes, but not for that reason *set* in the sense of causal outcome.

This I believe is roughly the situation in which we find ourselves with respect to neoliberal eliminationism. It has an identifiable character that includes central institutions such as politics, law, trade, finance, the military, health care, entertainment etc. and, of course, education. If the Marx-Minsky-environmentalist et al. picture is correct, this system we have created continues to grow along a fated trajectory that ends with human and environmental elimination. But there is no way to know with certainty whether or not these processes will run to completion. Right now it looks like they might. But: a) there might be random occurrences that are currently impossible to foresee and b) external environmental factors might conspire to knock the neoliberal endgame off its trajectory or stop it in its tracks. These two possibilities do not require mystery, theology or "spirituality," for they are the same possibilities to which any organism is subject as it survives and replicates. Though not exactly a matter of our own personal volition, this means that there always remains a measure of *Hope*: the only creature Pandora, the first woman on earth, was able to keep when all the others flew from her jar.

But the woman took off the great lid of the jar with her hands and scattered all these and her thought caused sorrow and mischief to men. Only Hope remained there in an unbreakable home within under the rim of the great jar, and did not fly out at the door; for ere that, the lid of the jar stopped her, by the will of Aegis-holding Zeus who gathers the clouds. But the rest, countless plagues, wander amongst men; for earth is full of evils and the sea is full. Of themselves diseases come upon men continually by day and by night, bringing mischief to mortals silently; for wise Zeus took away speech from them. So is there no way to escape the will of Zeus.[40]

Even though we cannot escape Zeus's will, we still may have Hope. This may not be much but it is something. In any event it is what we have.

While unforeseen random occurrences are by definition impossible to guess at, the category of eventuality that involves an "external environmental factor" allows for some speculation. As I have hinted, the leading candidate seems to me to be resource depletion, specifically regarding the fossil fuels without which our modern industrial economy could not survive in its present form: mainly oil, natural gas and coal (electricity). While there is uncertainty regarding the timing of so-called "peak oil," i.e. the point of maximum available oil, after which the finite resource can only grow scarcer, many analysts believe we already have or are soon to reach it.[41] Whatever the precise timing, though, the level of our dependency on this uncompromisingly finite set of resources is truly astonishing. There is a good argument to be made that we have largely in effect burned through a fossil fuel bonanza, an energy windfall beyond anything human beings have ever experienced, all in the last few centuries.

Worse, all of our major social systems depend upon its

continued abundance. As financial and energy analyst Chris Martenson explains:

> On the faulty assumption that fossil fuels will always be a resource we could draw upon, we fashioned economic, monetary, and other assorted belief systems based on permanent abundance, plus a species population on track to number around 9 billion souls by 2050.
>
> There are two numbers to keep firmly in mind. The first is *22*, and the other is *10*. In the past 22 years, half of all of the oil ever burned has been burned. Such is the nature of exponentially increasing demand. And the oil burned in the last 22 years was the easy and cheap stuff discovered 30 to 40 years ago. Which brings us to the number 10.
>
> In every calorie of food that comes to your table are hidden 10 calories of fossil fuels, making modern agriculture and food delivery the first type in history that consumes more energy than it delivers. Someday fossil fuels will be all gone. That day may be far off in the future, but preparing for that day could (and one could argue *should*) easily require every bit of time we have.[42]

Martenson then goes on to predict that

> the underlying rates of depletion will continue to fight the recent production gains in the US and elsewhere in the world until they soon come to a standstill, eventually swamping even heroic efforts. Steadily rising energy costs and decreasing net energy yields will simply not be able to fund the future economic growth and consumptive lifestyles that developed nations are depending on (and that developing nations are aspiring to).[43]

The synergy of scarcer oil and economic downturn (in my view powered primarily by the TRPF and in Martenson's view by rising net energy costs, i.e. the difference between the costs of extraction/production of the extracted energy and its value), has the potential to create an extreme amount of volatility in the world system generally. It may already have.

A recent snapshot from austerity-starved Greece illustrates how this economic-energy crisis dynamic can feed off of one another in devastating ways. In the winter of 2013, Greek forests were becoming denuded of trees because of illegal logging. The cause? Cash-strapped citizens were violating environmental laws and chopping down trees for fuel to heat their homes. Many of them can no longer afford their power bills. A Greek mother, Sofia, explains, "'At first we were shocked and disappointed that we had to do this,'" Sofia says, "'We've gone back 30 or 40 years with this. It's not war - or rather it is, but an economic war. We hope it'll last only one or two years because we have children, we have a future. We can't live like this, for God's sake.'"[44] Because of all the burning a wood smoke haze has descended on cities like Athens and Thessaloniki, choking and afflicting citizens with toxicity. "'The atmosphere has never been worse,'" said Marianna Filipopoulou, a social-anthropologist who has lived in Athens for four years. "'It's getting more and more difficult to breathe. Even our eyes hurt because of the smog.' She said the blame lies, not with families, but with their deplorable circumstances: 'There is no other way given the scarcity of money.'"[45] *Atlantic* reporter Derek Thompson summarizes: "It is the smog of austerity. Greece is literally breathing in the fumes of its recession."[46] In terms of economic eliminationism, Greece is our canary in an all-too real coal mine and the current experience of the thoughtless and cruel austerity being imposed upon them offers a glimpse at what may soon be coming elsewhere (along with the above 50% youth unemployment rate mentioned in Chapter 4). When basic costs of living such as energy or food (as in Egypt prior to the 2011 Tahrir Square uprisings) things can quickly spiral out of control and anything might happen politically. Not all of it is good, witness the post-austerity rise of Greece's neo-Nazi Golden Dawn party (now at a record 10% public support), distressingly reminiscent of how in the 1920s an austerity-plagued Germany gave birth to Hitler and the Nazis.

In terms of my present argument, all this illustrates how environmental wild cards can enter into the economic crisis equation in devastating ways, especially if we include the gravest long-term threats such as climate change, ocean acidification and resource depletion. This is certainly not "good news" and in no way do I mention this unholy mutualism as something for which oppositional forces should cheer and await gleefully. These conjoined phenomena represent misery full stop and are not good for anybody, certainly not in the short-term (which many may not live beyond). At the same time, such developments introduce vast new layers of complexity and, it is to be assumed, contingency into the future trajectory and overall sustainability of capitalism as currently constituted. This is not the same as a revolutionary cadre taking power into their own hands and seizing, by an act of collective will, the reins of power. It is not directly volitional in that manner. Rather, it represents an eventuality for which to prepare to the extent possible. It is like the situation in which a blizzard is bearing down on one's house. It makes no sense directly to oppose the blizzard in the sense of trying to prevent it from occurring or divert its course; this would be a foolish waste of time with a high opportunity cost regarding precious advance preparation time. The storm will come and it is much more productive to accept the fact and *prepare* accordingly. Fuel. Flashlights. Candles. Snow equipment. Whatever might be needed. In a way, those preparing in such a scenario could be criticized as being "pessimistic" because they are passively accepting the coming of the blizzard. The response can only be that if this is pessimism, an informed pessimism vis-à-vis that which cannot be changed is rational.

Compartmentalized pessimism and negative visualization

We live in the middle of things which have all been destined to die...
Mortal you have been born, to mortals you have given birth...
Reckon on everything, expect everything.
Seneca[47]

I am *defending* a *compartmentalized pessimism* regarding the prospects for altering the school system *in our society and the present time* in the direction of anything resembling social justice. I say "compartmentalized" because the pessimism is to be targeted toward social assemblages whose processes are so dependent on machinations in the underlying economy that those assemblages are unlikely really to move on their own. Our education system may change substantially, and there may be a dusting of oppositional grit in the gears, but the gears *will* end up turning as directed by the needs - or perceived short-term needs - of the owners of capital. All the while occupants of those systems, because they have lives to lead and mouths to feed, must "keep calm and carry on" and make the best of things for basic humane and ethical reasons obtaining in their immediate lifeworld. One cannot be indifferent to one's immediate environment but at the same time it is not advisable to delude oneself about how "radical" one's professional practice can actually be. You're not a hero. You have dirty hands. Get over it.

Part of the "getting over it" is, I think, allowing the pessimism to spill over a bit more generally. There is a bracing narrative that runs as a persistent undercurrent in Western intellectual history. (It is one of the main currents in Eastern traditions such as Buddhism and Taoism.) This undercurrent rejects what Richard Rorty calls the "metaphysical comfort" of imagining the world to be fundamentally benevolent, especially where the conviction of benevolence is bound up with a self-congratulatory anthropocentrism, the idea that human beings are the center of it all, whether it be as creatures in God's image, whom he has "chosen," at the top of a *scala naturae*, perfectible, blessedly rational and autonomous, or whatever "uniquely human" attribute it is imagined has been bestowed. This tradition has serious doubts about our alleged nobility, and even our uniqueness, and tends to counsel a certain rapprochement with reality - not a quietism or a disinclination to act in the world, but a certain acceptance of what we undergo and, as much as they are graspable by finite beings, of nature and the cosmos themselves.

A short list of those associated with this under-tradition might include Heraclitus, Socrates (arguably as distinct from Plato on this point), Sophocles, Lucretius, the Stoics, Shakespeare (in places), Spinoza, Nietzsche and many among today's structuralists and "object-oriented" philosophers - to name but a few. To risk a dangerously imprudent generalization, there is a strong sense, at least much of the time, from these thinkers and traditions, that human beings are not the Lords of Being, commanding all we survey. It is recognized that we are far more subject to forces beyond our grasp and unamenable to our provincial purposes than we are truly in control of anything. There is also no particular reason to hope for a metaphysical restitution or compensation in the form of Heaven, Justice or a Happily Ever After. The thought is that it would be best to mature beyond the infantile position of expecting the universe to cater to our desires and conform to our projections, no matter what our yearning or strategies of propitiation.

As time ultimately grinds all of our efforts to dust, perhaps the best we can do is try to see ourselves within the frame of some larger point of view, a narrative in which by definition we do not play a starring role. We can, for example, learn to view things as in some important sense rational and necessary - which is not the same as "accepting" an unjust status quo. This is what Spinoza means by viewing the world *sub specie aeternitatis* (literally "under the aspect of eternity,") taking the *really* long view;

finding consolation, not in our power and grandiosity but, along with Lucretius, in our very smallness against an infinitely larger backdrop, miraculous in that it affords us even partial access: "This dread, these shadows of mind, must thus be swept away/Not by rays of the sun nor by the brilliant beams of day,/But by observing Nature and her laws."[48] Within this under-tradition, an attitude of inquisitive humility premises all else.

This attitude I think is often missing from a left opposition that is constantly trying to *motivate*, to convince itself that, *really*, "another world is possible" and that "the people, united, can never be defeated," and so on. This sloganeering is under-standable. But perhaps, when "another world" recedes from grasp and "the people" are in fact defeated, the cheerleading becomes counter-productive to the point that it can sow the seeds of self-hatred. One of the key psychological elements of capitalism's great nefarious genius is to cause individuals to *internalize* their failures and to refuse to see their own problems with, say, debt or joblessness as part of a larger pattern afflicting countless others alongside them. The anti-capitalist left sometimes offers its own mirror image of this cruel psychology, this bright-siding, by proffering that the revolution would come about if only you were sufficiently radical, more devoted, or harder-working. (Or the green variants: you didn't sufficiently reduce your carbon footprint, off-grid homestead or "uncivilize" with enough vigor, etc.) Yet maybe there are certain areas where *it's just not going to happen* and the general run of life and surviving its periodic crises - family, health, money - is all one can do. Should one really be ashamed of this, that one didn't make it to the last rally? Used some fossil fuel? Took a nap? The bleak asceticism implicit in these admonitions seems every bit as unforgiving as it was for the medieval self-flagellators and horse shirt wearers. Maybe we activity addicts need a little of theologian Reinhold Niebuhr's *Serenity Prayer*, the one made programmatic by Alcoholics Anonymous, at least the part reading "grant me the serenity to accept the things I cannot change; the courage to change the things I can; and wisdom to know the difference."[49] They have become cliché, but these lines still strike me as containing a very worthy aspiration, one of those many bits of wisdom floating around that "everybody knows" but is very hard actually to put into practice.

For the putting into practice it is helpful to turn to Stoicism and in particular the Roman Stoic Seneca (4 BC-65AD). Seneca was a Renaissance Man *avant la lettre*: philosopher, proto-psychologist, financier, playwright, Hall of Fame belle-lettrist, political advisor (unfortunately to Nero, who eventually murdered him), among other things. He is best known for his essays and letters that might best be described as "practical ethical advice" as they explore every day experiences such as anger, jealousy, money, anxiety, health, fear of death, disaster preparation, mercy, and grief - to name but a few - from the point of view of Stoicism. Though no stranger to university syllabi, Seneca has been underrated for the past few generations. But a recent wave of interest in Stoicism has revived interest in his writings along with the rest of the Stoics. Aided by a group of capable popular authors, Stoicism now seems well-restored to one of its rightful places: into the world of affairs among practical people rather than sequestered in libraries as the exclusive possession of a few academics.[50] This popular Stoic revival is also interesting for what it may imply: a kind of premonition of the need to cope with structural decay and degeneration. This is consistent with the fact that Stoicism has also long appealed existentially to those engaged in dangerous occupations such as soldiers, police and fire fighters. These are individuals for whom a disaster-like situation might loom around any corner in the course of their duties. As US Army Major Thomas Jarrett, former Green Beret and practitioner of Stoicism, advises, "'Soldiers need a philosophy that enables them to suffer, and not even to see it as suffering, but instead as a form of service ... If your philosophy doesn't work in the most dire circumstances, then abandon it now, because it's a Starbucks philosophy.'"[51] One wonders, alongside the current popular fascination with apocalypticism - including the rage for zombies and such - a spike in interest in a proven disaster-ready worldview arises as yet another intimation of, if not the future itself, but a cultural preoccupation with the conceivability of what I have been calling eliminationism. Like other coping mechanisms, the appeal of Stoicism may be a *symptom*.

More explicitly along these lines, one powerful technique is what philosopher of Stoicism William B. Irvine terms "negative visualization," which he considers to be "the single most valuable technique in the Stoic's psychological tool kit."[52] Along with other notable Stoics like Marcus Aurelius and Epictetus, Seneca offers a deceptively simple bit of advice about, in effect, the need to stop and smell the roses. As with most of the practical advice from Stoicism, there is nothing esoteric here; it has the ring of good common sense. It is not an observation, frankly, that would be of huge conceptual interest as the object of an academic treatise. Where it becomes interesting is if you actually try to *experience* it: you, *yourself*, in the first person and not as an object of disinterested academic curiosity, analogous to the experiential difference between perusing an actuarial mortality table and being told by your doctor that you have six months to live. A *lived* appreciation of this distinction is, in fact, the gateway into the proper application of negative visualization for Seneca.

One of the biggest obstacles preventing the experience is that, somewhat like the teenager's notorious and often tragically false sense of his own immortality, the false comfort we provide ourselves that all of those bad things happening are "out there" in some separate realm from the one we inhabit (perhaps that of "TV news" or "the internet"). We "know" intellectually that this is not the case, yet we do not typically take such matters to heart because we are in the stance of consuming yet another information product in an endless stream of the same. (At the same time, this distancing is often sanity-preserving and not altogether unwelcome. Consider the philosopher Simone Weil, who was so sensitive to distant others that upon hearing the news of a famine in China, she broke down weeping. One wonders: is this touching - or crazy?[53]) Post-tragedy, how many times have we heard the interviewee say, as if on cue, "I never thought something like this could happen around here." Well now he knows. Seneca writes: "'I did not think it would happen.' Is there anything you think will not happen, when you know that it can happen, and your own eyes show it has happened already to many?"[54] What is false here is the deliberate psychological insulation, from the Stoic point of view, the childish insistence that denies, to quote a favorite line of Seneca's, "Whatever fate one man can strike can come to all of us alike."[55] "There but for the grace of God go I," as the expression goes.

So the first step is stripping away one's false existential sense of invulnerability. Toward that end, Stoic negative visualization counsels that one should conduct for oneself an admittedly morbid-sounding personal slideshow of worst-case scenarios. These can help make even more present to our minds the radical contingency of our lives, and indeed all lives. One should, for instance, imagine what one loves the most and imagine its removal. It could be one's child. (In fact, one of Seneca's most celebrated letters, from which I have been quoting, is his "Consolation to Marcia" upon the untimely death of her son.) The idea is that the more one considers such "unthinkable" eventualities: 1) One will be better able to bear it should the unthinkable occur. "The man who has anticipated the coming of troubles takes away their power when they arrive."[56] And 2) the more one will appreciate, say, one's daughter, and not take her for granted. "Seize the pleasures your children bring, let them in turn take enjoyment in you, and drink the cup of happiness dry without delay: you have been given no promise about tonight - I have granted too long an adjournment - no promise about this very hour."[57]

Seneca does not hold that one should not grieve or suffer the expected emotions. This would be unrealistic. He does think, however, if one has steeled oneself beforehand through steady mental practice, this will lessen the shock and, above all, the sense that some cosmic injustice has been done to you and yours. This is because there *is* no cosmic justice. It would be idiotic to *blame* the earthquake for its ravages, to be angry at it the same way one would be righteously indignant at a marauding neighbor who did the same damage. There is the famous story of the Persian Emperor Xerxes, on his way to Greece, ordering the waters of the Hellespont lashed 300 times because they "disobeyed" his will by "refusing" to calm for his army's crossing. Quite ludicrously un-Stoic. It goes back to the initial existential point of understanding that events are not really happening *to you* in the sense that *you* are the star of the cosmic drama - notwithstanding our perhaps natural biases toward ourselves. The earthquake and the Hellespont waters and the death of one's loved one just *happened*; they just *are*; they did not happen *to you*. Besides, with the loved one, if one had all along taken the Stoic advice to "drink the cup of happiness dry," then one would have had that many fewer regrets, that many fewer of those things that one *should* have done, *should* have said etc., such regrets constituting our truest haunting and restless ghosts. So, really, for Seneca, these *memento mori* have little to do with the dour and doleful; they are rather exhortations to live life more fully. This, I think, is part of what Nietzsche's Zarathustra meant when he spoke of the need, despite omnipresent suffering and misery, for a "Holy yes-saying."[58]

That is not all. It is necessary to go beyond Seneca on this point, though in a way that is true to his spirit. Negative visualization's potentially salutary effects are not to be confined to specific difficulties such as grief, but we are urged by Seneca to "apply this picture to your entrance into the whole of life."[59] Extrapolating from this dictum of expansion, it seems to me that there is little reason to hold that the contemplation of worst case scenarios needs to be confined to an individual's *personal* experiences. It stands to reason that the same logic and therefore the same benefits could be expected to apply from adopting this Stoic technique to *collective* experience as well, as group preparation for larger-scale and more widely-shared difficulties that might plausibly be imagined. Irvine notes that one traditional but sometimes under-appreciated function of the custom of saying grace at mealtime (I might add from my own experience the annual recitation of the Passover Haggadah in Judaism) is that it provides just such a shared appreciation of the contingency of what *is*. This is essentially what one is doing when one gives "thanks" for the food, the company, one's freedom etc., as doing so implies that things could well have been otherwise - actually, in the case of the Passover Seder, *have* been otherwise in the group's shared history. "Said with these thoughts in mind, grace has the ability to transform an ordinary meal into a celebration."[60]

It is warranted, I believe, to extend the idea still further. Our culture proselytizes against the lived consideration of finitude and mortality in myriad ways. Our popular culture, geared toward the rapid turnover of commodities and their planned obsolescence, tends to worship the "new new" thing and in so doing builds in a biased fascination toward youth. Due to a variety of factors including, surely, the ideals of nuclear family life and the economics of health care, we increasingly sequester elderly in assisted living and other retirement "communities," decreasing intergenerational contact and by extension the old style of encounter with the death of elders that tended to take place in the home amidst the everyday multigenerational closeness of family life. Contrary to all of human history save the last few generations, it seems increasingly proper to us that death should take place in a medical facility as an individual affair and is something from which to shield the children. Our largely unquestioned narratives of progress and confidence in techno-fixes tend also to place at a distance any serious consideration of the finitude and limitations of our culture at large. Such talk sounds whiny and defeatist, constitutive of that insufficiently bright-sided "positive" outlook, a character deficiency to be remedied by the prescription of psychoactive mood-altering drugs. As with the actuarial tables, everyone "knows" about death etc. but again it is that difference, long highlighted by thinkers such as Sartre and Heidegger, between knowing it as a factoid versus as an actual (shared) experience. Witness the strong tendency when informed of someone's illness to want to "medicalize" the discussion and thereby place matters at a psychologically safer remove. This seems natural to us. What else is one to talk about? Fate? The point of it all? The worth-whileness of the deceased - and survivors' - lives? Who needs *that* at a time of emotional crisis? As "natural" as all of this seems, however, as per the above, the Stoic position would be that this distancing stance is unhealthy not just for individuals but, by extension, whole societies.

For one thing, as Freud emphasized, thanatotic matters come back upon us long-term as a "return of the repressed" in various subconscious ways, from probably harmless recurrent tropes in popular culture like the horror and apocalyptic genres, to more troubling phenomena such as our denial of the gory details of our military adventures, environmental devastation, and catastrophic for-profit health care system (in the US especially), where the repressed return as blowback, at which point it is too late to do anything. We are ostriches, not only unable to act in anticipation of long-term difficulties (remembering from earlier chapters that this is Grantham's Achilles heel of capitalism), but actively shielding ourselves from them. This is simply irrational, like the person with white coat anxiety who puts off doctor's visits for fear of what she might hear and thereby missing out on an early diagnosis of an ailment that *would* have been treatable if caught in time. If only she had had a *slight* bit of the Stoic hypochondria of negative visualization, she could have been saved.

Similarly, when considering the largest threats we face, including TRPF-induced eliminationism, climate change and resource depletion, it seems advisable to adopt whatever pedagogies may be available to engage in a bit of salutary culture-wide negative visualization. As indicated earlier, we already do this, I think, at the subconscious level of the consumption of personal entertainments, as when we flip on the TV zombie drama *The Walking Dead* or curl up with *World War Z* or any of the many other options of this ilk.

It is not so great a step to interrogate the widespread interest in these themes more frontally, appreciating from a new angle Lucretius's prescience:

> *So who are you to balk*
> *And whine at death? You're almost dead in life, although you walk*
> *And breathe. You fritter away most of your time asleep. You snore*
> *With your eyes open; you never leave off dreaming, and a score*
> *Of empty nightmares fills your mind and shakes it to the core.*
> *Often, addled and dizzy, you don't even know what's wrong -*
> *You find yourself besieged at every turn by a whole throng*
> *Of cares, and drift on shifting currents of uncertainty*[61]

A serious communal examination of the "empty nightmares" of such as zombies (the "dead in life") might just help decrease their hold on us in the manner of cognitive behavior therapy or psychoanalysis.

A contemporary pedagogical agenda could arise from these old Stoic ruins. It would have to do with the possibility of forcing ourselves to confront the fact that our status on this planet is contingent - a fact greatly exacerbated by our own actions - and appreciate the corollary to this hard truth that we are not the lords of being who enjoy the special favor of a Metaphysical Guarantor. Yet, as The Dark Mountain Project's "post-environ-mentalist" *Manifesto* observes,

> Today, humanity is up to its neck in denial about what it has built, what it has become - and what it is in for. Ecological and economic collapse unfold before us and, if we acknowledge them at all, we act as if this were a temporary problem, a technical glitch. Centuries of hubris block our ears like wax plugs; we cannot hear the message which reality is screaming at us. For all our doubts and discontents, we are still wired to an idea of history in which the future will be an upgraded version of the present. The assumption remains that things must continue in their current direction: the sense of crisis only smudges the meaning of that 'must'. No longer a natural inevitability, it becomes an urgent necessity: we must find a way to go on having supermarkets and superhighways. We cannot contemplate the alternative.[62]

Hence the acute need for Stoic visualization, by which we might grapple with "the alternative" and thereby illuminate whatever possibilities may exist for ourselves, *without assuming that everything will always stay the same*. Toward this end, one might imagine a pedagogy of counterfactuals here, where learners of any age might be led to experience and reflect upon situations highlighting questions of "what would life be like were it not for X?" We already do this in various ways. A well-known maudlin version of such a counterfactual pedagogy is famously depicted in the classic film *It's a Wonderful Life*, where George Bailey is led to see what life would have been like without him. On a more manageable and "safer" pedagogical scale, it is common for schools to ask students to unplug their electronics (including mobiles!) for a time or write an essay on what they learned when the power went out after a storm for a couple of days. Or what it might like to be blind or otherwise physically disabled.

There are plenty of available examples. My family and I learned quite a bit once when on our farm the old well (our only one) caved in and we were without water for a couple of weeks. I highly recommend running water deprivation for anyone desiring a radical alteration of life caused by the removal of something previously taken for granted. We learned, quite experientially, how preoccupying water has been for human beings in history, and for many in the developing world today without proper access to it (over 2 *billion* people according to the World Health Organization).[63] In the spirit of the old truism that the burned hand teaches best, I would submit that these are lessons that are best learned - really *only* learned - upon the platform provided by experience. In order to be effective, then, a counterfactual pedagogy of negative visualization would be most effective as an *opportunistic* effort that builds upon peoples' actual experiences of coping with whatever it is that has been lost, the most traumatic of these things being, usually, those that are most vital and therefore taken for granted (like food, water, health and energy). It is not by accident that so many of Seneca's Stoic writings are written *to* individuals as "consolations" for them as they attempt to cope with something traumatic like the death of a child. These are not detached speculations.

I would stress that a pedagogy of loss such as this is not *just* the famous Heideggerian point from *Being and Time* about tools and how as "ready-to-hand" they only stand out to us as objects when they break down. Matters can go much deeper than that if we allow them to, if we allow them to illuminate our darkened landscape more fully.

In my well collapse experience, certainly the easy flow of water to which I'd been accustomed my entire life (in cities and suburbs) caused the entire phenomenon of groundwater to become an immediate and obsessive direct object of concern: literally a case of noticing for the first time the ground beneath one's feet. It was an inherently unlimited experience, though. I suppose it could have been possible to dig the new well and feel so traumatized that I didn't want ever to have to *think* about water again. But really, learning about the process had a way of leading to other things, a powerful spillover effect, if you will. I started having to consider the catchment basin for where to put the new well, worry about pesticides and other contaminants that might soak into the ground within the relevant circumference of the well site, because of those potential contaminants consider our farming, animal husbandry (we have horses and chickens) and septic methods, not to mention potentially urgent issues concerning natural gas fracking (we live in fracking-mad Pennsylvania) and on and on. The event also offered a kind of first-person entrée into history, as we very dramatically appreciated for the first time why the original builders hundreds of years ago would have placed the house near a stream (even at the risk of rising spring floods) and, thank Zeus, the little spring house the old-timers had built nearby - neglected and covered over with weeds until we discovered how much we needed it for almost everything (several gallons to: cook and clean up dishes, flush toilets, water the animals (lots!) and a million other little things needing water that one doesn't normally notice. For example, we learned very well an age-old fundamental truth that does not, it turns out, require advanced schooling: *water is heavy*. Hauling only a gallon or two on one occasion is no big deal. Hauling gallon after gallon, continually, day after day, many times a day, is quite another matter altogether. It will change the way you live. And that was just two weeks! *This* was a counterfactual pedagogy based on actual experience, one that could have been accomplished in any number of ways, that connected us more appreciatively to our environment and our history.

Given current and forecast conditions, we are likely to be

encountering a great many of these impromptu "teachable moments" involving our civilization's most frightening longer-term counterfactuals concerning climate change and resource depletion. The unfolding three-way race among these two and economic catastrophe will be one, literally, for the ages.

Hope among the ruins

There is no chance to move towards a better future if we misunderstand the situation we are currently in.
Steve Keen[64]

Just as the Stoics advocate negative visualization for individuals, I am advocating a negative counterfactual pedagogy on the group scale. What if *we* no longer had *this*? Or *that*? Economically. Environmentally. The kicker, though, is that, for reasons outlined above, it seems to me that a pedagogy that aims to consider societal collapse is unlikely to be successful via formal instruction taking place in regular schools. I would be highly suspicious of pedagogues creating workbooks and writing "lesson plans" on collapse (and educationists getting grants for the same). In this realm, the best teacher will be the actual experiences that are likely to unfold in the coming years. Therefore the *psychological* readiness for these events is just as important as material preparedness. There is already much to learn: the "storms of our grandchildren" may already be upon us and if so the open air "schools" of our collective negative visualization will be all-too vivid and their lessons all-too real.[65] As I have indicated in these pages, class is now in grim session from Greece to Spain, from Tahrir Square to the streets of London, from Kinshasa to Port-au-Prince and from the dry Great Plains to what used to be the beaches of the north Jersey Shore.

Compounding the urgency of an opportunistic and experiential pedagogy is the demise of possibilities within our increasingly constrained and resource-starved public schools and colleges. The venue for an education about what matters most seems increasingly possible only *outside* the formal educational assemblage. Here is a sliver of pedagogical good fortune upon which to capitalize: as the structural necessities extinguish what is possible on the "inside," the kind of learning that needs to take place is best accomplished on the "outside" anyway. There is the obnoxious cliché that one should "never let a good crisis go to waste" and, as Klein has illustrated, capitalism often evolves not in a smooth fashion but in a punctuated form through a "shock doctrine" where volatility opens possibilities. Seizing back that pedagogical momentum is central to the agenda of a revolutionary opportunism whose time is fated - yes *fated* - to arrive due to financialized capitalism's self-immolating character and its world-killing thirst for unsustainable growth at all costs. The shock doctrine can work both ways, as it started to when the 2008 financial crisis gave birth to the various occupy movements.

We are soon to face directly another period of imperative inevitability, where a harsh disjunction presents only one possible choice, as it did for Rosa Luxemburg when she offered the choice of "socialism or barbarism" before the First World War. (Her world chose the latter.) Trotsky amplified the motto in a way that eerily presaged the next world war, the nuclear age, and environmental destruction: "Capitalism, enveloped in the flames of a war of its own making, shouts from the mouths of its cannons to humanity: 'Either conquer over me, or I will bury you in my ruins when I fall!'"[66] With the rise of the *planetary* threats of nuclear war and environmental destruction that are preconditioned by the awesome power of capitalist production, we see now that there are worse things even than a reversion to "barbarism" which, from an environmental point of view, might not be the worst of all possible outcomes in the long run. Barbarism might at least leave us (and other creatures) with a habitable planet. Our primary need is to ensure the very existence of a long run.

Despite our best efforts, it may come to ruin - as in Marx's "mutual ruin of the contending classes" - but still, even with this strong possibility hanging over us, there is something to accepting fate, not denying it or wishing it away, and persevering in the fight. *Even when it is perceived as hopeless.* As Seneca writes, "Even in the case of shipwreck we should extol the helmsman whom the sea overwhelms as he still grips the rudder and does battle with the elements."[67] Besides, the fact of human fallibilism should mitigate absolute despair just as much as it does unjustified optimism. The helmsman may lose his battle with the sea yet still, somehow, survive. It is possible. There may be some factor unknown to us in the situation and, lacking even that, there may be such a thing as chance. Our inherent finitude and lack of omniscience is not just a limitation but may constitute a saving psychic grace as well.

That *one* creature that did not escape from Mother Pandora's jar, Hope, may lie in our adaptive capacity to learn, this time not clever external fixes, but about *ourselves* and the lies contained in the stories of which we have become collectively enamored. Especially the one about how we are allegedly inter-galactically chosen by the Big Other, specially favored, and placed at the center of the moral universe. The necessary lessons may thus be right there before us; but for that reason very far away. It is our fate that those lessons will always recede from us, the eternal Socratic insight being that true learning not only presupposes ignorance but continually generates more of it. Yet we persist; there is no other way for us. As our first poet instructs,

For the gods keep hidden from men the means of life.[68]

Notes

Epigraph

1. "The Broken Balance," *The Selected Poems of Robinson Jeffers* (Stanford, CA: Stanford University Press), 162.

Introduction

1. "The Locust Years," House of Commons (November 12, 1936). Available from http://www.churchill-society-london .org.uk/Locusts.html. (Accessed February 21, 2013)
2. Karl Marx, *Grundrisse* (New York: Penguin Books, 1973), 743.
3. Pierre Bourdieu, *Outline of a Theory of Practice* (London: Cambridge University Press, 1977), 191f.
4. Barbara Ehrenreich, *Bright Sided: How the New Positive Thinking is Undermining America* (New York: Picador, 2010).
5. Martin Heidegger, *The Question Concerning Technology and Other Essays* (New York: Garland Publishing, 1977), 17.
6. Henry A. Giroux, *Disposable Youth: Racialized Memories and the Culture of Cruelty* (New York: Routledge, 2012).
7. See Donella H. Meadows, Jorgen Randers and Dennis L. Meadows, *Limits to Growth: The 30-Year Update*. 3rd Ed., (Burlington, VT: Chelsea Green, 3rd Ed., 2004); Richard Heinberg, *The End of Growth: Adapting to Our New Economic Reality* (Gabriola Island, BC: New Society Publishers, 2011); James Hansen, *Storms of My Grandchildren: The Truth About the Coming Climate Catastrophe and the Last Chance to Save Humanity* (New York: Bloomsbury, 2010); and John Bellamy Foster, Brett Clark and Richard York, *The Ecological Rift: Capitalism's War on the Earth* (New York: Monthly Review Press, 2010).
8. On the low-hanging fruit of universal literacy, see Tyler Cowen, *The Great Stagnation* (New York: Penguin kindle edition, 2010), Chapter One.

9. Chris Hayes, *Twilight of the Elites.*

10. Naomi Klein, *The Shock Doctrine: The Rise of Disaster Capitalism* (New York: Picador, 2008).

11. Michael Huesemann and Joyce Huesemann, *Techno-fix: Why Technology won't Save Us or the Environment* (Gabriola Island, BC: New Society Publishers, 2011).

12. *Friedrich Nietzsche, The Gay Science, trans. Walter Kaufmann (New York; Vintage, 1974),* 276.

13. John Michael Greer, *The Long Descent: A User's Guide to the End of the Industrial Age* (Gabriola Island, BC: New Society Publishers, 2008).

Chapter I

1. *Media Matters with Robert McChesney* (Urbana, IL: WILL-AM Radio, July 17, 2012). Available from: http://wil.illinois .edu/mediamatters/. (Accessed February 20, 2013)

2. Karl Marx and Friedrich Engels, *The Communist Manifesto* in *The Marx-Engels Reader*, ed. Robert C. Tucker (New York: Norton, 1972), 476.

3. John Bellamy Foster, Brett Clark and Richard York, *The Ecological Rift*, 15.

4. See Nicholas B. Allen and Paul B. T. Badcock, "Darwinian models of depression: A review of evolutionary accounts of mood and mood disorders," *Progress in Neuro-Psychopharmacology and Biological Psychiatry* 30.5 (2006): 815–826.

5. Friedrich Nietzsche, *The Gay Science*, 344.

6. Paul Kingsnorth, "Confessions of a Recovering Environmentalist," *Orion* (January/February 2012). Available from: http://www.orionmagazine.org/index.php/articles/arti cle/6599. (Accessed February 21, 2013)

7. See Rockström, J., W. Steffen, K. Noone, Å. Persson, F. S. Chapin, III, E. Lambin, T. M. Lenton, M. Scheffer, C. Folke, H. Schellnhuber, B. Nykvist, C. A. De Wit, T. Hughes, S. van der

Leeuw, H. Rodhe, S. Sörlin, P. K. Snyder, R. Costanza, U. Svedin, M. Falkenmark, L. Karlberg, R. W. Corell, V. J. Fabry, J. Hansen, B. Walker, D. Liverman, K. Richardson, P. Crutzen, and J. Foley. "Planetary boundaries:exploring the safe operating space for humanity," *Ecology and Society* 14.2 (2009): 32. The boundaries are: climate change, ocean acidification, ozone depletion, phosphorous and nitrogen depletion, biodiversity loss, freshwater scarcity, land system change, aerosol loading and chemical pollution.

8. "Men are deceived into thinking themselves free, a belief that consists only in this, that they are conscious of their actions and ignorant of the causes by which they are determined. Therefore the idea of their freedom is simply the ignorance of the causes of their action." Baruch Spinoza, *Ethics* (Indianapolis: Hackett, 1982), 35.

9. "This workshop where *ideals are manufactured* - it seems to me it stinks of so many lies." Friedrich Nietzsche, *On the Genealogy of Morals*, trans. Walter Kaufmann (New York: Vintage, 1967), 47.

10. G.W.F. Hegel, *Philosophy of Right*, trans. T.M. Knox (London: Oxford University Press, 1952), 13.

11. See Chris Harman, *Zombie Capitalism: Global Crisis and the Relevance of Marx* (Chicago: Haymarket Books, 2009); Alex Callinicos, *Bonfire of Illusions: Twin Crises of the Liberal World* (London: Polity Press, 2010); Andrew Kliman, *The Failure of Capitalist Production: Underlying Causes of the Great Recession* (London: Pluto Press, 2012); and Guglielmo Carchedi, *Behind the Crisis: Marx's Dialectic of Value and Knowledge* (Chicago: Haymarket Books, 2012).

12. Available from: http://www.youtube.com/user/brendanmcooney. See especially "The Falling Rate of Profit 1 of 2" and "The Falling Rate of Profit 2 of 2." (Accessed June 1, 2012)

13. Andrew Kliman, *The Failure of Capitalist Production* 50.

14. See Michelle Alexander, *The New Jim Crow: Mass Incarceration*

in the Age of Colorblindness (The Free Press, 2012), 59-96.

15. I do not mean to oversell things vis-à-vis Marx. In fact it is a good maxim never to bet against him regarding whatever "new" economic phenomenon is alleged to have escaped his notice. Marx was more than aware of the potential for credit-fueled upward instability. He even, interestingly, saw in the development of credit "the latent abolition of capital ownership." Marx further explains that "[i]f the credit system appears as the principal lever of overproduction and excessive speculation in commerce, this is simply because the reproduction process, which is elastic and by nature, is now forced [once the credit system has developed] to its extreme limits; and this is because a great part of the social capital is applied by those who are not the owners, and who therefore proceed quite unlike owners who, when they function themselves, anxiously weigh the limits of their private capital." (Marx, *Capital, Volume III* (New York: Penguin Books, 1981), 572. Andrew Kliman points to this passage as an early discussion of the "moral hazard" that arises from commercial credit's operative long-term tendency to sever the direction of capital from its ownership, to separate financial reward from financial risk (e.g. CEO's earning bonuses for failing companies, too big to fail banks socializing their casino losses). See Kliman, *The Failure of Capitalist Production*, 19-20.

16. Available from: http://www.paulcraigroberts.org/2012/05/20/recovery-or-collapse-bet-on-collapse/ (Accessed February 21, 2013)

17. Available from: http://www.bankofengland.co.uk/publications/Documents/speeches/2010/speech433.pdf. (Accessed February 21, 2013)

18. Hyman P. Minsky, *Can "It" Happen Again? Essays on Instability and Finance* (Armonk, NY: M.E. Sharpe, Inc., 1982), 123.

19. Alan Greenspan, "The Challenge of Central Banking in a Democratic Society," Francis Boyer Lecture of The American Enterprise Institute for Public Policy Research, Washington, D.C. (December 5, 1996). Available from: http://www.federalreserve.gov/boarddocs/speeches/1996/19961205.htm. (Accessed February 21, 2013)

20. Steve Keen, *Debunking Economics*, rev. ed. (London: Zed Books, 2011), 354-355. Keen elaborates his "modern debt jubilee" proposal in Steve Kfile://localhost/een, "The Debtwatch Manifesto," Debtwatch.com (January 2, 2012). Available from/ http/::tinyurl.com:6nlxhyt.(Accessed February 21, 2013)

21. *Why Nations Fail: The Origins of Power, Prosperity and Poverty* (New York: Crown Business, 2012), 81.

22. "The Falling Time Cost of College: Evidence from a Half a Century of Time Use Data," *Review of Economics and Statistics* 93.2 (2011): 468-478.

23. Available from: http://www.aaup.org/AAUP/pubsres/acad eme/2012/MJ/Feat/Kuma.htm (accessed February 21, 2013); drawn from Kevin Kumashiro, *Bad Teacher! How Blaming Teachers Distorts the Bigger Picture* (New York: Teachers College Press, 2012).

24. Ibid.

25. "Dan Ariely: The Polar Bear and the Prius," available from: http://www.youtube.com/watch?v=aFlXgSkvslI&feature=pl ayer_embedded. (Accessed February 21, 2013)

26. Jeremy Grantham, *GMO Quarterly Letter* (February 2012). Available from: https://www.gmo.com/America/Library/Letters/ (Accessed June 1, 2012)

27. Ibid.

28. Ibid.

29. Andrew Nusca, "Rural U.S. Population Lowest in History, Demographers Say," *CBS News Smart Planet* (July 28, 2011).

Available from: http://www.smartplanet.com/blog/smart-takes/rural-us-population-lowest-in-history-demographers-say/17982

30. Tyler Cowen, *The Great Stagnation* (New York: Penguin kindle edition, 2011).

31. Ibid.

32. Ibid.

33. See John Bellamy Foster, "Marx's Theory of Metabolic Rift: Classical Foundations for Environmental Sociology," *The American Journal of Sociology* 105.2 (September 1999): 366-405; and John Bellamy Foster, Brett Clark, and Richard York, *The Ecological Rift*.

34. Foster, Clark and York, *The Ecological Rift*,14.

35. See James Howard Kunstler, *Too Much Magic: Wishful Thinking, Technology, and the Fate of the Nation* (New York: Atlantic Monthly Press, 2012).

36. Martin Heidegger, "On the Essence of Truth," in *Basic Writings*, ed. David Farrell Krell (New York: Harper & Rowe Publishers, 1977), 127.

37. See Marcel Mauss, *The Gift: Form and Reason and Exchange in Archaic Societies* (New York: W. W. Norton & Co., 2000) and Charles Eisenstein, *Sacred Economics: Money, Gift and Society in the Age of Transition* (Evolver Editions, 2011). I discuss internal norms peculiar to education in *Democratic Education Stretched Thin: How Complexity Challenges a Liberal Ideal* (Albany, NY: SUNY Press, 2007), 62-79.

38. Levi Bryant, "The Stakes of SR/NFM/OOO/Onticology: Who's Afraid of the Big Bad Wolves?" *Larval Subjects* (blog), June 5, 2012. Available from: http://larvalsubjects.word press.com/2012/06/05/the-stakes-of-srnfmoooonticology-whos-afraid-of-the-big-bad-wolves/#comment-135177. (Accessed June 5, 2012)

Chapter 2

1. *Capital, Volume* III, trans. David Fernbach (London: Penguin Books, 1981), 180.
2. The "wave" terminology is drawn from Ernest Mandel, *Late Capitalism* (London: Verso, 1978), 108-146.
3. See my *Democratic Education Stretched Thin*.
4. The language of "spheres" is developed in Michael Walzer, *Spheres of Justice: A Defense of Pluralism and Equality* (New York, Basic Books, 1984). Alasdair MacIntyre provides an influential account of institutional corruption, defined as when the "internal goods" structuring a practice of whatever sort (including education) give way to "external goods" such as money or power, in his *After Virtue: A Study in Moral Theory* (South Bend, IN; University of Notre Dame Press), Chs. 14-15. The *locus classicus* of the notion of regulatory capture is the free market economist George Stigler, "The Theory of Economic Regulation," *The Bell Journal of Economics and Management Science* 2.1 (Spring 1971): 3-21.
5. David Harvey, *The New Imperialism* (Oxford: Oxford University Press, 2003), 134-136.
6. Applied originally to Goldman Sachs, the famous vampire squid/blood funnel image is from Matt Taibbi, "The Great Bubble Machine," *Rolling Stone* (April 5, 2010). Available from: http://www.rollingstone.com/politics/news/the-great-american-bubble-machine-20100405. (Accessed February 21, 2013)
7. Harvey, *The New Imperialism*, 121-123.
8. The idea of "biopower" derives from the work of Michel Foucault on "biopolitics" (in such works as *The History of Sexuality, Volume 1* (New York: Vintage, 2000)), as appropriated by Michael Hardt and Antonio Negri, *Multitude: War and Democracy in the Age of Empire* (New York: Penguin Books, 2005).

9. Arthur Schopenhauer, *On the Principle of Sufficient Reason*, trans. Karl Hillebrand (New York: Prometheus Books, 2006).

10. Alex Callinicos, *Bonfire of Illusions: The Twin Crises of the Liberal World* (Cambridge: Polity Press, 2010), 45.

11. G. W. F. Hegel, *The Philosophy of Right*, trans. T.M. Knox (London: Oxford University Press, 1967), 12.

12. Ibid., 13.

13. Karl Marx, *Theses on Feuerbach* in Quinton Hoare, ed., *Karl Marx: Early Writings* (New York: Vintage, 1975), 423.

14. My translation, "Il faut toujours suivre ceux qui cherchent la vérité et toujours fuir ceux qui l'ont trouvée." This quote seems universally attributed to Gide, though I cannot find a specific source for it.

15. G.W.F. Hegel, *Phenomenology of Spirit*, trans. A. V. Miller (London: Oxford University Press, 1979), 49-50.

16. See John Michael Greer, *Apocalypse Not: Everything You Know About 2012, Nostradamus, and the Rapture is Wrong* (Berkeley, CA: Viva Editions, 2011).

17. Elaine Pagels, *Revelations: Visions, Prophecy and Politics in the Book of Revelations* (New York: Viking, 2012).

18. Naomi Klein, *The Shock Doctrine*.

19. Eric Hobsbawm, *How to Change the World: Tales of Marx and Marxism* (London: Abacus, 2011), 419.

20. There are further nuances not directly relevant to the present analysis, e.g. Marx distinguishes the "organic" from the "technical" composition of capital, where the latter is the ratio of the absolute *amounts* of variable to fixed capital (however that might be assessed) and the former is the ratio of the present market *values* of them.

21. Gary S. Becker, *Human Capital: A Theoretical and Empirical Analysis with Special Reference to Education*, 3rd ed. (Chicago: University of Chicago Press, 1964).

22. See John Bellamy Foster and Robert W. McChesney, "The Global Stagnation and China," *Monthly Review* 63.9: 1-28.

23. Samir Amin, *The Law of Worldwide Value* (New York: Monthly Review Press, 1978).

24. I allude to the classic tale of Chinese peasant workers by Pearl Buck, *The Good Earth* (New York: Simon & Schuster, 1980).

25. Foster and McChesney, "The Global Stagnation and China," 9.

26. Good catalogs of past and potential future technological "game changers" are to be found in Ray Kurzweil, *The Singularity is Near: When Humans Transcend Biology* (New York: Penguin Books, 2006); and Peter Diamandis and Steven Kotler, *Abundance: Why the Future is Better Than You Think* (New York: The Free Press, 2012).

27. Michael J. Bazyler, *Holocaust Justice: The Battle for Restitution in America's Courts* (New York: New York University Press, 2003), 60-62.28. Andrew Kliman, *The Failure of Capitalist Production*.

29. Karl Marx, *Capital: Volume III* (New York: Penguin, 1981), 346.

30. See Ari Levaux, "The Latest Raw Milk Raid: An Attack on Food Freedom?" *Atlantic Monthly* (August 15, 2011). Available from: http://www.theatlantic.com/health/archive /2011/08/the-latest-raw-milk-raid-an-attack-on-food-freedom/243635/. (Accessed February 21, 2013)

31. *Monopoly Capital: An Essay on the American Social and Economic Order* (New York: Monthly Review Press, 1966).

32. Samir Amin, *The Law of Worldwide Value*, 110-111. Andy Higginbottom helpfully defines imperialist rent as "the above average or extra profits realised as a result of the inequality between North and South in the global capitalist system. Imperialist rent is a case of above average super-profits or monopoly profits. Since normal profits derive from surplus value and the exploitation of workers, the presence of super-profits indicates intensified or additional

mechanisms of exploitation." Andy Higginbottom, "'Imperialist Rent' in Practice and Theory," paper presented at "Workshop: Trade Unions, Free Trade and the Problem of Transnational Solidarity," Center for the Study of Social and Global Justice, University of Nottingham (UK) (December 11-12, 2011), 2. Available from: http://andreasbieler.net/work shop/. (Accessed February 21, 2013)

33. Higginbottom, "'Imperialist Rent' in Practice and Theory," 17-24.

34. Alex Callinicos, *Bonfire of Illusions*, 45.

35. See Samir Amin, *Ending the Crisis of Capitalism or Ending Capitalism?* (Oxford: Pambazuka Press, 2011).

36. Marx, *Capital: Volume III* (London: Penguin, 1991), 367. As cited in Andrew Kliman, *The Failure of Capitalist Production*, 21.

37. Karl Marx, *German Ideology* (1846) in *The Marx-Engels Reader*, Ed. Robert C. Tucker (New York: Norton, 1978), 172-173.

38. See Michael B. Katz, *The Irony of Early School Reform: Educational Innovation in Mid-Nineteenth Century Massachusetts* (Cambridge, MA: Harvard University Press, 1968).

39. Raj Patel, *Stuffed and Starved: The Hidden Battle for the World's Food* (New York: HarperCollins, 2009).

40. "Homo suburbiensis" is from Australian poet Bruce Dawe's poem of the same name, available in his *Sometimes Gladness: Collected Poems 1954 to 1997* (Victoria: Pearson Australia, 2001).

41. Richard Wolff, *Capitalism Hits the Fan: The Global Economic Meltdown and What to Do About It* (North Hampton, MA: Olive Branch Press, 2009)

42. *This American Life*, Episode 355 (National Public Radio: Original air date May 9, 2008). Available from: http://www.thisamericanlife.org/radio-archives/episode/355/the-giant-pool-of-money. (Accessed

February 21, 2013).

43. James Galbraith, *The Predator State: How Conservatives Abandoned the Free Market and Why Liberals Should Too* (New York: Free Press, 2008).

44. Among the many analyses of this process, economist Michael Hudson's work is especially helpful. A recent relevant paper is "Scenarios for Recovery: How to Write Down the Debts and Restructure the Financial System," paper given at *Paradigm Lost: Rethinking Economics and Politics,* hosted by the Institute for New Economic Thinking, (Berlin, April 13, 2012). Available from: http://ineteconomics.org/sites/inet.civicactions.net/files/hudson-michael-berlin-paper.pdf. Accessed February 21, 2013).

45. David Harvey, *The New Imperialism.*

46. Stephen P. Broughman et al., "Characteristics of Private Schools in the United States: Results from the 2009–10 Private School Universe Survey" (Washington DC: National Center for Education Statistics, US Department of Education, 2011), 2. Available from: http://nces.ed.gov/pubs2011/2011339.pdf. (Accessed February 21, 2013)

47. Wen Tiejun et al., "Ecological Civilization, Indigenous Culture, and Rural Reconstruction in China," *Monthly Review,* 63.9 (February 2012): 31.

48. Slavoj Žižek, as cited in Rebecca Mead, "The Marx Brother," *The New Yorker* (May 5, 2003).

49. Andrew Kliman, *The Failure of Capitalist Production,* 26-27.

Chapter 3

1. Hyman P. Minsky, *Can "It" Happen Again? Essays on Instability and Finance* (Armonk, NY: M.E. Sharpe, 1982)?, 284.

2. Hans Magnus Enzensberger, *Civil Wars: From L.A. to Bosnia* (New York: The New Press, 1995), 36.

3. Karl Marx, *Capital: Volume III* (London: Hammondsworth,

1976), 198. As quoted in Alex Callinicos, *The Revolutionary Ideas of Karl Marx* (Chicago: Haymarket Books, 1983).

4. Michael Hudson, "Paul Krugman's Economic Blinders," *Michael-Hudson.com* (May 14, 2012). Available from: http://michael-hudson.com/2012/05/paul-krugmans-economic-blinders/

5. Hyman P. Minsky, *Can "It" Happen Again?*, 66.

6. Ibid.

7. Hyman P. Minsky, *Stabilizing an Unstable Economy* (New Haven: Yale University Press, 1986), 10.

8. See Steve Keen, *Debunking Economics: The Naked Emperor Dethroned?* (London: Zed Books, 2011), 319-356.

9. "...the massive destruction of capital value that took place during the Great Depression and World War II set the stage for the boom that followed." Andrew Kliman, *The Failure of Capitalist Production*, 23.

10. "Here at last monopoly capitalism finally found the answer to the 'on what' question? On what could government spend enough to keep the system from sinking into the mire of stagnation? On arms, more arms, and ever more arms." Paul Baran and Paul Sweezy, *Monopoly Capital*, 213.

11. Nietzsche, *The Gay Science*, 125.

12. Chris Harman, *Zombie Capitalism: Global Crisis and the Relevance of Marx* (Chicago: Haymarket Books, 2009).

13. Michel Houellebecq, *The Possibility of an Island* (New York: Vintage, 2007). *Booklist* memorably - and relevantly - describes the novel as concerning a cult of sexually promiscuous health fanatics who achieve immortality through cloning.

14. Plato, *Republic*, 540b.

15. Robert H. Frank and Philip J. Cook, *The Winner-Take-All Society: Why the Few at the Top Get So Much More Than the Rest of Us* (New York: Penguin, 1996).

16. Gary S. Becker, *Human Capital*, 16.

17. Ibid., 17.

18. Mikhail Bakunin, "On the International Workingman's Association and Karl Marx (1872)." Available from: http://www.marxists.org/reference/archive/bakunin/works/1872/karl-marx.htm.

19. John Marsh, *Class Dismissed: Why We Cannot Teach or Learn Our Way Out of Inequality* (New York: Monthly Review Press, 2011), 160.

20. David J. Blacker, "The Institutional Autonomy of Education," *Journal of Philosophy of Education* 32.2 (May 2000): 229-246.

21. A sobering recent meditation on this phenomenon is found in Henry A. Giroux, *Education and the Crisis of Public Values* (New York: Peter Lang, 2011).

22. This is *not* a criticism of Freirean pedagogies because Freire and many inspired by him, such as the Brazilian Landless Workers Movement (MST) in Brazil, presuppose that very larger social movement of resistance within which to situate their pedagogical efforts. See the interview with Rebecca Tarlau, conducted by Sasha Lilly, "Efforts by Brazil's Landless Worker's Movement (MST) to Transform Education," *Against the Grain* (radio program and podcast), KPFA.org, July 3, 2012. Available from: http://www.kpfa.org/archive/id/82063.

23. John Marsh, *Class Dismissed*, 178.

24. Ibid., 168, 169.

25. Joan Robinson, *Economic Philosophy: An Essay on the Progress of Economic Thought* (New York: Doubleday Anchor, 1964), 45.

26. Henry A. Giroux, *Disposable Youth: Racialized Memories and the Culture of Cruelty* (New York: Routledge, 2012), 4; Michelle Alexander, *The New Jim Crow: Mass Incarceration in the Age of Colorblindness* (New York: The Free Press, 2010).

27. Daniel Jonah Goldhagen, *Worse Than War: Genocide,*

Eliminationism and the Ongoing Assault on Humanity (New York: PublicAffairs, 2009); Arno Mayer, *Why Did the Heavens Not Darken? "Final Solution" in History* (Verso, 1990).

28. For statistics on race and incarceration in the U.S., see *The Sentencing Project* (available from: www.sentencing project.org); for the number of African-American males with records, see Alexander, *The New Jim Crow*, 7.

29. Slavoj Žižek, "Philosopher, Cultural Critic and Cyber-Communist" (interview), *JAC Online: A Journal of Rhetoric, Culture and Politics* 21.2 (2011): 257. Available from: http://jaconlinejournal.com/archives/vol21.2/olson-zizek.pdf. (Accessed February 21, 2013)

30. National Center for Education Statistics, "Fast Facts," (Washington, DC: U.S. Department of Education, 2011). Available from: http://nces.ed.gov/fastfacts/. (Accessed February 21, 2013).

31. For an excellent case study of Chicago along these lines, see Pauline Lipman, *The New Political Economy of Urban Education: Neoliberalism, Race and the Right to the City* (London: Routledge, 2011).

32. Istvan Meszaros, "The Dialectic of Structure and History: An Introduction," *Monthly Review* 63.1 (May 2011): 26-27.

33. Immanuel Kant, *Critique of Pure Reason* (London: Cambridge University Press, 1999), A51/B75.

34. Immanuel Kant, *Grounding of the Metaphysics of Morals* (Indianapolis: Hackett, 1983), 35-36.

35. Classic accounts are found in Samuel Bowles and Herbert Gintis, *Schooling in Capitalist America: Educational Reform and the Contradictions of Economic Life* (Chicago: Haymarket Books, reprint ed., 2011); Pierre Bourdieu, *Reproduction in Education, Society and Culture* (London: Sage, 1977); and Paul Willis, *Learning to Labor: How Working Class Kids Get Working Class Jobs* (New York: Columbia University Press, 1981).

36. *Discourse on Colonialism* (New York: Monthly Review Press,

2001), 21.

37. Isaiah Berlin, *Two Concepts of Liberty* (London: Clarendon Press, 1966), 2.

38. Mohammad Fadel, "Special Analysis: Religion and the Arab Spring," *The Islamic Monthly* (Summer/Fall 2011). Available from: http://onlinedigeditions.com/display_article.php?id=8 32740. (Accessed February 21, 2013).

39. Keith Hart, Jean-Louis Laville and Antonio David Cattani, eds., *The Human Economy* (Cambridge: Policy Press, 2010); and Jan Breman, *Outcast Labour in Asia: Circulation and Informalization of the Workforce at the Bottom of the Economy* (London: Oxford University Press, 2010).

40. Mike Davis, *Planet of Slums* (London: Verso, 2006).

41. Jan Breman, *The Labouring Poor in India: Patterns of Exploitation, Subordination and Exclusion* (London: Oxford University Press, 2003), as quoted in Mike Davis, *Planet of Slums*, 199.

42. David Simon, "Few opportunities for an actress from the other America,'" *Baltimore Sun* (March 12, 2011). Available from: http://articles.baltimoresun.com/2011-03-12/news/bs-ed-simon-statement-20110312_1_drug-prohibition-drug-arrest-drug-economy. (Accessed February 21, 2013).

43. Wendy Brown, "American Nightmare: Neoliberalism, Neoconservatism, and De-Democratization," *Political Theory* 34 (2006): 705.

44. Mike Judge, Director, *Idiocracy* (Hollywood: 20th Century Fox, 2007).

45. Michel Foucault, *Discipline and Punish: The Birth of the Prison* (New York: Vintage, 1995), 257f.

46. The dropout rate is near 70% in some urban areas. Source: *Yes We Can: The Schott 50 State Report on Public Education and Black Males* (Cambridge, MA: Schott Foundation for Public Education, 2010). Available from: http://www.blackboys-report.org/bbreport.pdf. (Accessed February 21, 2013.) On

incarceration rates, "By their mid-30's, 6 in 10 black men who had dropped out of school had spent time in prison." Erick Eckholm, "Plight Deepens for Black Men, Studies Warn," *New York Times* (March 20, 2006).

47. Michelle Holder, "Unemployment in New York City During the Recession and Early Recovery: Young Black Men Hit the Hardest" (New York: Community Service Society, 2010). Available from: http://b.3cdn.net/nycss/ea8952641d08e68fbb_c4m6bofb0.pdf. (Accessed February 21, 2013)

48. Soren Kierkegaard, *Diary of a Seducer* (London: Continuum, 2006).

49. Ebenezer C. Brewer, *The Wordsworth Dictionary of Phrase and Fable* (Ware, Hertfordshire: Wordsworth Editions, 2001), 437.

50. I allude to the Massachusetts General School Act (1647), commonly referred to as the *Old Deluder Satan* act. It reads in pertinent part: "It being one chief project of the old deluder, Satan, to keep men from the knowledge of the Scriptures, as in former times by keeping them in an unknown tongue, it is therefore ordered that every township in this jurisdiction, after the Lord has increased them [in] number to fifty householders, shall then forthwith appoint one within their town to teach all such children as shall resort to him to write and read, whose wages shall be paid either by the parents or masters of such children, or by the inhabitants in general." See Lawrence A. Cremin, *American Education: The Colonial Experience, 1607-1783* (New York: Harper & Row, 1970), 180.

Chapter 4

1. Dmitry Orlov, *Reinventing Collapse: The Soviet Experience and American Prospects*, rev. ed. (Gabriola Island, BC: New Society Publishers, 2011), 112.

2. Michael Hudson, "Debts that Can't Be Paid, Won't Be," *Michael-Hudson.com* (April 10, 2012). Available from: http://michael-hudson.com/2012/04/debts-that-cant-be-paid-

wont-be/

3. See Michael B. Katz, *Irony of Early School Reform*.

4. I am drawing from Martin Heidegger's analysis of tool-use from *Being and Time* (New York: Harper & Row, 1962).

5. "Chris Hedges on Capitalism's 'Sacrifice Zones.'" *Bill Moyers & Company* (July 20, 2012). http://billmoyers.com/segment/chris-hedges-on-capitalism's-'sacrifice-zones'/

6. Paul Conklin, *A Revolution Down on the Farm: The Transformation of American Agriculture since 1929* (Lexington, KY: University Press of Kentucky, 2008), 3.

7. Almost alone among industrialized countries, the U.S. has no formal *national* provision of education at any level. Though the federal government asserts in various ways - mostly via statute and constitutional law - the states enjoy plenary power over their education system. They are only limited formally by indirect constitutional considerations that may come into play (e.g. are they violating basic rights?) and practically by their entirely contingent desire to obtain federal funding through categorical aid. Most federal statutes in education, such as *Title IX* (sex discrimination), *IDEA* (disabilities education) and *No Child Left Behind* (testing) are not direct mandates but rather are contingent upon states' desire to secure federal funding; in principle, absent that desire they would not apply.

8. "New Home for Innovation: JP Morgan Chase Innovation Center Opens at UD," *UDaily*, University of Delaware, Newark, DE, October 17, 2011. Available from: http://www.udel.edu/udaily/2012/oct/innovation101711.html. (Accessed February 21, 2013). The University's news organ reports, the "Innovation Center was built as part of the strategic JPMorgan Chase-University of Delaware collaboration established in December 2009 focused on *building a pipeline of technology talent through University curriculum*, enriching internships and joint research projects to drive

innovation [emphasis added]."

9. Immanuel Wallerstein, "Cities in socialist theory and capitalist praxis," *International Journal of Urban and Regional Research*, 8.1 (1984), 64.

10. For a provocative statement, see "Russ" (2011) at the blog "Volatility," (available from: http//attempter.wordpress .com): "Contrary to propaganda, there's nothing modernistic about corporations. On the contrary, they're a carryover phenomenon from feudalism. This feudal vestige persisted through the early heyday of capitalism, soon becoming the preferred mode of organization to prevent the full textbook logic of capitalism from developing. The result was that the economy never evolved beyond a feudal-capitalist hybrid. And once capitalism reached its terminal stage starting in the 1970s, where the combination of Peak Oil and the terminally declining profit rate threatened to attenuate forms of economic domination completely, the corporation became the basic unit of class war, and the anti-social, anti-political, anti-sovereign form around which full feudalism is intended to be restored." See also M. Zafirovski, "Neo-Feudalism in America? Conservatism in Relation to European Feudalism," *International Review of Sociology* 17.3 (2007): 393.

11. Istvan Meszaros, "The Dialectic of Structure and History: An Introduction," *Monthly Review* 63.1 (2011), 26-7.

12. J. Medaille, "Neo-Feudalism and the Invisible Fist," *The Distributist Review* (blog), August 23, 2010. Available from: http://distributistrview/com/mag/2010/08/neo-feudalism-and-the-invisible-fist. (Accessed February 21, 2013)

13. Charles Hugh Smith, *Why Things are Falling Apart and What We Can Do About It* (Amazon Digital Services: kindle edition, 2012).

14. Available from: http://studentloanjustice.org, http://occupys-tudentdebt.com, and http://forgivestudentdebt.com. (All

accessed January 23, 2012)

15. R. Applebaum, "Want a real economic stimulus and jobs plan? Forgive student loan debt!," Available from: http://signon.org/sign/want-a-real-economic.

16. See David Graeber, *Debt: The First 5000 Years* (London: Melville House, 2011): 2, 82.

17. For more detail, see *FinAid: The SmartStudent Guide to Financial Aid*, available from: http://www.finaid.org/loans (accessed January 23, 2012)

18. See lawyers.com, "Student Loans in Bankruptcy," available from: http://bankruptcy.lawyers.com/consumer-bankrupt cy/Student-Loans-In-Bankruptcy.html. (Accessed January 23, 2012).

19. M. Pilon, "The $55,000 Student-loan Burden: As Default Rates on Borrowing for Higher Education Rise, some Borrowers See No Way Out; 'This is Just Outrageous Now,'" *Wall Street Journal*, February 13, 2010. Available from: http://online.wsj.com/article; Cameron Huddleston, "What Happens When You Default on Student Loans," *Kiplinger* (August 30, 2010). Available from: http://www.kiplinger .com/columns/kiptips/archives/what-happens-when-you-default-on-student-loans.html. (Accessed February 21, 2013).

20. United Nations, Office of the United Nations High Commissioner for Human rights,, *Supplementary Convention on the Abolition of Slavery, the Slave Trade, and Institutions and Practices Similar to Slavery* (Geneva: The United Nations, 1956). Available from: http://www2.ohchr.org/english/law/ slavetrade.htm.

21. Andrew Ross, "Andrew Ross Speaks to Occupy Wall Street on Student Debt," *SocialText* (September 6, 2011). Available from: http://socialtextjournal.org/periscope/2011/09/andrew -ross-speaks-to-ows-on-student-debt-php; and Jeffrey Williams, "Academic Freedom and Indentured Students:

Escalating Student Debt is a Kind of Bondage," *Academe* 98.1 (January-February 2012). Available from: http://www.a aup.org/AAUP/pubres/academe/2012/JF.

22. In Sara Jaffe, "OWS Education Activists Launch Student Debt Refusal Pledge," *Alternet* (November 21, 2011). Available from: http://www.alternet.org/newsandviews/arti cle/737128.

23. "The labor force participation rate for all youth - the proportion of the population 16 to 24 years old working or looking for work - was 59.5 percent in July, the lowest July rate on record. The July 2011 rate was down by 1.0 percentage point from July 2010 and was 18.0 percentage points below the peak for that month in 1989 (77.5 percent)." U.S. Department of Labor, Bureau of Labor Statistics, "Employment and Unemployment Among Youth Summary" (August 2012). http://www.bls.gov/news.release/youth.nr0. htm.

24. Dmitry Orlov, *Reinventing Collapse*, 112-113.

25. Ken Lawrence, "Karl Marx on American Slavery," *Sojourner Truth Organization* (1972). Available from: http://www. sojournertruth.net.marxslavery.pdf.

26. Gary S. Becker, *Human Capital*, 16.

27. *Brown v. Board of Education*, 347 U.S. 493 (1954).

28. Recent U.S. Bureau of Labor Statistics data on employment status and educational attainment may be found at http://www.bls.gov/news.release/empsit.t04.htm (accessed January 23, 2012). Unsurprisingly, the data show that employment rates are significantly higher for those with more college.

29. Samir Amin, "The Right to Education," *Pambazuka News* 557 (November 10, 2011). Available from: http://pambazuka.org /en/category/features/77838.

30. Anthony Grafton, "Our universities: Why are they failing?," *New York Review of Books* 59.1 (January 12, 2012).

31. Carey Nelson, "From the President: One Last Chance," *Academe* (January-February 2011). Available from: http://aaup.org/AAUP/pubres/academe/2011/JF/col/ftp.htm.

32. Friedrich Engels, *Principles of Communism* (Moscow: Progress Publishers, 1969 [1847]), 85.

Chapter 5

1. This motto of "enlightened absolutism" is discussed in Immanuel Kant's "An Answer to the Question: What is Enlightenment? (1784)" Available from: http://www.columbia.edu/acis/ets/CCREAD/etscc/kant.html.

2. Nassim Nicholas Taleb, *Antifragile: Things That Gain from Disorder* (New York: Random House, 2012).

3. Katie Kindelan, "Ohio School Lets Gay Student Wear Controversial T-Shirt," *ABC News*, April 5, 2012. http://abcnews.go.com/blogs/headlines/2012/04/ohio-school-agrees-to-let-gay-student-wear-controversial-t-shirt-for-one-day/.

4. This folktale is related in Alan Watts, *Tao and the Watercourse Way* (New York: Pantheon Books, 1975), 31. There is also a wonderful children's book that expresses the same theme for the preschool set: Margery Cuyler, *"That's Bad! That's Good!"* (New York: Henry Holt, 1993).

5. *Plessy v. Ferguson*, 163 U.S. 559 (1896).

6. See, e.g. *Cummings v. Richmond County Board of Education*, 175 U.S. 528 (1899).

7. *Wallace v. Jaffree*, 472 U.S. 38 (1985).

8. Jan Crawford Greenberg, *Supreme Conflict: The Inside Story of the Struggle for Control of the United States Supreme Court* (New York: Penguin Books, 2007), 118.

9. *New Jersey v. TLO*, 469 U.S. 325 (1985), *Vernonia School District v. Acton*, 515 U.S. 646 (1995), and *Board of Education v. Earls*, 536 U.S. 822 (2002).

10. *Goss v. Lopez*, 419 U.S. 565 (1975).

11. *Board of Education of Westside Community Schools v. Mergens,* 496 U.S. 226 (1990), which upholds the federal *Equal Access Act* (1984).

12. Reynolds Holding, "Ruling 'Bong Hits' Out of Bounds," *Time* (June 25, 2007). Available from: http://www.time.com/time/nation/article/0,8599,1637131,00.html.

13. *Tinker v. Des Moines Independent Community School District,* 393 U.S. 503 (1969).

14. There is one more preliminary consideration for whether expression is eligible for constitutional protection that will be addressed later in the chapter.

15. The classic work on the perennial capitulation of school administrators to outside interests is Raymond E. Callahan, Education and the Cult of Efficiency (Chicago: University of Chicago Press, 1962).

16. Originally from Justice Oliver Wendell Holmes, the "marketplace of ideas" metaphor used in *Tinker* quotes Justice William Brennan's majority opinion in *Keyishian v. Board of Regents,* 385 U.S. 589, 603 (1967): "'The vigilant protection of constitutional freedoms is nowhere more vital than in the community of American schools.' *Shelton v. Tucker,* 364 U.S. 479, 487 (1960). The classroom is peculiarly the 'marketplace of ideas.' The Nation's future depends upon leaders trained through wide exposure to that robust exchange of ideas which discovers truth 'out of a multitude of tongues, [rather] than through any kind of authoritative selection.'"

17. James E. Ryan, "The Supreme Court and Public Schools," *Virginia Law Review* 86.7 (2000): 27. Ryan continues, "In short, the Court's approach can be defended, at least generally, on the grounds of necessity. Schools need some constitutional room to achieve their goals, and the Court needs to ensure that students do not shed all of their constitutional rights at the schoolhouse door. A defensible way to resolve this dilemma is to identify the core, universal function of schools,

and to use this function as a guide to determine the circumstances in which schools will be granted deference."

18. Section 894 (Article 94) of the *Uniform Code of Military Justice* reads in pertinent part: "Mutiny or Sedition: (a) Any person subject to this chapter who - (1) with intent to usurp or override lawful military authority, refuses, in concert with any other person, to obey orders or otherwise do his duty or creates any violence or disturbance is guilty of mutiny. (b) A person who is found guilty of attempted mutiny, mutiny, sedition, or failure to suppress or report a mutiny or sedition shall be punished by death or such other punishment as a court-martial may direct."

19. *Bethel School District No. 403 v. Fraser*, 478 U.S. 675 (1986).

20. Supreme Court Justice Potter Stewart once famously (or infamously) admitted the difficulty in defining pornography, but then added, "I know it when I see it." This is, of course, as Potter himself later recognized, untenable as a legal standard. See *Jacobellis v. Ohio*, 378 U.S. 184 (1964).

21. An additional area of concern involves the potential advocacy of violence, particularly in this post-Columbine and Newtown era of heightened school safety concerns. There are probably too many gray areas here, but generally speaking the judgment will be whether the alleged threat contained in the message is established as real and direct enough. So, for example, a school would be on firmer ground disallowing a "KKK" symbol than it would a message bearing the words "white power," because the Ku Klux Klan has an unambiguous track record of intimidation and violence, whereas the "white power" message, however obnoxious, does not have that level of specificity. The analysis in such cases is really that due to the threat of violence it carries, the message constitutes conduct rather than speech, and therefore it is outside the scope of First Amendment protection. Allowing state statutes prohibiting

cross burning, the Court directly affirms the threat-like nature of this practice in *Virginia v. Black et al.* 538 U.S. 343 (2003) - this latter being authored, interestingly, by none other than Justice Thomas.

22. *Bethel v. Fraser*, 478 U.S. 683.

23. *Hazelwood School District et al. v. Kuhlmeier et al.*, 484 U.S. 260 (1988).

24. An exception might be where the "educational purpose" of the field trip is inherently very broad, for example, a trip to see a political candidate or governmental official who, by virtue of his or her position (or sought position), is legitimately the object of many kinds of citizens' grievances or "petitions." For this reason, an event such as one where school students are sent to watch a presidential motorcade might be thought to constitute more of a public forum.

25. *Morse v. Frederick*, 393 U.S. 423.

26. Ibid., 424.

27. Timing is crucial in jurisprudence. While it is not in itself unreasonable to question whether something has a constitutional basis, it is unreasonable to reject out of hand that basis where there is a well-established line of precedent. Thomas's argument would have been reasonable (though perhaps wrong) in 1969, just as Justice Hugo Black's *Tinker* dissent was reasonable at the time. The Court does change course and reverse itself from time to time. But even the majority opinions associated with dramatic reversals usually offer some legal rationale for how the reversal is not really a reversal but is somehow consistent with the relevant Court case law. (For example, *Brown v. Board of Education*, 347 U.S. 483 (1954) overturned *Plessy v. Ferguson*, 163 U.S. 637 (1896) on the constitutionality of de jure racial segregation on the premise that since education had become more important in 1954 than it was in 1896, it was now worthy of Fourteenth Amendment consideration.) This is wholly rational for an

institution whose legitimacy derives in large part from *stare decisis* deference to precedent.

28. *Morse v. Frederick*, 393 U.S. 410.
29. Connecticut in 1818 became the final state to abandon an official establishment of religion. See Leonard W. Levy, *The Establishment Clause: Religion and the First Amendment* (Chapel Hill: University of North Carolina Press, 1994), 49.
30. *Morse v. Frederick*, 393 U.S. 412.
31. Jonathan Zimmerman, "Got Discipline?" *Los Angeles Times* (June 28, 2007). Available from: http://www.latimes.com/news/opinion/commentary/la-oe-zimmerman28jun28,1,6696557.story.
32. Henry Mark Holzer, "Justice Clarence Thomas and Utopian Originalism," presented at the Heritage Foundation (Washington, DC), November 14, 2007.
33. *Morse v. Frederick*, 393 U.S. 412.
34. Aside from the area directly concerning school-sponsored religious exercises (which has a complicated post–World War II history), the only direct students' rights precursor to *Tinker* would be the sort of beachhead of freedom of conscience in circumscribed areas, most notably the right to opt out of the Pledge of Allegiance (*West Virginia State Board of Education v. Barnette*, 319 U.S. 624 [1943]). Realizing this, Thomas would probably want to set back the clock a few decades earlier, at least to the 1930s.
35. *Tinker v. Des Moines*, 393 U.S. 510.
36. Clarence Thomas, quoted in Adam Liptak, "Reticent Justice Opens Up to a Group of Students," *New York Times*, April 14, 2009, A11.
37. Svetlana Boym, *The Future of Nostalgia* (New York: Basic Books, 2001), xviii.
38. Ibid., 49.
39. Ibid.
40. Benedict Anderson, *Imagined Communities: Reflections on the*

Origin and Spread of Nationalism (New York: Verso, 1991).

41. Boym, *The Future of Nostalgia*, 41.

42. One blogging wit posts: "You can almost picture Thomas with a paddle in his hand, ordering some mischievous child of yore to bend over for a good, compassionate Republican spanking. Thomas's ideal school seems to be Dotheboys Hall in Nicholas Nickleby." Available from http://nomore-hornets.blogspot.com/ 2007/06/bong-hits-4-thomas.html. (Accessed February 21, 2013)

43. Thomas seems to suggest as much in his recent autobiography, *My Grandfather's Son: A Memoir* (New York: Harper, 2007). In his review of this book, William Grimes writes that Thomas "portrays himself as a persecuted, almost Christlike figure singled out by the liberal establishment, at the behest of his civil rights enemies, not just for criticism but also for total annihilation" (Grimes, "The Justice Looks Back and Settles Old Scores," *New York Times*, October 10, 2007; available from: http://www.nytimes.com/2007/10/10/books/10grim.html). If, following Boym, a conspiracy-seeking mindset is a key indicator of a dangerous form of restorative nostalgia, the paranoia evident from Thomas's own pen certainly makes him look worse in this regard. (However germane it may be to the nostalgia discussion, one should be mindful that Thomas's autobiography, where he speaks merely as "a book author," is, strictly speaking, irrelevant to the legal hermeneutics argument.)

44. I make an argument along these lines in Blacker, *Democratic Education Stretched Thin*, 26–28.

45. Svetlana Boym, "Nostalgia and Its Discontents," *The Hedgehog Review* 9.2 (2007), 9.

46. Friedrich Nietzsche, *Birth of Tragedy*, trans. Walter Kaufmann (New York: Vintage, 1967), 18.

47. See *Ahlquist v. City of Cranston*, No. 11-138 (D. Rhode Island 2012012); and "Will Phillips, 10-Year-Old, Won't Pledge

Allegiance to a Country that Discriminates Against Gays," *Huffington Post*, March 18, 2010. Available from: http://www.huffingtonpost.com/2009/11/12/10-year-old-wont-pledge-a_n_355709.html. (Accessed February 21, 2013.) The CNN interview of Phillips is required viewing for anyone dismissive of young children's moral-political autonomy.

Chapter 6

1. Samir Amin, "The Right to Education," *Pambazuka News* 557 (November 10, 2011). Available from: http://pambazuka .org/en/category/features/77838. (Accessed February 21, 2013)
2. David Harvey, *The Enigma of Capital and the Crises of Capitalism* (London: Profile Books, 2010), 239.
3. A pirated clip of this bit from a show in New York City (10/23/2012) may be found at http://www.youtube.com /watch?v=c5_56uV8Xk8. (Accessed February 21, 2013). I heard him deliver it at the Merriam Theater, Philadelphia, PA, January 18, 2013. Louis C.K.'s website is https://buy.louisck.net/.
4. See my *Dying to Teach: The Educator's Search for Immortality* (New York: Teachers College Press, 1997).
5. John Marsh, *Class Dismissed*.
6. Chris Hayes, *Twilight of the Elites: America After Meritocracy* (New York: Crown, 2012).
7. Ray Kurzweil, *The Singularity is Near: When Humans Transcend Biology* (New York: Penguin Books, 2006).
8. For more on capitalism and monsters, see David McNally, *Monsters of the Market: Zombies, Vampires and Global Capitalism* (Chicago: Haymarket Books, 2012).
9. Ben O'Brien, "G&A Exclusive: An Inside Look at Hornady Zombie Max Ammo," *Guns & Ammo* (October 14, 2011). Available from: http://www.gunsandammo.com/2011/10/14/

hornady-zombie-max-ammo/#ixzz2IphJKA1Q. (Accessed February 21, 2013)

10. Andy Campbell, "Zombie Bullets: Z-Max Ammunition Top Seller After Cannibal Attacks," *The Huffington Post*, June 13, 2012. Available from: http://www.huffingtonpost.com/2012 /06/13/zombie-bullets-z-max-ammunition_n_1594226.html. (Accessed February 21, 2013)

11. Translation altered by the author. Jean-Paul Sartre, *Nausea*, trans. Lloyd Alexander (New York: New Directions, 1964), 128-129.

12. Eugene Thacker, *In the Dust of this Planet: Horror of Philosophy Vol. 1* (Winchester: Zero Books, 2011), 9.

13. Definition available from: http://en.wikipedia.org/wiki /Downcycle. (Accessed February 21, 2013)

14. Libby Sander, "Freshman Survey: Even More Focused on Jobs," *Chronicle of Higher Education*, January 24, 2013. http://chronicle.com/article/Freshman-Survey-This-Year/136787/.

15. Note that in the U.S. the recipient of the right to education is broader than "the citizenry" as, via the Equal Protection Clause of the U.S. Constitution's Fourteenth Amendment, all "persons" residing within the jurisdiction of the United States are eligible. The broadest consequence of this conception is that it has secured education rights for undocumented immigrant children. See *Plyler v. Doe*, 457 U.S. 202 (1982).

16. A classic analysis of this process during the advent of U.S. public schooling is Michael B. Katz, *The Irony of Early School Reform*.

17. Tyler Cowen, *The Great Stagnation*.

18. "...the Lord gave, and the Lord hath taken away; blessed be the name of the Lord." Job 1: 20-21 (KJV).

19. See Michelle Alexander, *The New Jim Crow* and Henry Giroux, *Disposable Youth*.

20. Kenneth J. Saltman, *Capitalizing on Disaster: Taking and Breaking Public Schools* (New York: Paradigm Publishers, 2007), 5.

21. Ibid.

22. Interview for *Women's Own* (September 23, 1987). Interview transcript available from the Margaret Thatcher Foundation, http://www.margaretthatcher.org/speeches/displaydocument.asp?docid=106689. (Accessed February 21, 2013)

23. See "Full Transcript of the Mitt Romney Secret Video," *Mother Jones* (September 19, 2012). Available from: http://www.motherjones.com/politics/2012/09/full-transcript-mitt-romney-secret-video#47percent. (Accessed February 21, 2013)

24. This quote is widely attributed to Gandhi but the attribution lacks proof. The closest thing is perhaps this far more subtle, even dialectical, sentiment: "If we could change ourselves, the tendencies in the world would also change. As a man changes his own nature, so does the attitude of the world change towards him. ... We need not wait to see what others do." See Brian Morton, "False Words Were Never Spoken," *New York Times*, August 29, 2011. Available from: http://www.nytimes.com/2011/08/30/opinion/falser-words-were-never-spoken.html. (Accessed February 21, 2013)

25. Jean-Paul Sartre, *Being and Nothingness* (New York: Citadel Press, 1956).

26. Terry Eagleton, *Why Marx Was Right* (New Haven: Yale University Press, 2011), 30.

27. Eric Hobsbawm, *How to Change the World)*, 109.

28. Karl Marx& Friedrich Engels, *Manifesto of the Communist Party* (1848). Available from: http://www.marxists.org/archive/marx/works/1848/communist-manifesto/ch01.htm.

29. Ibid.

30. Eric Hobsbawm, *How to Change the World*, 120.

31. Étienne Balibar, *The Philosophy of Marx* (London: Verso,

2007), 91.

32. See Herman Cappelen, *Philosophy Without Intuitions* (New York: Oxford University Press, 2012).

33. Michael Huesemann and Joyce Huesemann, *Techno-Fix: Why Technology Won't Save us or the Environment* (Gabriola Island, BC: New Society Publishers, 2011), 71f.

34. See Richard Martin, *SuperFuel: Thorium, the Green Energy Source for the Future* (New York: Palgrave Macmillan, 2012); and Robert Hargreaves, *THORIUM: Cheaper than Coal* (Createspace: 2012).

35. See the detailed report by the Global Campaign for Education, *Gender Discrimination in Education: The Violation of Rights of Women and Girls* (Committee on the Elimination of Discrimination Against Women: A Johannesburg, South Africa: February 2012). Available from: http://campaignforeducation.org/docs/reports/GCE_INTERIM_Gender_Report.pdf.

36. Many ideas, proposals and activism news along these lines may be found at occupystudentdebt.com and occupystudentdebtcampaign.com.

37. See Larry Cuban, *Teachers and Machines: The Classroom Use of Technology Since 1920* (New York: Teachers College Press, 1986).

38. Gilles Deleuze and Felix Guattari, *A Thousand Plateaus: Capitalism and Schizophrenia* (Minneapolis: University of Minnesoat Press, 1987), 4; Bruno Latour, *Reassembling the Social: An Introduction to Actor-Network-Theory* (New York: Oxford University Press, 2005).

39. I model this process as a kind of "contextualism" in my *Democratic Education Stretched Thin*, 99-115.

40. Latour, *Reassembling the Social*, 166.

41. Jason W. Moore, "Wall Street is a Way of Organizing Nature," *Upping the Anti* 12 (2011), 42.

42. Foster et al.'s notion (from the later Marx of *Capital Volume*

III) of "metabolism" and "metabolic rift" gestures toward this conception and is a welcome antidote to the anthropocentric myopia afflicting many Marxists. See Foster et al., *The Ecological Rift*. A more direct appreciation of the artificiality of the society/nature divide may be found in Jason W. Moore, "The Socio-Ecological Crises of Capitalism," in Sasha Lilley, ed., *Capitalism and Its Discontents: Conversations with Radical Thinkers in a Time of Tumult* (Oakland, CA: PM Press, 2011), 136-152. Moore writes that "in the world left today, in a sense we do see a convergence around a dialectical sense of how mature and society are interwoven. There was a time when industrial struggles in large factory settings were regarded as social and peasant struggles or conservation movements were seen as environmental. But in fact what we see today and nowhere more clearly than the ongoing struggles for justice around world agriculture, is a fusing of all of these moments. There is an emergent sensibility that Wall Street is a way of organizing global nature - every bit as directly as a farmer or mine albeit with specific forms." (p. 138)

43. The reference is to historian Lynn White Jr.'s famous "stirrup thesis" in *Medieval Technology and Social Change* (New York: Oxford University Press, 1966) that the invention of the stirrup made feudalism possible owing to how central it made "the man on horseback" (i.e. mounted knight) and consequently the elaborate social structure necessary to maintain that expensive compound creature.

Chapter 7

1. "Barclays and the Limits of Financial Reform," *The Nation* 295.5&6 (July 30/August 6, 2012), 9. These are the late author's last words from his long running *Nation* column "Beat the Devil."

2. See Antonio Gramsci, *Prison Notebooks*, ed. Quentin Hoare

and Geoffrey Hoare Smith (New York: International Publishers, 1971), 175, n75: "Romain Rolland's maxim 'Pessimism of the intelligence, optimism of the will' was made by Gramsci into something of a programmatic slogan as early as 1919, in the pages of *Ordine Nuovo*." This is commonly said to be on the paper's "masthead," although a Google images search of actual editions of *L'Ordine Nuovo* seems not to confirm this.

3. "Dark Ecology," *Dark Mountain* 3 (Croydon, UK: The Dark Mountain Project, Summer 2012), 23.

4. Here I am echoing Graham Harman's categorization of the primary strategies for devaluing the ontological status of objects, what he calls "undermining" (their reality consists only in their sub-parts) and "overmining" (their reality consists only in the larger whole of which they are part). Graham Harman, *The Quadruple Object* (London: Zero Books, 2011), 8-12.

5. Frederic Jameson, *Postmodernism, or, The Cultural Logic of Late Capitalism* (London: Verso, 1991), 5.

6. Ibid.

7. John Michael Greer provides a salutary antidote to the apocalyptic tendency, on this specific topic and generally. See *The Long Descent* and *Apocalypse Not*.

8. George S. Counts, *Dare the School Build a New Social Order?* (Carbondale, IL: Southern Illinois University Press, 1978 [1932].

9. See http://www.whywaldorfworks.org/ and http://www.waldorflibrary.org/. (Both accessed February 21, 2013)

10. See http://www.reggiochildren.it/ and http://reggiochildren-foundation.org/. (Both accessed February 21, 2013)

11. See http://www.summerhillschool.co.uk/. (Accessed February 21, 2013)

12. There was a famous incident where the U.K's Office for Standards in Education, Children's Services and Skills

(Ofsted) tried unsuccessfully to close down Summerhill. See Jessica Shepherd, "So, kids, anyone for double physics? (But no worries if you don't fancy it): Official approval at last for school where almost anything goes," *The Guardian* (November 30, 2007). Available from: http://www. guardian.co.uk/uk/2007/dec/01/ofsted.schools.

13. Blacker, *Dying to Teach* (New York: Columbia University Teachers College Press, 2007).

14. As reported by Mike Cole and Sara C. Motta, here is what truly substantive educational change looks like: "Pre-Chávez, Venezuela's higher education system was notoriously exclusionary and elitist, reproducing a culture of clientelism and personalism. Not surprisingly, it developed frameworks of education and learning that were heavily influenced by the dominant ideas of the West, and the US in particular. To counter this, one of 21st-century socialism's central features is the extended role of the educative society, accompanied by mass intellectualism from birth to death (Chávez has described Venezuela as "a giant school"). A central objective of this is to develop the conditions for the production of autonomous and relevant ideas for the development needs of the majority of Venezuelans. It is also a means to overcome the traditional division of labour present within Venezuelan society and politics, in which there were thinkers (the dominant economic and intellectual elite) and doers (those who produced, yet were unable to control or receive the fruits of production). "Opinion: The Giant School's Emancipatory Lessons," *Times Higher Education* (March 11, 2011). Available from: http://www.timeshighereducation.co.uk/story.asp?storycode=414858. I thank Alpesh Maisuria for suggesting this.

15. James V. Wertsch, *Voices of Collective Remembering* (New York: Cambridge University Press, 2002), 141. Thanks to Eugene Matusov for this example.

16. William B. Irving, *A Guide to the Good Life: The Ancient Art of Stoic Joy* (New York: Oxford University Press, 2009), 103.

17. John Holloway, *Crack Capitalism*, 9.

18. Ibid., 11.

19. Ibid., 9.

20. In Charles H. Kahn, *The Art and Thought of Heraclitus*, (New York: Cambridge University Press, 1979), #104.

21. Kenny Rogers, "The Gambler," On *The Gambler* (Capitol Records: Nashville, TN, 1978).

22. Blacker, *Democratic Education Stretched Thin*.

23. There are plenty of further examples. One might add certain versions of Marxism that have fueled a sense of destiny among adherents and, a very different sort of example, the Mongols of the Genghis Khan period (and later) who felt that it was divinely ordained that they should rule all peoples. In fact, it seems to me that this fatalism-activism combination is much more common than the fatalism-quiescence combination, though the latter, I think, does exist - though, it seems more likely at the level of the individual psyche. Even there, though, there are famous counter examples like Stoicism, which is not known for generating passive types (more on Stoicism later).

24. Plato, *Republic*, trans. Robin Waterfield (New York: Oxford University Press, 1993), 617c.

25. (New York: Oxford University Press, 2010).

26. G. A. Cohen, "Historical Inevitability and Human Agency in Marxism," *Proceedings of the Royal Society of London* 402.1832 (September, 1986), 77-78.

27. "What does the Spartacus League Want? (New York: Monthly Review Press, 1971 [1919]). Available from: http://www.marxists.org/archive/luxemburg/1918/12/14.htm.

28. Robert C. Solomon, "On Fate and Fatalism," *Philosophy East and West*, Vol. 15, No. 4 (October 2003), 438.

29. Fragment #104, in Charles Kahn, *The Art and Thought of*

Heraclitus (Cambridge: Cambridge University Press, 1979). As quoted in Solomon, 445.

30. Robert C. Solomon, "On Fate and Fatalism," 442.

31. Friedrich Nietzsche, *The Gay Science* (New York: Cambridge University Press, 2001), 270. Nietzsche is himself borrowing from one of the Roman poet Pindar's *Odes*.

32. Robert C. Solomon, "On Fate and Fatalism," 443-444.

33. Ibid., 452.

34. Jean-Paul Sartre, "Itinerary of a Thought," *New Left Review*, 1.58 (November-December 1969). Available from: http://newleftreview.org/I/58/jean-paul-sartre-itinerary-of-a-thought.

35. Arthur Schopenhauer, *Two Fundamental Problems of Ethics* (New York: Oxford University Press), 81.

36. Ibid.

37. Plato, *Meno*, in *Five Dialogues*, trans. G.M.A. Grube (Indianapolis: Hackett, 1981), 100b.

38. Nicholson Baker, *Human Smoke: The Beginnings of World War II, the End of Civilization* (New York: Simon & Schuster, 2009).

39. Martin Heidegger, "Only a God Can Save Us (1966)," in Sheldon Wolin, ed. *The Heidegger Controversy: A Critical Reader* (Cambridge, MA: MIT Press, 1993), 91.

40. Hesiod, *Works and Days*, 90-105. http://www.perseus.tufts.edu/hopper/text?doc=Perseus%3Atext%3A1999.01.0132%3Acard%3D83

41. There is a wealth of sources to consult here. To get a flavor of the debate, I would recommend Chris Martenson, *The Crash Course: The Unsustainable Future of Our Economy, Energy and Environment* (New York: Wiley, 2011) and his blog, *Peak Prosperity*, www.peakprosperity.com. There are also many relevant works by peak oil expert Richard Heinberg, such as *Peak Everything: Waking Up to the Century of Declines* (Gabriola Island, BC: New Society Publishers, 2010). Two very active sites on peak oil are *The Oil Drum:*

Discussions about Energy and Our Future, www.the oildrum.com, *The Association for the Study of Peak Oil and Gas*, www.peakoil.net, and the Post Carbon Institute, www.postcarbon.org. For a dissenting view, see Daniel Yergin, "There Will Be Oil," *The Wall Street Journal*, September 17, 2011, available from http://online.wsj.com/article/SB10001424053111904060604576572552998674340.html; and his *The Quest: Energy, Security and the Remaking of the Modern World* (New York: Penguin, 2012).

42. Chris Martenson, "The really, really big picture: There isn't going to be enough net energy for the economic growth we want," Post-Carbon Institute (January 13, 2013). Available from: http://www.postcarbon.org/blog-post/1402948-the-really-really-big-picture-there. (Accessed February 21, 2013)

43. Ibid.

44. Mark Lowen, "Crisis –hit Greeks Chop Up Forests to Stay Warm," *BBC News Europe*, January 27, 2013. Available from: http://www.bbc.co.uk/news/world-europe-21202432.

45. Derek Thompson, "How this Smoke Cloud Becomes the Ultimate Symbol of Greece's Depression," *The Atlantic Cities*, January 31, 2013. Available from: http://www.theatlanticcities.com/jobs-and-economy/2013/01/how-smoke-cloud-became-ultimate-symbol-greeces-depression/4561/.

46. Ibid.

47. This is a mash-up of lines from Seneca's "On Anger" and "Consolation to Marcia," available in Seneca, *Dialogues and Essays*, trans. John Davie (New York: Oxford University Press, 2007), compiled and placed together as "A Senecan Praemeditatio," in Alain de Botton, *The Consolations of Philosophy* (New York: Vintage Books, 2000), 91.

48. Lucretius, *The Nature of Things*, trans. A. E. Stallings (New York: Penguin, 2007), BkI, 46-148.

49. See http://www.aahistory.com/prayer.html. (Accessed February 21, 2013)

50. This is a rewarding area of study, as there are easily available high quality translations (much of which can be found free online), and excellent scholarly secondary sources, including masterful works by A. A. Long, Brad Inwood, Pierre Hadot, John M. Cooper, Martha Nussbaum, and many others. Truly notable, though, is the recent spate of popular books (some by professional philosophers, some not). Among the most notable: Alan de Botton, *The Consolations of Philosophy* (New York: Vintage, 2001), Jules Evans, *Philosophy for Life and Other Dangerous Situations* (London: Rider, 2012), William B. Irvine, *A Guide to the Good Life: The Ancient Art of Stoic Joy* (New York: Oxford University Press, 2009), and (this is not a mistake), Timothy Ferriss, *The 4-Hour Workweek: Escape the 9-5, Live Anywhere, and Join the New Rich* (New York: Harmony, 2009). This heterogeneity is consistent with ancient Stoicism as a school, which contained high-end philosophers like Chrysippus, more popular figures such as Seneca and politician and orator Cato the Younger, and also middle spectrum types, most famously the slave Epictetus, the Senator Cicero and the Emperor Marcus Aeurelius.

51. As quoted in Jules Evans, *Philosophy for Life and Other Dangerous Situations,* 70.

52. William B. Irvine, *A Guide to the Good Life,* 68.

53. A point like this was made to me by the late philosopher Peter Winch. The story about Weil is related in Simone de Beauvoir, *Memoirs of a Dutiful Daughter* (New York: Harper, 2005).

54. Seneca, *Dialogues and Essays,* 61.

55. Ibid. This line is attributed to a playwright contemporaneous with Seneca.

56. Ibid.

57. Ibid., 62.

58. Friedrich Nietzsche, *Thus Spoke Zarathustra* (New York: Penguin Books, 1978), 4.31.

59. Seneca, *Dialogues and Essays*, 71.

60. William B. Irvine, *A Guide to the Good Life*, 77.

61. Lucretius, *The Nature of Things*, BkIII, 1044-1052.

62. *Uncivilisation: The Dark Mountain Manifesto* (2009). http://dark-mountain.net/about/manifesto/.

63. World Health Organization, "Health through safe drinking water and basic sanitation," *Project on Water Sanitation Health* (2013). Available from: http://www.who.int/water_sanitation _health/mdg1/en/index.html.

64. "The Debtwatch Manifesto," *Steve Keen's Debwatch*, available from http://www.debtdeflation.com/blogs/2012/01/03/the-debtwatch-manifesto/. (Accessed February 18, 2013)

65. I allude to James Hanson's *Storms of My Grandchildren: The Truth About the Coming Climate Catastrophe and Our Last Chance to Save Humanity* (New York: Bloomsbury, 2009).

66. Leon Trotsky, "Socialism or Barbarism (1917)," available from: www.marxists.org/history/etol/newspape/fi/vol9/no6 /trotsky.html.

67. Seneca, *Dialogues and Essays*, 59.

68. Hesiod, *Works and Days*, trans. Hugh G. Evelyn-White. (Cambridge, MA: Harvard University Press, 1914), 42.

Index

Contemporary culture has eliminated both the concept of the public and the figure of the intellectual. Former public spaces – both physical and cultural – are now either derelict or colonized by advertising. A cretinous anti-intellectualism presides, cheerled by expensively educated hacks in the pay of multinational corporations who reassure their bored readers that there is no need to rouse themselves from their interpassive stupor. The informal censorship internalized and propagated by the cultural workers of late capitalism generates a banal conformity that the propaganda chiefs of Stalinism could only ever have dreamt of imposing. Zer0 Books knows that another kind of discourse – intellectual without being academic, popular without being populist – is not only possible: it is already flourishing, in the regions beyond the striplit malls of so-called mass media and the neurotically bureaucratic halls of the academy. Zer0 is committed to the idea of publishing as a making public of the intellectual. It is convinced that in the unthinking, blandly consensual culture in which we live, critical and engaged theoretical reflection is more important than ever before.